COMBATING INJUSTICE

COMBATING INJUSTICE

THE NATURALISM OF
FRANK NORRIS, JACK LONDON
& JOHN STEINBECK

JON FALSARELLA DAWSON

Louisiana State University Press
Baton Rouge

Published by Louisiana State University Press
lsupress.org

Designer: Barbara Neely Bourgoyne
Typeface: Sentinel

Cover illustration: Protestors parading with picket signs during the San Francisco General Strike of 1934. Courtesy San Francisco History Center, San Francisco Public Library.

Portions of chapter 3 first appeared as "'I Pray the Lord My Work's All Right': Economic Themes in Jack London's 'The Apostate'" in *Excavatio* 25 (2015). Portions of chapter 5 first appeared as "Solidarity Forever: The Historical Background of John Steinbeck's *In Dubious Battle*" in *Steinbeck Review*, vol. 12, no. 2 (2015), pp. 130–48, copyright © Jon Falsarella Dawson, and is used with permission of The Pennsylvania State University Press.

Library of Congress Cataloging-in-Publication Data
Names: Dawson, Jon Falsarella, author.
Title: Combating injustice : the naturalism of Frank Norris, Jack London, and John Steinbeck / Jon Falsarella Dawson.
Description: Baton Rouge : Louisiana State University Press, [2022] | Includes bibliographical references and index.
Identifiers: LCCN 2021047216 (print) | LCCN 2021047217 (ebook) | ISBN 978-0-8071-7712-9 (cloth) | ISBN 978-0-8071-7761-7 (pdf) | ISBN 978-0-8071-7762-4 (epub)
Subjects: LCSH: American fiction—20th century—History and criticism. | Working class in literature. | Social change in literature. | Naturalism in literature. | Norris, Frank, 1870–1902—Criticism and interpretation. | London, Jack, 1876–1916—Criticism and interpretation. | Steinbeck, John, 1902–1968—Criticism and interpretation. | LCGFT: Literary criticism.
Classification: LCC PS374.W64 D39 2022 (print) | LCC PS374.W64 (ebook) | DDC 813/.509355—dc23/eng/20211222
LC record available at https://lccn.loc.gov/2021047216
LC ebook record available at https://lccn.loc.gov/2021047217

For Stella

CONTENTS

ACKNOWLEDGMENTS

Combating Injustice is the culmination of a decade of work, and this project benefited from the assistance of numerous individuals. First I want to thank James Nagel for his insight, guidance, and encouragement. Dr. Nagel has taught me what it means to be a scholar and a professional, and I am incredibly grateful. I am also deeply indebted to Hugh Ruppersburg, Richard Menke, and Kristin Boudreau for their guidance throughout the project. I also wish to acknowledge Geoffrey Green, Michael Krasny, Gayle Davies, Mary-Kay Gamel, William Nickell, and Lloyd Laub. They have provided me with invaluable assistance throughout my academic career that helped me to become the scholar that I am today. I would especially like to thank Eric Solomon, who encouraged me to work on American naturalism and to find my own voice as a writer without regard to whatever theoretical trends happened to be fashionable at the moment.

I owe a debt of gratitude to the research librarians at the Bancroft Library at the University of California, the Henry E. Huntington Library, the Martha Heasley Cox Center for Steinbeck Studies, and the National Archives at San Francisco. These librarians helped me find the periodical sources that form the foundation of this study, and their advice guided this project in directions that I never would have considered. I would like to acknowledge my editor at Louisiana State University Press, James W. Long, and the readers who evaluated the manuscript. Their feedback and suggestions for revision improved this study immensely. I would like to thank Elizabeth Gratch for her skilled copyediting of the manuscript and James Wilson for making sure that the book reaches the largest possible audience. I would also like to express my gratitude to *Excavatio* for permission to reprint material from "'I Pray the Lord My Work's All Right': Economic Themes in Jack London's

'The Apostate'" and the *Steinbeck Review* for permission to reprint material from "Solidarity Forever: The Historical Background of John Steinbeck's *In Dubious Battle.*"

This book also benefited from the support and insights of my colleagues at San Francisco State University, the University of Georgia, and the University of North Georgia. Most notably, I would like to thank Nicole Camastra, Cameron Crawford, Shannon Gilstrap, Joe Lease, Spenser Simrill, Elizabeth Steere, Sara Steger, and Kurt Windisch for their advice and encouragement as I grappled with various stages of the project. I especially want to express my gratitude to Sooyun Lew, who not only kept me alive throughout my first round of graduate school but also provided me with a place to stay as I was conducting research for this project at the Huntington Library. I would also like to acknowledge Eric Boucher, Rob Cavestany, Greg Graffin, Brett Gurewitz, Chris Hannah, Steve Harris, Gary Holt, and John Mellor for their constant inspiration, and I would be remiss if I did not thank the 2010, 2012, and 2014 San Francisco Giants.

I am grateful to my parents, Bob, Derrick, Laurie, and Marcia, for all they have done for me and all they have put up with from me. I would especially like to thank my mother, Laurie Dawson, for introducing me to the writers I discuss in this study and offering incisive feedback on countless drafts at every stage of development. I also owe a profound debt of gratitude to my wife, Alisha Topete-Cromwell. Without her love, encouragement, and impressive command of American history, I would not have been able to complete this book, and she has helped me throughout this process in ways that are too numerous to articulate. Finally, I would like to thank my daughter, Stella, for giving me enough time to write each day while also reminding me that not every aspect of life revolves around naturalist fiction. Her intellectual curiosity and creativity are constant sources of inspiration, and she reminds me why it is imperative that we continue to fight for a better world.

COMBATING INJUSTICE

INTRODUCTION

In "The Novel with a 'Purpose,'" Frank Norris asserted that the highest form of literature "must tell something, must narrate vigorous incidents and must show something, must penetrate deep into the motives and character of type-men, men who are composite pictures of a multitude of men. It must do this because of the nature of the subject, for it deals with elemental forces, motives that stir whole nations."[1] Norris understood the role that authors played in shaping public opinion; as a result, he felt that writers had an obligation to engage with the major issues of their eras in a manner that expressed fundamental truths about their world. Developing this point, Norris claimed that fiction could be used "for the good of the people, fearlessly proving that power is abused, that the strong grind the faces of the weak, that an evil tree is still growing in the midst of the garden . . . that the races of men have yet to work out their destiny in those great and terrible movements that crush and grind and rend asunder the pillars of the houses of the nations."[2] Instead of merely entertaining or diverting the reader, Norris argued that the novel should explore the inner workings of man and society, examine the forces that shape the actions of individuals, and represent these observations in a manner that directs readers to purposeful action.

This view of fiction also animated the output of two other dominant figures in American naturalism: Jack London and John Steinbeck. In his introduction to *The Cry for Justice* (1915), London highlighted the social significance of literature, which can illustrate that "this fair world so brutally unfair, is not decreed by the will of God nor by any iron law of Nature" and that "the world can be fashioned a fair world indeed by the humans who inhabit it, by the very simple, and yet most difficult process of coming to an understanding of the world."[3] This emphasis on injustice resulting not from "the will of God or any iron law of Nature" but from human action indicates the impulses underlying London's social fiction as these works promote the very process of understanding that he deemed essential to creating a just world. Steinbeck advocated a comparable purpose in his 1962 Nobel Prize acceptance speech. He observed that a writer is "charged with exposing our many grievous faults and failures, with dredging up to the light our dark and dangerous dreams for the purpose of improvement."[4] During the 1930s, Steinbeck had a particular focus for these endeavors, observing in 1938 that every "effort I can bring to bear is and has been at the call of the common working people to the end that they may eat what they raise, wear what they weave, use what they produce and in every way and in completeness share in the works of their hands and their heads."[5] For Steinbeck, literature could play an important role in the struggle for social justice by illuminating the harmful practices that constrain the development of the masses, which could provide an impetus for action.

These passages elucidate a central premise of American naturalism. Critics have often viewed this literary tradition as the application of nineteenth-century science to literature, focusing on the philosophical and artistic contexts of naturalism as they trace how these writers engaged with the insights of biology, psychology, and sociology from fin de siècle America.[6] *Combating Injustice* proposes an alternate focus for American naturalism. This book argues that social criticism offers a unifying thread in the fiction of Norris, London, and Steinbeck, whose major fiction portrays the symptoms of injustice and identifies their causes with the aim of creating a more equitable society. Drawing on original periodical sources for works from *McTeague: A Story of San Francisco* (1899) to *The Grapes of Wrath* (1939), this study analyzes how Norris, London, and Steinbeck engaged with central economic issues of nineteenth- and twentieth-century America. Most notably, these writers drew attention to the concentration of resources, including the ownership of the land; industrial expansion and the rise of mechanization; widespread poverty; and extreme economic inequality.[7] Norris, London, and Steinbeck highlight the dangers of these developments through their impact on the central characters, whose fates result from the practices of powerful institutions and affluent individuals. These depictions showcase the need for social change as they expose the causes of injustice so that their audience could address these conditions before they engendered tragedies similar to those in naturalist works.

The previous scholarship on naturalism has often avoided viewing the movement in terms of social criticism, asserting that such concerns are incompatible with the ideas of determinism within this tradition. Malcolm Cowley contends that naturalists "have no faith in reform, whether it be the reform of an individual by his own decision or the reform of society by reasoned courses of action. The changes they depict are the result of laws and forces and tendencies beyond human control."[8] As a result, the central characters are nothing more than "'human insects' whose brief lives are completely determined by society or nature. The individual is crushed in a moment if he resists; and his struggle, instead of being tragic, is merely pitiful or ironic."[9] V. L. Parrington advances a related view. He observes that for a naturalist, "the individual is impotent in the face of things. Hence it is as the victim, the individual defeated by the world, and made a sardonic jest of, that the naturalist chooses to portray man."[10] Cowley and Parrington contend that naturalists fail to advance a meaningful social critique since they present individuals as the helpless victims of broader forces. Charles Child Walcutt also finds determinism to be inconsistent with ideas of social progress. In *American Literary Naturalism: A Divided Stream* (1956), Walcutt argues that the opposing tendencies of determinism and reform cause a fundamental instability in naturalist novels since an emphasis on characters governed by seemingly insuperable forces does not appear congruent with a belief in human agency.

Many of the major studies of naturalism also obscure the centrality of social criticism to this movement and present deterministic ideas in a manner that does not address the socioeconomic outlook of many naturalist works. Donald Pizer, for instance, asserts that naturalism involves an opposition "between the individually significant and the deterministic" that affirms the importance of the values threatened by the conditioning forces of life.[11] In *Twentieth-Century American Literary Naturalism: An Interpretation* (1982), Pizer contends that naturalists "appeared to be saying that we live in a trivial, banal, and tawdry world which nevertheless encloses us and shapes our destinies. We seek to escape from this world into the inner life because only there do we find the richness of feeling denied us in experience."[12] While this position effectively counters Walcutt's claims about alleged philosophical inconsistencies within naturalism, Pizer's readings de-emphasize the operations of the social structures that are often responsible for shaping the actions of the central characters. This tendency is also apparent in John J.

Conder's *Naturalism in American Fiction: The Classic Phase* (1984) and Lee Clark Mitchell's *Determined Fictions: American Literary Naturalism* (1989). Conder places his argument in philosophical terms, analyzing determinism through the ideas of Thomas Hobbes and Henri Bergson. Conder, however, elides the social significance of naturalist works, and his analysis removes the genre from its ideological origins. Mitchell posits that naturalist writers express deterministic ideas through stylistic devices that call autonomous selfhood into question. Despite this innovative approach to naturalist fiction, Mitchell's focus on style obfuscates the institutional pressures that shape the actions of the central characters.

Other studies have argued that naturalist writers, while appearing to challenge social hierarchies, actually reinforce the ethos of consumer capitalism. In *The Gold Standard and the Logic of Naturalism: American Literature at the Turn of the Twentieth Century* (1987), Walter Benn Michaels examines how naturalist novels operate within a broader cultural framework, arguing that naturalist texts do not advance a meaningful critique of the economic system since they are inextricably linked to the fundamental assumptions of the socioeconomic order they attempt to subvert. Michaels strives "to map out the reality in which a certain literature finds its place and to identify a set of interests and activities that might be said to have as their common denominator a concern with the double identities that seem, in naturalism, to be required if there are to be any identities at all."[13] While texts are undoubtedly shaped by their cultural framework and express meanings beyond those envisioned by their authors, Michaels's approach entails tracing allusions to financial issues in the novels of Norris, Theodore Dreiser, and Edith Wharton, which distorts the complexity of their aesthetic achievements and neglects the actual socioeconomic perspectives they advance. June Howard's *Form and History in American Literary Naturalism* (1985) and Mark Seltzer's *Bodies and Machines* (1992) are more successful in their analyses of how naturalist works often reinforce the classist assumptions of their eras. However, *Combating Injustice* will argue that representations of dehumanized proletarians are embedded within the social criticism of naturalism, offering illustrations of the consequences produced by the present economic system.

Two recent monographs have emphasized the role of social criticism in American naturalism: Ira Wells's *Fighting Words: Polemics and Social Change in Literary Naturalism* (2013) and Cecelia Tichi's *Jack London: A*

Writer's Fight for a Better America (2015). Wells perceives naturalist fiction as an inherently polemical genre, arguing that "the naturalists were helping to chart some of the fundamental coordinates of twentieth-century political and cultural life. . . . The naturalists must be studied because the world they invented in their 'creative writing' is the political world that we inhabit today."[14] Wells focuses on environmental issues in *The Octopus;* abortion and birth control in *An American Tragedy* (1925); and domestic terrorism in *Native Son* (1940), reinforcing assumptions that naturalists were frequently wrong or naive as they often championed positions that modern audiences would find questionable, such as Dreiser's support for euthanasia. By contrast, *Combating Injustice* explores the portrayal of economic issues in naturalism, arguing that Norris, London, and Steinbeck offer insight regarding conditions that remain prevalent in the United States. Tichi makes the case for viewing London as a public intellectual. She contends that this perspective is "fundamental to an understanding of his work and its significance to America's historical development" and that "renewed attention to London's career reveals how a figure of enormous popular appeal and astonishing output in fact exerted great leverage for social change in a critically vital historical moment."[15] Toward this end, Tichi examines London's thought through comparisons with representative figures and discussions of important events rather than analyses of London's fiction. *Combating Injustice,* on the other hand, centers on close readings of London's novels and stories, which were his primary means of fighting injustice, and this study analyzes the economic arguments of these works, connecting them to the treatment of similar themes from Norris and Steinbeck.

Combating Injustice will argue that economic determinism is central to the social criticism in American naturalism. In their portrayals of injustice, Norris, London, and Steinbeck present a conception of determinism that engages with Perry Westbrook's definition of the term as the "doctrine that all occurrences in the universe are governed by inexorable laws of cause and effect."[16] This emphasis on depicting the underlying causes of phenomena reflects the practice of many naturalists. As Émile Zola noted in *Le Roman expérimental* (1880), writers within this tradition "show the mechanism of the useful and the useless, we disengage the determinism of the human and social phenomena so that, in their turn, the legislators can one day dominate and control these phenomena. In a word, we are working with the whole country toward that great object, the conquest of nature and the increase

of man's power a hundredfold."[17] Norris, London, and Steinbeck often identify these causative relations through the practices of those individuals and
institutions that preside over the economic system, delineating how these
agents influence the outcomes available to the protagonists. In this context,
determinism should not be confused with fatalism: these authors are not
suggesting that the forms of injustice are inevitable and immutable; instead,
they demonstrate that such outcomes result from the practices of men and
thereby can be altered by human action. As George Wilbur Meyer observed,
naturalism "is based on the old idea of progress and the perfectibilitarian
principle that man has an infinite capacity for improving himself and his
environment. The purpose of Naturalism, moreover, is primarily utilitarian—
that of stimulating and strengthening man's ability to better his society."[18]
Toward this end, deterministic themes and representations of the forces that
impel the protagonists to ruin supply a means to lay bare the operations of
the socioeconomic system, offering readers a greater awareness of the plight
facing the working class to become agents of social change.

These ideas of determinism provided an effective means to engage with
the social issues that plagued the United States during the nineteenth and
twentieth centuries. Nelson Lichtenstein asserts that during this time,
"industrial and financial institutions secured ever-greater economic and
political power, [and] ordinary Americans of all ethnic backgrounds found
themselves increasingly subject to forces beyond their control. . . . Workers'
earnings and the prices they paid for goods were subject to the impersonal
mechanisms of world trade and to decisions made on behalf of profit in re-
mote corporate boardrooms."[19] These conditions resulted from the transformation of the American economy as the nation shifted from agriculture
to industry, with its reliance on mass production and unskilled labor, and
workers moved from rural areas to the urban environment. This migration
was initiated by the collapse of commodity prices during the final decades
of the nineteenth century: wheat sold for $2.50 a bushel in the late 1860s,
$1.25 in the late 1870s, $1.00 in 1884, and $0.56 in 1894; corn fell from $0.66
in 1866 to $0.21 in 1896; and cotton dropped from $0.24 a pound in 1870 to
less than $0.10 from 1891 to 1903.[20] The workers flooding into cities found
employment in the manufacturing sector, where the majority of employees
earned wages that barely covered basic requirements. While skilled laborers, a group that comprised roughly 15 percent of industrial employees, had
annual incomes that allowed for high standards of living, 45 percent of the

manufacturing workforce during the 1880s barely subsisted on incomes slightly above the poverty line of $500 yearly; 40 percent struggled to survive below this threshold, a quarter of whom lived in destitution.[21] As a result of these circumstances, American workers seemed powerless to impact their fates, which resulted not from their own actions but from the complicated processes of those institutions and individuals that dictated the development of American capitalism.

These concerns emerge in the immediate sources for the major works of Norris, London, and Steinbeck, which originate from events and social conditions in California.[22] From the gold rush to the Great Depression, this state has provided dramatic examples of the central issues that have shaped American life and created drastic consequences for the population. This focus on California stems from the fact that all three writers had strong connections to the state. Though Norris was born in Chicago, he moved to San Francisco in 1884 and, after stints in Paris and New York, spent much of his adult life in the Bay Area. London was born in San Francisco in 1876; spent his formative years in Oakland; and moved to Glen Ellen after he became a successful writer, residing there until his death in 1916. Steinbeck was born in Salinas in 1902, and he lived throughout the state before moving to New York in 1941. These authors long recognized the literary potential of California. In "An Opening for Novelists," for instance, Norris called for writers to "get at the heart of us, the blood and bones and fiber of us, that shall go a-gunning for stories up and down our streets and into our houses and parlors and lodging houses and saloons and dives and along our wharves and into our theatres."[23] In this locale, the novelist could explore a broad cross section of society, especially among those individuals who deviated from middle-class conventions. From events in the Golden State, Norris saw the basis for a literature that could reflect the complexity of modern life and illuminate the forces that animated the unseemly aspects of the human enterprise.

In their use of California history, Norris, London, and Steinbeck present the state as a microcosm for conditions throughout the nation, illuminating the economic issues that influenced American society. Norris, for instance, based *The Octopus: A Story of California* (1901) on the Mussel Slough tragedy of May 11, 1880, a gunfight between ranchers and representatives of the Southern Pacific Railroad in a dispute over land prices. Norris augmented the particulars of this incident with press accounts of the company's manipulation of freight rates during the 1890s, gleaning pertinent details from the

San Francisco Chronicle and *Examiner.*[24] These sources supplied the empirical foundation for Norris's treatment of the causative forces that diminished the opportunities for the working class, and this representation of the railroad's control over California suggests the rise of monopoly capitalism throughout the United States. By the turn of the twentieth century, American Telephone and Telegraph dominated the nation's means of communication, International Harvester made 85 percent of all farm machinery, Standard Oil controlled 90 percent of the refining capacity in America, and consolidation shaped commerce throughout the country.[25] Through presenting the consequences engendered by monopolies, *The Octopus* underscores concerns that were significant to a national audience, which Norris intensifies through his focus on wheat, the staple crop of American farming.

Many of London's works also incorporate events from California into representations of the societal pressures that impact the central characters, and the author would often develop his themes with material that placed occurrences in a national or international context. For instance, "The Apostate" (1906) originated from London's employment as a factory worker at the R. Hickmott Canning Company in Oakland.[26] London supplemented these recollections with periodical accounts of child labor, specifically Juliet Wilbor Tompkins's "Turning Children into Dollars" and Owen R. Lovejoy's "The Modern Slaughter of Innocents," to portray his protagonist's experiences in the workforce and to illustrate the consequences when production is organized around profit rather than human need. "The Dream of Debs" (1909) also had its immediate origins in California, incorporating elements from a 1901 strike in San Francisco that provided background for the fictional general strike. London expanded the focus of the narrative through additional references to labor history, including the rise of the Industrial Workers of the World, within the frame of Eugene Victor Debs's vision of social progress. The dystopia in *The Iron Heel* (1908) also reflects London's America. The author used incidents from well-known labor disputes of the period, including the Haymarket massacre and the Colorado labor wars, and material from Robert Hunter's *Poverty* (1904), Ernest Untermann's *Science and Revolution* (1905), and Henry George's *The Menace of Privilege* (1905).[27] From these sources, London depicted the Iron Heel as the logical extension of elements within his society, expressing the need to check their development before they take the forms presented in the novel.

Steinbeck also utilized events in California that spoke to national issues, which he connected to more universal themes and concerns. *In Dubious Battle* (1936) originated from numerous strikes throughout the state, including one at the Tagus Ranch in August 1933 and another that spread throughout the cotton fields of the San Joaquin Valley that October.[28] These events occurred during a period of intense labor strife throughout the nation. During 1933, there were 1,695 strikes nationwide, a twofold increase over the previous year; in 1934, there were another 1,856 work stoppages that featured 1.5 million individuals.[29] By incorporating multiple walkouts from a period of massive labor upheaval, Steinbeck universalizes the narrative from a depiction of a particular conflict to a broader treatment of labor issues. This focus enabled Steinbeck to expose the conditions that result from the landowners' control over resources, which allows them to pay their workers low wages and subject them to substandard conditions. Steinbeck used a similar approach in *The Grapes of Wrath.* For this novel, he drew on reports written by Tom Collins, head of the Farm Security Administration camp at Arvin, California; accounts of the Salinas lettuce strike of 1936; episodes from the Visalia floods of 1938; and firsthand interactions with itinerant workers.[30] From these sources, Steinbeck's depiction of a representative migrant family presents the exodus to California as the result of economic conditions prevalent throughout the United States while also situating *The Grapes of Wrath* within the contours of American history.

In their artistic responses to these issues, Norris, London, and Steinbeck demonstrate the impact of such practices on the central characters, whose tragedies reflect the plight of the working class within capitalist society. Norris and his contemporaries emphasize those "twisted from the ordinary, wrenched out from the quiet, eventful round of every-day life, and flung into the throes of a vast and terrible drama, that works itself out in unleashed passions, in blood, and in sudden death."[31] In these portrayals, Norris posits that writers should examine the "great, terrible dramas... among the lower—almost the lowest—classes; those who have been thrust or wrenched from the ranks, who are falling by the roadway."[32] Through these characters, naturalists offer powerful illustrations of the tribulations facing marginalized individuals. Accordingly, writers within this tradition present women driven to prostitution through poverty, factory workers reduced to appendages of the machines they tend by modern industrial processes, farmers forced from their ancestral land by large banks, and workers ruthlessly exploited by capital. Although Shelgrim in *The Octopus* and the bankers in *The Grapes of Wrath* attribute such effects to abstract laws of the marketplace, these men orchestrate the practices that create such drastic consequences. The plight of Norris's ranchers, for instance, results from the railroad officials fixing the price of land and setting freight rates to maximize profits. Similarly, the Joads' predicament results from the operations of the banks that force the migrants off their land in Oklahoma, and the family is further exploited by the large growers in California. Through this influence over economic activity, these individuals and institutions bear ultimate responsibility for the plight of the poor.

The social criticism of Norris, London, and Steinbeck further emerges in their characters' attempts to address inequitable circumstances, and these efforts often involve resistance against dominant power. While their protagonists' actions are shaped by environmental pressures and societal forces, these characters are not wholly stripped of agency: they have the capacity to act in pursuit of their interests.[33] Accordingly, Norris, London, and Steinbeck emphasize the defiant conduct that temporarily allows the principals to challenge their exploitation, illustrating both ineffective and potentially effective strategies of resistance. Regarding the former, *McTeague* and *The Octopus* accentuate the limitations of responses to injustice that prioritize the interests of isolated individuals or small groups over the broader constituencies that also suffer under the existing economic structure. Rather than acquiesce to his economic subordination, McTeague lashes out at those whom he deems responsible for his plight, Trina and Marcus Schouler, unaware of the systemic forces that have conditioned his downfall. The ranchers in *The Octopus* actively oppose the Pacific and Southwestern Railroad, first through legal means but then through the bribery scheme, before being driven into the disastrous gunfight. In these works, the principals cannot ultimately forestall their demise, yet these results do not signify the futility of struggle and instead express the need for broader resistance.

London's and Steinbeck's protagonists also resist their exploitation, refusing to accept the constraints of the deterministic world as the only basis for life and attempting to create new models of development through collective action. In "The Apostate," Johnny rejects the factory system, *The Iron Heel* emphasizes the violent conflict between the Oligarchs and the revolutionists, the general strike in "The Dream of Debs" enables the workers to destabilize the hierarchies that have governed American society, and Martin Eden struggles against the restrictions of both his working-class milieu and the bourgeois world. London's proletarians in *The Iron Heel* and "The Dream of Debs" exhibit far greater control over their lives through the collective action that causes them to confront their adversaries from a position of relative strength, options that are not available to the individualistic Martin Eden or the dehumanized protagonist in "The Apostate." Steinbeck's Depression-era fiction also demonstrates the necessity of such resistance. The pickers of *In Dubious Battle* use the organizational structure of the union to defy the growers and their emissaries, while the Joads challenge the prerogatives of private wealth and seek to diminish their adverse effects through acts of compassion. Further, the undertakings of both the union and the migrant family indicate the value of concerted action as a vehicle for progressive change, one that allows the downtrodden to take on those institutions and individuals that misuse their authority.

These depictions reflect the fact that naturalist fiction was primarily directed at middle-class readers who needed to recognize both the ravages of American capitalism and the tenuous nature of their class positions. As Cecelia Tichi notes, the middle class "enjoyed leisure time to read and sufficient income to buy books and to subscribe to magazines that published the facts about child labor, wretched wages, poor housing, and workplace hazards. The bourgeoisie, in addition, held authoritative positions of responsibility and civic leadership in their communities. They wielded power and exerted influence. Any activist efforts to shape public opinion to redirect the socioeconomic future must in some measure include them."[34] For Norris, London, and Steinbeck, the middle class could play a central role in the process of social change as their privileged class position would allow them significant opportunities to confront the powerful and impact policy. First, however, this audience would need to be exposed to the effects of contemporary conditions and recognize the urgency to challenge the existing basis of economic power. This idea is central to *The Iron Heel*. The novel focuses on Avis's conversion to socialism from her privileged background when she witnesses the plight of the working class and the impediments to their progress, which helps her understand the need for systemic change. By aligning the text with the perspective of one who initially parallels a privileged audience and showing how she becomes a committed revolutionist, London highlights the necessary transformation that individuals must undergo to work toward meaningful change. Norris, London, and Steinbeck also direct their appeals to the economic self-interest of their audience. Toward this end, *The Iron*

Heel also offers the examples of affluent groups that do not heed these lessons through the farmers and minor industrialists who are ruined by the predatory practices of the Oligarchy. Such portrayals highlight how the prosperous could also be victimized by the current economic order and indicate that they need to align themselves with labor in the broader struggle against capital.

In developing the social criticism in their major works, Norris, London, and Steinbeck engage with what became known as the American Dream. Though this concept dates back to some of the earliest European settlements in North America, the term itself first appears in Walter Lippmann's *Drift and Mastery* (1914).[35] The American Dream gained its clearest expression in James Truslow Adams's *Epic of America* (1931) as "the dream of a land in which life should be fuller for every man, with opportunity for each according to his ability or achievement" that results from "a social order in which each man and each woman shall be able to attain to the fullest stature of which they are innately capable, and be recognized by others for what they are, regardless of the fortuitous circumstances of birth or position."[36] According to Jennifer Hochschild, the American Dream "promises that everyone, regardless of ascription or background, may reasonably seek success through action and traits under their own control."[37] In such formulations, the American Dream is predicated on the beliefs that people can shape their destinies, that conditions in the United States would allow the higher aptitudes of men and women to germinate in the pursuit of prosperity, and that their potential for progress would be limited only by their willingness to apply themselves through diligent labor.

In this context, the California settings in the fiction of Norris, London, and Steinbeck have an additional resonance due to the popular representations of the state as a land of opportunity. Beginning with the gold rush of 1848, California has symbolized the possibilities at the center of the American imagination since the abundant land and plentiful resources of the state seemed to offer the potential for greater economic opportunities. The initial accounts of prospectors reflected the central virtues of the American Dream, reinforcing the idea of labor as the guarantor of advancement. In the spring of 1850, a correspondent for the *Belleville (IL) Advocate* claimed that no "one should think of coming here to pick up a fortune without work; but, whoever is willing to live on flap-jacks, and pickled pork, and can carry dirt in a bag half of a day and 'rock the cradle' the other half, the chances are 99 to 1, that he will make from 5 to 10 thousand dollars every year he stays in California."[38]

While the discourse surrounding the gold rush reflected conventional formulations of the American Dream, developments in California shifted this
concept from its historical moorings. H. W. Brands contends that the "old
American dream, the dream inherited from ten generations of ancestors, was
the dream of the Puritans, of Benjamin Franklin's Poor Richard, of Thomas
Jefferson's yeoman farmers: of men and women content to accumulate their
modest fortunes a little at a time, year by year by year. The new dream was
the dream of instant wealth, won in a twinkling by audacity and good luck."[39]
This newfound emphasis on accumulation contributed to a socioeconomic
order with few opportunities for all workers. The majority of migrants to California found that their dreams of affluence resulted in poverty and exploitation, which reflected the circumstances facing the working class throughout
the nation. The experiences of working people during the nineteenth and
twentieth centuries have troubling implications for the validity of the American Dream, suggesting that individuals have limited control over their economic fates as their opportunities are increasingly thwarted by dominant
social institutions.

Norris, London, and Steinbeck expose the discrepancy between a dominant concept of the American experience and its application to life in the
United States, expressing the need to alter the structures that often impede
mobility so that the nation can live up to its ideals. While "The Apostate"
and *In Dubious Battle* present characters who cannot gain economic mobility, Norris, London, and Steinbeck often take a more nuanced approach. In
some instances, these writers emphasize the plight of characters who cannot maintain their social standing because of economic pressures. In *The
Octopus,* the growers occupy a tenuous position within the economic order
because of the dominance of the Pacific and Southwestern Railroad, which
undermines the gains made by the ranchers. In *The Iron Heel,* London traces
the impact that an intensification of current conditions would have on the
middle class, whose members are victimized by the Oligarchy's manipulation of the socioeconomic system. These texts engage with concerns of immediate relevance to many readers, suggesting that all individuals within
capitalism are susceptible to economic pressures.

The Grapes of Wrath and *Martin Eden* (1909)provide more complex illustrations of these themes. In the former, the Joads have fallen from an independent existence as landowners, and they must leave Oklahoma in search
of brighter opportunities. Nonetheless, the family is relatively fixed in its

economic position: no matter what they do and where they go, the Joads lack the means to improve their lives. This focus on a group of people whose prospects do not really change expresses a heightened realism in *The Grapes of Wrath*. *Martin Eden* differs from the other texts by centering on a figure who becomes affluent through his incessant labor to become a writer. However, Martin's individualistic aims allow for acquisition but do not lead him to realize the romantic and intellectual aspirations that he defines as the measures of success, and the narrator connects the young man's failure to achieve his true objectives to his alienation from his fellow workers, which turns his apparent success into a broader failure. In the portrayal of Martin's resulting disillusionment, London advances a powerful indictment of the bourgeoisie through representing the intellectual and moral bankruptcy of a socioeconomic order that reduces all human endeavors to commodities.

The works of Norris, London, and Steinbeck are aligned with these struggles for justice against the practices of powerful social institutions that often dictate the opportunities available to the working class. Through an engagement with the conditions facing American laborers, these authors complicate conventional narratives of progress in order to address the underlying economic causes that influence human behavior. By portraying how these causative agents adversely impact the general population and connecting the outcomes to significant developments in U.S. history, Norris, London, and Steinbeck illustrate the need for the transformation of the socioeconomic system in a manner that will improve the material circumstances of the general population.

1

TWISTED FROM THE ORDINARY

Economic Determinism in Frank Norris's McTeague

Frank Norris played a central role in the development of American natural-ism. Reflecting on this broader significance, Joseph R. McElrath Jr. observes that "Norris registered dramatically the transition from the age of Emerson, Thoreau, and Whitman to that of Fitzgerald and Steinbeck. More specifi-cally, he signaled the movement away from Victorian cultural values—and especially from the defunct metaphysical idealism that Zola so despised to the more positivistic and pragmatic modern sensibility at the turn of the century."[1] Norris's contributions to naturalism are evident in *McTeague,* which focuses on a former miner who has started a dental practice in San Francisco and whose fortunes are bolstered when his fiancée, Trina Sieppe, wins five thousand dollars in the lottery. This emphasis on advancement situates the narrative within the national success story as McElrath notes that McTeague "is the kind of individual one might point to when celebrat-ing the American Dream" in the first half of the work.[2] However, the second half of the novel traces the couple's deterioration as a result of economic pressures after McTeague is forced to close his dental office. According to Lawrence E. Hussman, *McTeague* suggests the emptiness of the American Dream "as a subset of the pervasive disillusionment that always follows hard on the single-minded pursuit of the objects of our desires."[3] Norris's engage-ment with the American Dream reflects his thematic preoccupation with the workings of heredity and environment, connecting his characters' plights to financial pressures that activate remnants of man's animal past.[4] Through this emphasis on economic determinism, *McTeague* illustrates that individ-uals rarely transcend the restrictions of their surroundings. This portrayal of ideas related to the American Dream helps to develop the social criticism of the novel, highlighting the consequences of poverty on the individual and expressing the dangers of acquisition when severed from ethical constraints.

Norris is a unique figure in American literature since he, unlike his contemporaries, discussed his works in relation to naturalism. In a letter to Isaac Frederick Marcosson explaining the Epic of Wheat trilogy he envisioned, Norris wrote that in *The Octopus,* "I am going back *definitely* to the style of MacT. and stay with it right along. . . . The Wheat series will be straight naturalism with all the guts I can get into it."[5] Norris's conception of naturalist fiction stems from his immersion in the work of Émile Zola, to whom Norris referred in numerous articles.[6] In "Zola as Romantic Writer," Norris observed that the "world of M. Zola is a world of big things; the enormous, the formidable, the terrible is what counts; no teacup tragedies here."[7] The reference to "teacup tragedies" establishes a contrast between Zola and the realism of William Dean Howells, with its portrayals of average, middle-class individuals in a manner that would be appropriate for all readers.[8] This tension between Zola and Howells establishes a primary component of Norris's conception of naturalism as a synthesis of the verisimilitude of realism and the philosophical depth associated with romanticism. Norris asserts that romanticism "is the kind of fiction that takes cognizance of variations from the type of normal life. Realism is the kind of fiction that confines itself to the type of normal life."[9] For Norris, this practice illustrates the surface of existence rather than the impulses and forces that animate experience, which thereby offers a limited examination of terrestrial life. Norris identifies romanticism as a means of transcending this approximation of superficial forms to trace "the unplumbed depths of the human heart, and the mystery of sex, and the problems of life, and the black, unsearched penetralia of the soul of man."[10] In this view, novelists should not confine themselves to reproducing the tangible world with photographic accuracy; instead, they should strive to reveal the forces that govern the actions of men and women. This understanding explicates the ideas underlying Norris's fiction.

Norris does not portray naturalism as a primarily aesthetic enterprise but as a means to develop a deeper understanding of human affairs, to expose injustice, and to ultimately engender meaningful change. In "The Novel with a 'Purpose,'" Norris claims that the best class of books "proves something, draws conclusions from a whole congeries of forces, social tendencies, race impulses, devotes itself not to a study of men but of man."[11] This desire to probe the inner workings of people and society speaks directly to the central premise of naturalist fiction, with its basis of explaining the forces that govern individuals and limit their possible outcomes. Norris further contends that in these narratives, the "social tendencies must be expressed by means of analysis of the characters of the men and women who compose that society, and the two must be combined and manipulated to evolve the purpose—to find the value of *x*."[12] In "The Responsibilities of the Novelist," Norris declares that the people "have a right to the Truth as they have a right to life, liberty, and the pursuit of happiness. It is *not* right that they be exploited and deceived with false views of life, false characters, false sentiment, false morality, false history, false philosophy, false emotions, false heroism, false notions of self-sacrifice, false views of religion, of duty, of conduct, and of manners."[13] For Norris, writers must be conscious of the social function of their works, and literature should reveal a fundamental truth about experience as it appears to the author, who should represent these observations in a manner that informs and directs readers to purposeful action.

The California setting of *McTeague* supplied an appropriate background for an examination of these concerns. Discussing the literary possibilities of the Golden State, Norris wrote, "I think there is a chance for somebody to do some great work with the West and California as a background, and which will be at the same time thoroughly American."[14] These ideas also emerge in "The Literature of the West," in which Norris responded to William R. Lighton's call for propriety to guide depictions of the region. Norris argued that such idealized depictions pose a broader problem since this part of the country has "the material, Homer found no better, the heroes, the great fights, the play of unleashed, unfettered passionate humanity, and we let it all go, this national epic of America, the only one we shall ever have," in favor of outmoded European models and formulaic tales of adventure, like Deadwood Dick.[15] For Norris, California could provide the basis for an epic national literature if writers would probe beneath superficial respectability to the forces that animate this area and its inhabitants. Toward this end, the writer needs to understand the history of the state to grasp the reality of current circumstances as this past continues to shape the present. Norris asserts that under the surface of the prosperous, respectable westerner, one will find "the Forty-niner. There just beneath the veneer is the tough fibre of the breed, whose work since the beginning of the nineteenth century has been the subjugating of the West."[16] For Norris, the pressures unleashed by the gold rush still played a pivotal role in modern California, and severing these elements from the texts about this locale would compromise their validity.

As Norris asserted, the gold rush shaped modern California, with implications for the nation as a whole. Kevin Starr notes that in "just about every way possible—its internationalism, its psychology of expectation ... its rapid creation of a political, economic, and technological infrastructure—the Gold Rush established, for better or for worse, the founding patterns, the DNA code, of American California."[17] These elements began to emerge when James W. Marshall discovered gold in January 1848, which initiated an influx of migrants to the West after the press accentuated the possibility for instant wealth in California. According to one story, gold was *"so abundant that there is not necessity for washing the earth; $700 per day is the amount by each man."*[18] Other stories exaggerated the potential for prosperity in California, with accounts that captured the popular imagination through the references to El Dorado, *La Bonanza,* "the Age of Gold," Hernán Cortés, Francisco Pizarro, and Ponce de León, which connected Marshall's findings to the mythic associations of California.[19] In the year following President James Polk's announcement that the precious metal had been discovered, the non–Native American population of the state increased from less than ten thousand in 1848 to 255,000 by 1851.[20] Describing the 49ers, Hubert Howe Bancroft observed that those the gold rush brought into California were "the toiling farmer, whose mortgage loomed above the growing family, the briefless lawyer, the starving student, the quack, the idler, the harlot, the gambler, the hen-pecked husband, the disgraced; with many earnest, enterprising honest men and devoted women."[21] In pursuit of this seemingly limitless wealth, these individuals braved the treacherous path to California, which would claim the lives of one traveler in twelve.[22] Initially, the potential rewards seemed to outweigh these risks as $594 million in ingots, or $10 billion in 2001 dollars, was extracted from the goldfields over the next decade.[23]

The experiences of those who came to California during this period did not reflect the dominant narrative of progress. Instead of providing widespread prosperity, the material benefits of this period were concentrated among a narrow segment of the population. Opportunities for economic expansion were available in 1848, when some 6,000 miners discovered nearly $10 million in gold, and this sum tripled in 1849, yet the number of gold seekers increased to over 40,000; in 1852, the peak year, the output was $80

million, but there were 100,000 people working claims.[24] As a result, most
prospectors found themselves laboring harder for less income, which decreased from a high of $20 a day in 1848, to $16 in 1849, to $10 in 1850, and
down to $3 by 1856.[25] Although such figures seem high by the standards of the
nineteenth century, these earnings were often insufficient to cover the high
prices of goods and services in the mining districts. Reflecting on his experiences in a camp near Mariposa, one prospector explained that the "price
of provisions had become so high that our paltry earnings were not nearly
sufficient to pay for the food we required to keep us alive. Flour was $1 a lb,
pork the same, Chilian [sic] jerky (dried beef) half a dollar to 75 cents, tea
$5, coffee $3, frijoles (dried beans) about half a dollar, and everything else in
the same proportion."[26] Californians had no relief in San Francisco, where a
pick or shovel sold for $10, a tin pan or wooden bowl for $5, a butcher's knife
for $30, a loaf of bread for 50 cents, and a hard-boiled egg for a dollar.[27] The
high costs of essential goods and services undermined the ability of average
individuals to attain prosperity or to even live decently as they continued to
work long hours for decreasing returns.

As opposed to ushering in a new era of general prosperity, the gold rush
produced conditions of desperation and poverty that aroused the worst aspects of human nature. David Vaught asserts that as "the prospects for individuals to strike it rich declined and all but disappeared by 1852, depression
and disillusionment descended over the picked-over goldfields, where elation
and dreams had abounded only a short time before."[28] This disenchantment
is reflected in the miners' journals, which are replete with incidents of crime
and its consequences. On August 29, 1851, a miner named Garrett Low wrote
that it "is an everyday occurrence . . . to see a coffin carried on the shoulders
of two men, who are the only mourners and only witnesses of the burial of
some stranger whose name they do not know."[29] Another prospector, William
Perkins, observed that it "is surprising . . . how indifferent people become to
the sight of violence and bloodshed in this country."[30] These accounts do not
represent isolated incidents; rather, they are indicative of life in the mining communities and larger cities that emerged during this time. As John
Boessenecker has demonstrated, the murder rate during this period was
astronomically high: Sonora had 506.6 homicides per 100,000 inhabitants
in 1850–51, which was fifty times the national homicide rate for 1999.[31] Outside of the gold regions, conditions were also quite dangerous: in San Francisco between 1849 and 1856, the figure was 49 per 100,000, six times that

for 1997; in Los Angeles between 1850 and 1851, the number peaked at 1,240 per 100,000.[32] The material promise of the gold rush had transformed into a scramble for riches that left many behind, which would also characterize conditions throughout the following decades.

These developments in California had a significant impact on American ideology. As Kevin Starr observes, the economic activity of California was characterized by "an essential selfishness and an underlying instability, a fixation upon the quick acquisition of wealth, an impatience with the more subtle premises of human happiness. These were American traits, to be sure, but the gold rush intensified and consolidated them as part of a regional experience."[33] As a result of the immense gains possible for some in California, capital accumulation began to be seen as the goal in itself, and the institutional structure that emerged over the following decades prioritized acquisition over more humane concerns. Glenn Porter observes that these changes undermined the values that once defined the nation: the "belief in competition and democracy, the goals of producing and saving, the idea that individuals could rise by their own efforts to wealth and power—or at least to something close to self-sufficiency—all seemed overshadowed by the giant corporations whose influence came to be felt in virtually every city and town across the land."[34] Commenting on the ethos that emerged during the following period, Ray Ginger notes that no "personal feelings or humanitarian considerations should be allowed to interfere with the duty of making a profit," and Walter Licht posits that production and consumption "became totally oriented toward selling and buying in the marketplace and that everything—goods, land, labor, even time—became valued accordingly by the calculus of supply and demand and the cash nexus."[35] This pursuit of wealth unhindered by ethical strictures drastically changed the nature of the national mythos and had a significant impact on the opportunities available to the general population.

These concerns are central to *McTeague,* which traces the fictive possibilities of California and explores the socioeconomic conditions that emerged in the state following the gold rush. The inspiration for *McTeague* stems from a homicide in San Francisco on October 10, 1893, when Patrick Collins killed his estranged wife in the cloakroom of a kindergarten where she worked as a charwoman after she refused to give him money. The newspaper reports suggest the plot of Norris's novel and correspond to many of its central themes. These connections emerge through the portrayal of Collins: "Whenever he got drunk he beat [his wife], and if she did not give him money he knocked her down."[36] This element of the coverage evokes the protagonist's violence toward Trina, and the economic context of this abuse mirrors Norris's representation. *McTeague* has further parallels to accounts of Collins's crime as a reporter for the *San Francisco Chronicle* declared that the killer continues "to bear himself with a stolid, brutish indifference that marks him as a type of all that is low in humanity."[37] A correspondent for the *San Francisco Examiner* advanced similar ideas, asserting that Collins's "face is not degraded, but brutish. That is to say, he is not a man who has sunk, but one who was made an animal by nature to start with. The face is broad, the brown eyes are set wide apart, the nose is flattened at the bridge and as broad as a negro's. The jaw is heavy and cruel."[38] This passage expresses the primary characteristics of McTeague, whom the narrator describes through extensive animal imagery, and the reference to the pronounced jaw found its way into the text as it reinforces Cesare Lombroso's beliefs about physical markings of criminality. This piece also features a possible source of the parallel between the dog fight and the conflict between McTeague and Marcus Schouler, the dentist's erstwhile friend and rival for Trina's affection. The writer closed by stating that one has "seen a chained bulldog bare his teeth and growl softly when a kind word was tossed to him. That is Collins."[39] However, the writer attempts to understand the deed from Collins's perspective and to comprehend the circumstances that gave rise to the killing, a strategy that anticipates Norris's approach in the book.

The Collins case provided the initial conception of *McTeague*, which Norris developed in eight student themes while studying at Harvard University under Lewis E. Gates. These assignments, written between January 7 and March 8, 1895, chiefly emphasize the protagonist's drunkenness and brutality toward Trina. The last installment provides a synopsis for the narrative that expresses the economic themes of the work, linking the protagonist's fate to financial pressures rather than biological forces as his drinking stems from the loss of his profession and his violence results from increasing poverty.[40] These thematic concerns are also evident through the dentist's return to the mines where he spent his youth, a movement that conveys his inability to transcend the restrictions of his early environment. Despite these connections, many significant aspects of *McTeague* are not present in this early summary, most notably Trina's compulsive avarice. Further, Norris had apparently not conceived of the two subplots since they do not appear in the outline; he does not present the McTeagues' courtship; and he does not mention Marcus, although this character appears in a previous episode. Other installments present embryonic versions of scenes that Norris would develop in *McTeague:* a theme focuses on the protagonist's Sunday routine in a form similar to that in the novel; one describes the central character at the gallery opening that appears in chapter 10; and another presents Trina's death in a manner consistent with chapter 19. These projects represent the earliest treatment of the materials that would become *McTeague,* yet Norris did not complete the manuscript until the fall of 1897. He submitted the text to Doubleday & McClure in early 1898, shortly after he began working for the firm; however, publication was delayed until February 1899 because of qualms about the realistic content and sordid nature of the narrative.

From the raw materials of the Collins case and ideas explored in the Harvard themes, Norris created an exploration of the extent to which people are masters of their fates. The opening of the novel seems to establish the protagonist as a figure for the progress possible in nineteenth-century America as McTeague has ascended from the working class to a lower-middle-class existence. The narrator refers to the protagonist's mother, a cook in his father's mining camp, as "an overworked drudge, fiery and energetic for all that, filled with the one idea of having her son rise in life and enter a profession."[41] This passage presents America as an open society where men and women from all ranks could achieve mobility, and Norris further underscores this development through McTeague's ethnic background. Hugh Dawson identifies the dentist as an Irishman because *Teague* was often employed as a derogatory term for those of Celtic ancestry, and his propensity for alcohol situates him within nineteenth-century representations of this group.[42] As such, the arc of McTeague's life evokes the ideas of material advancement that appealed to immigrants to the United States, who had left their homelands for opportunities to attain higher living standards or to enable such outcomes for their progeny. Norris further develops the potential for mobility in the United States by emphasizing the intellectual limitations of the central character, whose mind is "heavy, slow to act, sluggish," and who is animated by unconscious drives rather than rational thought (6). These references seem to suggest that one's ability to rise in America is not predicated on innate qualities and that the restrictions governing human potential are inapplicable to the New World for those willing to labor diligently.

However, Norris destabilizes McTeague's material progress through the economic context that frames the actions of the characters, and even the references to his mobility highlight the tensions that imperil his social position. The narrator observes that McTeague's hands were "hard as wooden mallets, strong as vises, the hands of the old-time carboy" and that "he suggested a draught horse, immensely strong, stupid, docile, obedient." The association between the dentist and a draft horse links McTeague to his former occupation as these animals were often used in the early days of the mining industry. The narrator heightens this connection by noting that McTeague "dispensed with forceps and extracted a refractory tooth with his thumb and finger" (6). The strength developed in his previous environment helps him in his new profession yet makes him out of place within middle-class society. These elements emerge in the opening paragraphs, which outline the protagonist's Sunday routine and introduce the prominent imagery of consumption that unifies the narrative. Describing this routine, the narrator states that "McTeague took his dinner at two in the afternoon at the car conductors' coffee-joint on Polk Street. He had a thick, gray soup; heavy, underdone meat, very hot, on a cold plate; two kinds of vegetables; and a sort of suet pudding, full of strong butter and sugar. On his way back to his office, one block above, he stopped at Joe Frenna's saloon and bought a pitcher of steam beer" (5). This description reflects the central attributes of McTeague through references to the words "thick," "heavy," and "strong," which appear throughout the text in relation to the dentist, indicating that he is governed by the basic animal instinct for food, a desire that intensifies in the second movement of the novel.

The narrator juxtaposes this imagery of consumption with the first references to gold, which serve as an important motif throughout the work.[43] In describing the dental parlors, the narrator refers to the aesthetic objects in McTeague's possession, most notably the canary in its gilded cage. The imprisonment of this bird alludes to both the economic framework that confines the central characters and the protagonist's earlier life as canaries were once used in mines to indicate the presence of poisonous gases.[44] The narrator further accentuates the importance of gold to the narrative when he mentions McTeague's purchase of "a steel engraving of the court of Lorenzo de' Medici, which he had bought because there were a great many figures in it for the money" (6). As Nan Morelli-White observes, the inclusion of Medici is significant in that he presided over the golden age of Florence, and this context connects the engraving to the broader patterns that Norris employs in this chapter, while McTeague's emphasis on obtaining a bargain reflects the preoccupation with material concerns that animates each of the principal characters, to varying degrees.[45] Norris underscores this point through linking the dentist to this precious metal through the mats that he uses in his patients' fillings and his prominent crop of yellow hair, elements that make him the figurative embodiment of gold and suggest its power over his life.

Norris further develops the economic context of *McTeague* when he describes Polk Street, which provides a microcosm for dominant society and expresses how class relations shape human interactions. When McTeague looks out his window at the street below, he observes

> drug stores with huge jars of red, yellow, and green liquids in their windows, very brave and gay; stationers' stores, where illustrated weeklies were tacked upon bulletin boards; barber shops with cigar stands in their vestibules; sad-looking plumbers' offices; cheap restaurants, in whose windows one saw piles of unopened oysters weighted down by cubes of ice, and china pigs and cows knee deep in layers of white beans. At one end of the street McTeague could see the huge power-house of the cable line. Immediately opposite him was a great market; while further on, over the chimney stacks of the intervening houses, the glass roof of some huge public baths glittered like crystal in the afternoon sun. (7)

This description privileges the manifestations of middle-class life through the commodities that demonstrate one's social position, and the acquisition of these articles animates the inhabitants. As David McGlynn posits, Norris stresses the confining nature of these interests through images of bars that allude to the canary's cage from the roof of the baths, the cables of the streetcar line, and the goods in the shop windows.[46] In this framework, Norris introduces McTeague's desire for the gilded molar to present an outward sign of his professional status.[47] However, the "enormous prongs" of the molar also evoke bars, which offer another parallel to the canary's enclosure and indicate that the dentist is trapped within the material aspirations of his surroundings. The class-based temporal and spatial relations on Polk Street reinforce this sense of confinement. The narrator observes that each day begins with the appearance of the newsboys and common laborers, who are followed by the street and municipal workers, the shop clerks and office employees, and then the "ladies from the great avenue a block above Polk Street made their appearance, promenading the sidewalks leisurely, deliberately" (8). This description of nearly two pages not only emphasizes the rigid order of this locale but also illustrates that monetary concerns dictate people's roles within the panorama of existence.

These impulses determine the perspectives of the central characters, who act in accordance with the economic imperatives of their surroundings. The narrator situates Trina in this fiscal climate through her wedding preparations when she "spent the morning between nine and twelve o'clock down town, for the most part in the cheap department stores" and would meet McTeague "breathless from her raids upon the bargain counters" before showing him what she had purchased, while discussing at length the prices of these items (76). Norris locates these excursions during the couple's period of domestic tranquility, yet the focus on acquisition reflects the tensions responsible for their fates later in the novel. The narrator links Trina's thrift to her genetic inheritance, asserting that she "had all the instinct of a hardy and penurious mountain people—the instinct which saves without any thought, without idea of consequence—saving for the sake of saving, hoarding without knowing why" (78–79). While the narrator emphasizes hereditary determinism through Trina's Swiss-German ancestry, the initial presentation of this idea is framed by the dictates of a commodity culture. This connection implies that environmental forces trigger this impulse for accumulation, and this reading gains further credence through the intensification of her hoarding after McTeague is prohibited from practicing dentistry.

Norris parallels this theme through Maria Macapa, who works as a cleaning lady in McTeague's building and also operates in line with the desires of dominant society. The narrator describes Maria's routine of collecting useless items that she would sell to Zerkow, a junk dealer, in exchange for money to spend "on shirt waists and dotted blue neckties, trying to dress like the girls who tended the soda-water fountain in the candy store" who "were elegant, they were debonair, they had their 'young men'" (23). Maria's yearning for these articles displays the controlling power of her environment, which limits her vision to the extent that she views shop girls as barometers of achievement and provides her with few opportunities for mobility. Maria's oft-repeated tale of the golden dinner service functions in this context, representing the outward forms of affluence to signal a higher class position, and she has been shaped by this milieu to the point that even her delusions originate within this framework.

These motifs of consumption frame McTeague and Trina's coupling, suggesting that their interactions operate within economic considerations rather than the biological impulses often employed to explain their behavior. George M. Spangler assigns a central role to sexual determinism as the primary force that necessitates the fates of the central characters. Spangler asserts that in "the first part the overall idea is that man's instincts, especially his sexual desire, have great power to trap and degrade him," while the second section of the novel reveals that "female sexuality is threatening and finally destructive to men."[48] Although McTeague and Trina act in accordance with biological drives, Norris situates these appetites within patterns of commodification. The narrator identifies Trina in the context of the "younger women of Polk Street—the shop girls, the young women of the soda fountains, the waitresses in the cheap restaurants" and notes that "Trina was McTeague's first experience. With her the feminine element suddenly entered his little world. It was not only her that he saw and felt, it was the woman, the whole sex, an entire new humanity, strange and alluring, that he seemed to have discovered. How had he ignored it so long? It was dazzling, delicious, charming beyond all words. His narrow point of view was at once enlarged and confused, and all at once he saw that there was something else in life besides concertinas and steam beer. Everything had to be made over again. His whole rude idea of life had to be changed" (19). The association of Trina with those who sell the consumer goods that impressed McTeague early in the novel indicates that his lust is connected to his desire to consume. In this context, the importance of objects stems from the value individuals attribute to them rather than any intrinsic worth. A similar logic governs McTeague's relationship with Trina since he wants not a particular woman but "the whole sex, an entire new humanity," which makes Trina as replaceable as any of the products that line Polk Street.

McTeague emphasizes Trina's function within the domestic economy, viewing her as a sexualized commodity to be consumed in the gratification of male desire. Norris heightens this development when McTeague spends the night at the home of Trina's family after their first date. As he opens Trina's closet to rummage through her clothes, the narrator observes that it "was not only her hair now, it was Trina herself—her mouth, her hands, her neck," and that, "seized with an unreasoned impulse, McTeague opened his huge arms and gathered the little garments close to him, plunging his face deep amongst them, savoring their delicate odor with long breaths of luxury and supreme content" (47–48). McTeague defines Trina in terms of her clothes, comparable to the garments that populate the stores on Polk Street, which further reduces her to the status of an object to satisfy his carnal appetites. Norris exhibits this idea of subjugation through the juxtaposition between the "huge arms" of the protagonist and the "little garments" of Trina, and the resulting dialectic between strength and frailty reinforces the nature of their courtship, with McTeague's gathering of the garments anticipating his later crushing embraces of the heroine. Describing the methods employed to win Trina, the narrator states that "he only had to take her in his arms, to crush down her struggle with his enormous strength, to subdue her, conquer her by sheer brute force" (52). This focus on McTeague's aspiration to possess Trina irrespective of her conscious wishes signifies her status as a sexualized commodity. This perspective demonstrates the extent to which interactions in the narrative are shaped by market forces, and Norris's emphasis on acquisition in this relationship prefigures the central tensions responsible for the characters' deterioration.

The narrator develops the economic themes of *McTeague* through the lottery, which provides for the advancement of the couple, yet Norris reinforces the tenuous nature of their progress through juxtaposing it against conventional formulations of the American Dream. When Trina learns that she has won five thousand dollars, the assembled neighbors and the agent recount "the legends and myths that had grown up around the history of the lottery" and conclude that "it was the needy who won, the destitute and starving woke to wealth and plenty, the virtuous toiler suddenly found his reward in a ticket bought at a hazard; the lottery was a great charity, the friend of the people, a vast beneficent machine that recognized neither rank nor wealth nor station" (67–68). This account reveals the contours of the national success story, presenting this sweepstakes as an embodiment of the narrative of progress with riches as the reward for virtuous conduct. The emphasis on achievement with regard to "neither rank nor wealth nor station" denotes the potential for mobility due to individual initiative within a social structure that does not lock people into the positions of their births.[49] However, the fact that this movement does not manifest through human efforts underscores the shifting nature of American life. In this formulation, fortunes occur independently of merit, transpiring purely as a result of luck, as a mere gamble with the odds stacked against the aspirant. The role of the lottery as a vehicle for prosperity further highlights the problematic basis of such an occurrence, which stems from the operations of chance and only pertains to a lucky few.

The relative absence of labor in *McTeague* also accentuates the transforming basis of the American Dream and undermines the apparent progress of McTeague and Trina. The descriptions of the employees on Polk Street emphasize those in the service economy, providing no images of people heading to the factories to produce essential commodities. Despite the fact that some minor figures are connected to manufacturing and McTeague is briefly employed by a firm that makes dental equipment, Norris seldom presents his principals in the process of working. Although the initial chapters are set primarily in the protagonist's parlors, these episodes stress the limited ability of McTeague, who spends more time reclined on his operating chair than engaged in his profession, and Norris further destabilizes McTeague's career through his lack of a license to practice dentistry. Trina is shown carving figurines for her uncle Olbermann's toy company; however, the narrator largely focuses on the "non-poisonous" paint that causes the loss of several fingers and necessitates the shift to another position. Maria and Zerkow operate in a slightly different context, serving as figurative miners who sift through refuse for potentially valuable items in a manner that evokes those who preceded them to California in order to find gold. Norris also links both individuals to this precious metal with Maria stealing mats from McTeague and Zerkow ransacking his rooms for the illusory dinner service. The representations of the central characters' occupations stem from the function of Polk Street as a business district rather than an industrial one, yet the emphasis on this segment of the population draws attention to an environment where acquisition is severed from production and has become the objective for its own sake.

The McTeagues' advancement culminates during the chapters surrounding their marriage, which situate these characters within the middle class through conventional markers of affluence while also illustrating the material tensions that will be responsible for the pair's deterioration. Norris highlights this striving for bourgeois respectability through the depiction of the couple's flat. As Don Graham notes, the descriptions of their first dwelling, with the Grandma and Grandpa pictures and assorted bric-a-brac, "express perfectly the infantile, sentimental quality of Trina's mind. They echo a motif developed at length in the meeting and courtship of McTeague and Trina: the childlike state of their sexual awareness."[50] This representation of innocence correlates to a broader economic context based on accumulating objects. The wallpaper, with its hundreds of Japanese mandarins, reflects Trina's concern with numbers. This reference implies her future interest in counting her gold pieces, and this effect is intensified by the cramped apartment teeming with decorative items. The account of the wedding banquet further underscores the emphasis on consumption through illustrations of gluttony. This tendency is most apparent in McTeague, who "ate for the sake of eating, without choice; everything within reach of his hands found its way into his enormous mouth" (97). This passage reinforces the protagonist's unreasoned existence in the context of naturalistic treatments of individuals governed by forces that they cannot control, evident through the dentist's lack of choice. Further, the focus on food suggests McTeague's central preoccupation with gratifying his animal instincts. His desire to eat without knowing why anticipates Trina's irrational impulse to hoard her savings and prefigures the primary conflict between the characters in the second half of the novel.

The narrator further reveals the problematic nature of McTeague and Trina's coupling through imagery that pertains to warfare and death. When Mr. Sieppe leads the groom to the ceremony, the narrator states that it "was like King Charles summoned to execution" and that the procession "moved at a funereal pace," while the song that follows the reception "became a dirge, a lamentable, prolonged wail of distress" (93, 99). These associations anticipate the fates of McTeague and Trina, whose union will become a prolonged battle as a result of the economic pressures that govern their actions. Norris reinforces this point through the aftermath of the wedding banquet as the narrator observes the skeleton of the roast goose; the calf's skull; and the empty champagne bottles referred to as "dead soldiers" on the mantelpiece; noting that the scene "was a devastation, a pillage; the table presented the appearance of an abandoned battlefield" (99). This representation of destruction during what should be a joyous event underscores the fissures that compromise the stability of the McTeagues' union, and the use of these images to describe the feast depicts the cause of this conflict in the tension between consumption and the satisfaction of human needs.

This focus animates the subsequent chapters, which trace the McTeagues' attempts to enhance their social position. These impulses are initially apparent through Trina's efforts to remove the lingering traces of McTeague's common origins and to further situate him within the bourgeoisie. Trina makes her husband give up his usual Sunday routine in favor of activities more properly befitting their current economic standing, with walks in the park to display the idleness enabled by their relative affluence. This transformation manifests further when McTeague starts to drink better beer, trades in his frayed cuffs for new ones, and begins to "observe the broader, larger interests of life, interests that affected him not as an individual, but as a member of a class, a profession, or a political party." These changes to his appearance and the awakening of broader concerns indicate his cultivation of qualities suitable for his station. These aspirations gain their clearest expression through McTeague's yearning for property. The dentist wants a "little home all to themselves, with six rooms and a bath, with a grass plat in front and calla-lilies." Expanding on the significance of a house, the narrator states that McTeague "would have a son, whose name would be Daniel, who would go to High School, and perhaps turn out to be a prosperous plumber or house painter. Then this son Daniel would marry a wife, and they would all live together in that six-room-and-bath house; Daniel would have little children. . . . The dentist saw himself as a veritable patriarch surrounded by children and grandchildren" (109). McTeague's aspiration for a conventional middle-class life reflects central features of the American Dream through the hopes of parents, such as McTeague's mother, for their children to have better, easier lives than the previous generation. However, Norris locates this interest in a home within the financial context that undergirds the narrative, following this discussion with a description of the couple looking in shop windows on Market and Kearney Streets. The narrator notes that the pair "stopped before the jewelers' and milliners' windows, finding a great delight in picking out things for each other, saying how they would choose this and that if they were rich" (111). This passage denotes that even the leisure of these characters is occupied with the desire for commodities, yet the irony is clear: the McTeagues are now well-off by the standards of the 1890s and have the resources to obtain the objects they covet.

However, the narrator undermines the solidity of the McTeagues' class position through Trina's incipient acquisitive mania. Her refusal to use her lottery money reflects the thrift central to earlier versions of the American Dream since she only spends what the couple can earn without recourse to her five thousand dollars. While Trina's capital seems to offer a protection against economic need, her behavior involves a significant departure from the national success story. The narrator states that the heroine "clung to this sum with a tenacity that was surprising; it had become for her a thing miraculous, a god-from-the-machine, suddenly descending upon the stage of her humble little life; she regarded it as something almost sacred and inviolable" (89). The reference to the "god-from-the-machine," the convention of classic drama in which a deity is introduced to solve a seemingly insoluble dilemma, highlights Trina's exalted view of her riches. The narrator destabilizes this perspective by noting that it "was a passion with her to save money. . . . Each time she added a quarter or half a dollar to the little store she laughed and sang with a veritable childish delight. . . . She did not save this money for any ulterior purpose, she hoarded instinctively, without knowing why" (107). Trina's covetous impulses stem not from a rational desire for financial security, evident through the fact that she does not save for "any ulterior purpose," but from unreasoned impulses that make her winnings the focal point of her existence, apparent through her exclamations of joy. Further, the use of "passion" in relation to her savings anticipates her eroticization of the gold coins later in the novel. The problematic character of her hoarding is manifest when she refuses to rent a particular house in their neighborhood, which represented the "ideal home" that they dreamed of inhabiting, because the payment aroused "every instinct of her parsimony" (114, 116). Norris provides a further illustration of this point when Trina is unwilling to send her parents fifty dollars to stave off the impending failure of their business. This refusal to draw on her funds in order to attain a more comfortable existence or to assist her family indicates that monetary concerns have superseded more humane considerations. Trina's avarice signifies the potential for wealth to alienate individuals from their humanity, and her actions convey the destructive nature of greed.

Trina's greed intensifies when McTeague loses his practice after Marcus reports his rival to the authorities for practicing dentistry without a license, which threatens the McTeagues' middle-class status and reiterates the role of environment in framing the characters' actions. Prior to the late nineteenth century, there were no licensing requirements for dentists, who could operate without risking legal sanction even if they had no prior training. Few options for professional instruction existed until the second half of the century. In 1875, there were only seven dental colleges in the United States, a number that increased to forty-seven by 1900, and practitioners had to obtain certification from an accredited school in order to operate.[51] When McTeague learns that he is prohibited from seeing patients, he initially fails to process the significance of what has occurred; instead, he takes recourse in his experience, although it makes no difference within the professionalization of American life. As McTeague occupies himself in arranging his parlors for clients who will never come again, Trina perceives this alteration in monetary terms, exclaiming "now we're paupers, beggars. We've got to leave

31

here—leave this flat where I've been—where *we've* been so happy, and sell all the pretty things; sell the pictures and the melodeon" (149). The loss of the commodities that display the couple's class position reflects the decline of their social standing, and this process is exacerbated by Trina's refusal to spend her savings in order to meet the physical requirements of the pair.

The narrator develops McTeague's descent through the loss of the refined habits associated with his ascension and the resumption of his earlier customs. The narrator states that McTeague "slipped back into the old habits (that had been his before he knew Trina) with an ease that was surprising. Sundays he dined at the car conductors' coffee-joint once more, and spent the afternoons lying full length upon the bed, crop-full, stupid, warm, smoking his huge pipe, drinking his steam beer, and playing his six mournful tunes on his concertina" (159). The reference to McTeague's original routine locates his regression in the economic context of Polk Street and Trina's pervasive avarice, ironically juxtaposing his past condition against his present one. Norris provides a parallel illustration of this reversion through the protagonist's new occupation working for a manufacturer of dental instruments. This job mirrors his previous vocation, yet McTeague no longer controls the particulars of his labor. Further, the narrator emphasizes the protagonist's reversion to a state based solely on gratifying his animal instincts in the context of the struggle for survival, evident through the references to food throughout the description of his new position.

The representation of Trina's miserliness further illustrates the destructive potential of greed within an economic system that privileges wealth. McTeague's deterioration, as apparent through his alcoholism and subsequent violence toward Trina, emerges in response to his wife's avarice.[52] The narrator observes that "Trina's stinginess had increased to such an extent that it had gone beyond the mere hoarding of money. She grudged even the food that she and McTeague ate, and even brought away half loaves of bread, lumps of sugar, and fruit from the car conductors' coffee-joint" (164). The references to food link the conflict between the couple to the patterns of consumption throughout the work and illuminate the central tension between Trina and McTeague: he emphasizes the necessities that would allow him to live with a measure of comfort, whereas she prioritizes acquisition divorced from any practical purpose, hoarding from blind compulsion. McTeague's violence toward Trina originates from what he perceives to be the denial of his humanity, which initially emerges through her refusal to provide him carfare in spite of an impending rainstorm. When Heise buys McTeague a drink to stave off illness, the narrator states that the whiskey "roused the man, or rather the brute in the man, and now not only roused it, but goaded it to evil. McTeague's nature changed. It was not only the alcohol, it was idleness and a general throwing off of the good influence that his wife had had over him in the days of their prosperity" (169). This focus on preserving her savings awakens her husband's animal nature, demonstrating the extent to which his behavior stems from economic pressures rather than hereditary or biological ones. The narrator further develops this point by noting that the protagonist "drank no more whiskey than at first, but his dislike for Trina increased with every day of their poverty, with every day of Trina's persistent stinginess" (171). The former dentist's preferred mode of torture, biting his spouse's fingertips, operates in the context of this desire to consume: he devours Trina when she diminishes his ability to possess the commodities that express prosperity and begrudges him the nourishment necessary to sustain his existence.

Norris further highlights the consequences of avarice through the erotic charge of money, which illustrates that a singular focus on acquisition undermines human relationships. The narrator states that the heroine "loved her money with an intensity that she could hardly express. She would plunge her small fingers into the pile with little murmurs of affection, her long, narrow eyes half closed and shining, her breath coming in long sighs" (170). Instead of viewing the money as a means to obtain requirements, Trina regards it with an intimacy that she does not display with her husband, evident when she refers to the coins as her "beauties" and declares "I *love* you" to these objects, in contrast to her exchanges with McTeague (196). The narrator provides a parallel illustration of this point when the former dentist absconds with his wife's savings, and she exclaims: "He's gone, my money's gone, my dear money—my dear, dear gold pieces that I've worked so hard for. Oh, to have deserted me—gone for good—gone and never coming back—gone with my gold pieces. Gone—gone—gone. I'll never see them again, and I've worked so hard, so *so* hard for him—for them" (191). Trina's concern is not with the disappearance of McTeague but with the fact that he has stolen her funds, evident through her continual shifting from him to her lost riches, which expresses the displacement of her affection from a person to mere things. The narrator reinforces this concept when he notes that Trina's "avarice had grown to become her one dominant passion; her love of money for the money's sake brooded in her heart, driving out by degrees every other natural affection" (194). Trina's exalted view of wealth has caused the values of the marketplace to replace conventional bonds between individuals, alienating her from her husband, her family, and her friends, a development that further dramatizes the perils of greed. This process culminates when Trina spreads "all the gold pieces between the sheets, and had then gone to bed, stripping herself, and had slept all night upon the money, taking a strange and ecstatic pleasure in the touch of the smooth flat pieces the length of her entire body" (198). Trina's response to the touch of her gold coins displays how her passions are governed by material considerations, which shape her relations with others and condition her eventual fate.

Zerkow also operates in this context, and his actions are governed by an acquisitive instinct that mirrors Trina's controlling passion. Norris writes that it "was impossible to look at Zerkow and not know instantly that greed—inordinate, insatiable greed—was the dominant passion of the man. He was the Man with the Rake, groping hourly in the muck-heap of the city for gold, for gold, for gold. It was his dream, his passion" (28). The reference to the "Man with the Rake," borrowed from John Bunyan's *Pilgrim's Progress* (1678), is significant in that it designates one who has rejected salvation to focus on filth. This characterization is appropriate for Zerkow, who roots through junk heaps in search of gold, an object that has transcended any other concern. The preeminent role of this precious metal to Zerkow manifests when Maria unveils the fillings made from this material; the narrator states that "Zerkow drew a quick breath as the three pellets suddenly flashed in Maria's palm. There it was, the virgin metal, the pure, unalloyed ore, his dream, his consuming desire" (28–29). The language of virginal innocence and purity suggests the nature of Zerkow's investment in this valuable resource and the displacement of his sexual desires from individuals to money. Norris further develops this theme through Zerkow's reactions to Maria's tale of the dinner service, which he hears "as if some hungry beast of prey had scented a quarry," and the narrator describes the junkman's reaction in terms associated with orgasm as the story "ravished Zerkow with delight," causing him to "breath[e] short" as he "gnawed at his bloodless lips," and the process culminates in a "spasm of anguish" as he begs to "have it all over again" (29–31). This episode, which echoes Trina rolling on the bed with her coins, provides a parallel illustration, through the subplot of Zerkow and

Maria, of the main themes of the central narrative and an indication of the McTeagues' probable fates.

Although the Maria and Zerkow story line has a clear connection to the central narrative, the episodes with Miss Baker and Old Grannis, who are elderly residents of the McTeagues' building who share an unspoken and unrequited love, supply a counterpoint to these plots by presenting figures who are not governed by the fiscal impulses that dictate the actions of the other couples.[53] Rather than centering their lives on acquisition and prioritizing wealth, Grannis and Miss Baker focus on obtaining necessary commodities, and currency thereby serves as a means to an end rather than the objective in itself. Miss Baker does not raid the bargain counters of the large department stores and instead buys only what she needs to live with some degree of comfort. Grannis offers an even stronger contrast in that he purchases the McTeagues' wedding photograph from the auction as a present for them, which indicates that he sees a greater worth in compassion than in the purely monetary valuation that Trina places on her former possessions. Norris clarifies the function of Grannis when he sells his book-binding apparatus and disrupts his ordered routine with Miss Baker. The narrator states that the elderly man "had sold his happiness for money; he had bartered all his tardy romance for some miserable bank-notes" (178). His regret over this sale reflects the broader economic tensions responsible for the destruction of the other characters; however, this transaction enables Grannis to attain a deeper degree of intimacy with Miss Baker, and he is not motivated solely by financial gain. As such, this subplot highlights the values that have been superseded by the focus on accumulation. The example of Grannis and Miss Baker further reveals that money need not necessarily serve a destructive function. Rather, the importance that the other characters place on capital and the role of such perspectives in governing conduct contribute to negative outcomes.

The novel further displays the alternatives to this focus on acquisition through juxtaposing McTeague's existence with Trina against his fishing trips, which convey his desire for more expansive spaces and anticipate his eventual flight to the mines. Describing these excursions, the narrator states that the protagonist "liked the solitude of the tremendous, tumbling ocean; the fresh, windy downs; he liked to feel the gusty Trades flogging his face, and he would remain for hours watching the roll and plunge of the breakers with the silent, unreasoned enjoyment of a child" (183). This account of the natural world recalls McTeague and Trina's courtship at the Oakland Estuary, yet the absence of his wife from this scene underscores their growing estrangement. The reference to the "unreasoned enjoyment of a child" offers an important connection to the heroine since the narrator employs this phrase earlier in relation to her hoarding. This repetition reinforces that Trina's attachment to her money denies McTeague the ability to live decently, which provides the impetus for his movement toward surroundings free from the constraints that now characterize his existence.

The narrator combines these elements through McTeague's fishing. This act enables him to meet his requirements for sustenance and also causes him to remember "how often he used to do this sort of thing when he was a boy in the mountains of Placer County, before he had become a car-boy at the mine. The instincts of the old-time miner were returning. In the stress of his misfortune McTeague was lapsing back to his early estate" (183). While McGlynn views this scene as an illustration of a broader conflict between the city and the country, Norris does not seem to be operating within this binary framework.[54] This shift to the perspectives and activities of McTeague's youth suggests his inability to transcend his previous environment, the influence of which has always lurked beneath the surface and prefigures the return to his "early estate." Norris develops this theme through following this episode with a return to Trina and the economic pressures that govern their lives. Most notably, the end of the chapter involves McTeague selling the gilded molar that once embodied his professional ambitions as this object has become a mockery of these aspirations through its placement within Zerkow's squalid flat.

McTeague's murder of Trina operates in this economic context, and Norris emphasizes this framework by reiterating the motifs that have characterized their relationship. After Trina does not aid McTeague, he states, "I—I—wouldn't let a *dog* go hungry," which articulates a measure of compassion that contrasts his wife's avarice (199). Further, the impetus for the killing is the sale of her estranged husband's "beloved concertina, that he had had all his life" (203). This passage alludes to the couple's fundamental disagreement during the disposal of their household goods after the loss of McTeague's profession, with the dentist viewing his possessions as records of his experiences, while Trina attributes only monetary value to these objects. These textual elements situate McTeague's actions within a clearly demarcated monetary context that the narrator reinforces when Trina does not assist her husband. When she refuses to give McTeague "every nickel" of her money, he states, "You ain't going to make small of me this time" (205). This statement appears repeatedly throughout the novel: in response to the Orpheum ticket agent in chapter 6, following the fight with Marcus in chapter 8, after he has lost his ability to practice in chapter 13, in reply to the other dentist's offer for the gilded molar in chapter 14, and prior to his initial beating of Trina in chapter 15. In these instances, the declaration has reflected McTeague's urge to assert his worth in a hostile and complex environment that he seems powerless to alter. When directed at Trina, this expression takes on a broader significance by demonstrating a desire to recapture the self-possession that has been lost as a result of his poverty and desperation. Through the context that sets up the homicide, the narrator illustrates the consequences of greed, which gain further credence through Zerkow's slaying of Maria since this act is informed by a similar set of financial concerns.

McTeague's subsequent flight to the Sierra Nevada reiterates the economic constraints that govern the world of the text. The narrator develops this point through the operations of the Big Dipper Mine, observing that "one heard the prolonged thunder of the stamp-mill, the crusher, the insatiable monster, gnashing the rocks to powder with its long iron teeth, vomiting them out again in a thin stream of wet gray mud. Its enormous maw, fed night and day with the car-boy's loads, gorged itself with gravel, and spat out gold, grinding the rocks between its jaws, glutted, as it were, with the very entrails of the earth, and growling over its endless meal, like some savage animal, some legendary dragon, some fabulous beast, symbol of inordinate and monstrous gluttony" (209). This passage contextualizes the imagery of consumption throughout the novel, locating these motifs within a general framework of acquisition. The machinery practices on a large scale what the central characters have performed on a smaller one in their attempts to extract gold from their surroundings heedless of the consequences. The narrator explicitly connects McTeague to the processes of the stamp mill: the "long iron teeth" evoke his former occupation as a dentist, and the acts of "grinding the rocks between its jaws" and gnashing "the rocks to powder" recall his act of biting Trina's fingers. The strength and power of the equipment also correlate to McTeague since these attributes are frequently associated with him. Further, the section about the car boys feeding the apparatus expresses McTeague's role within this environment, one that shaped him physically and emotionally. Norris further highlights the relationship between McTeague's life in San Francisco and his return to Placer County through the description of the office at the mine. The telephone reflects the complex urban realm McTeague has fled, while the revolver and cartridge belt allude back to the rifle manufacturer's calendar in his dental parlors and anticipate the final confrontation with Marcus. Most important, the handgun hangs from a nail that also holds a bag of gold dust, which further links the violence in the work to a desire for financial gain, and a chromolithograph of Jean-François Millet's *Angelus,* a representation of the pastoral world that has been superseded by the industrial order.[55] These elements underscore the outcomes unleashed by emphasizing wealth over any broader belief system.

The final chapters of *McTeague* offer a parallel illustration of the forces that have circumscribed the protagonist's possible mobility and establish a dialectic between the imperatives of dominant society and the need for self-preservation. While critics have argued that the conclusion deviates from the primary orientation of the narrative, Norris insisted that the ending was appropriate and responded to Howells: "I agree in every one of your criticisms always excepting the anti climax, the 'death in the desert' business. I am sure that it has its place."[56] The ending serves an important structural function by reinforcing the economic themes of the work within a final summation of its causative pressures. Norris continues the focus on gold that has animated the rest of the novel through the introduction of Cribbens, who partners with McTeague to search for gold, and the discovery of a claim that would enable the protagonist to transcend his instability. The narrator, however, juxtaposes this find with the development of McTeague's sixth sense, which signifies his further reversion to the instincts of his primitive forebears as an adaptation to his new surroundings. The narrator states that "McTeague felt the mysterious intuition of approaching danger; an unseen hand seemed reining his head eastward; a spur was in his flanks that seemed to urge him to hurry, hurry, hurry" (227). These impulses are not merely the products of his animal inheritance; instead, these elements emerge in relation to the dictates of environment.

Norris clarifies this point through the reappearance of Marcus Schouler, who has been deputized as part of the posse sent to apprehend McTeague following Trina's murder. Marcus continues to be motivated by pecuniary matters: his primary concern is Trina's five thousand dollars, a sum that he claims "belongs to me by rights" (237). This emphasis on wealth shapes the interactions between the men during the last section of *McTeague,* highlighting both the possibility for renewal that emerges outside the economic framework of dominant society and the inevitable tragedy that results from an exclusive interest in financial gain. After the mule carrying the last of their water makes his escape, "the sense of enmity between the two had weakened in the face of a common peril," and they join in pursuit of the animal, realizing that their possibility for survival depends on this collective endeavor (241). This tension mirrors McTeague's earlier flight from his strike, which has less value than his continued existence, and Norris suggests that fiscal considerations are of little importance next to one's desire to live. The novel reiterates the underlying basis of the conflict between these characters when they stand over the mule that Marcus has killed with his final bullet: in "an instant the eyes of the two doomed men had met as the same thought simultaneously rose in their minds. The canvas sack with its five thousand dollars was still tied to the horn of the saddle" (242). The renewed emphasis on Trina's money reflects the tensions that have framed the text, and Marcus's violent death coupled with McTeague's certain demise provide a further representation that one cannot escape the confines of the deterministic world, a theme that Norris intensifies through the closing image of the canary in his gilded prison.

Rather than illustrating antiquated theories of biological determinism, *McTeague* reflects on a conception central to the American experience through its examination of the extent to which citizens can shape their material circumstances.[57] Through its representation of the forces that limit opportunities for economic advancement, the narrative demonstrates that an inability to realize such progress often stems from not the failings of the individual but structures rooted within one's environment. As such, the novel expresses the discrepancy between American ideals and their application to life in the United States, contextualizing the experiences of those who do not attain mobility while suggesting that a different set of social conditions might engender different outcomes.

2

TENTACLES OF CAPITAL

The Historical Background of The Octopus

The Octopus further develops Norris's treatment of the limitations to advancement in America. Describing his planned Epic of Wheat, which would start with *The Octopus,* Norris outlined a plan "to write three novels around the one subject of *Wheat.* First, a story of California, (the producer), second, a story of Chicago (the distributor) third, a story of Europe (the Consumer) and in each to keep to the idea of this huge, Niagara of wheat rolling from West to East." He determined that the first volume would involve a conflict between wheat ranchers and the Southern Pacific Railroad, a subject so vast that he would be able to get "at it from every point of view, the social, agricultural, & political,—Just say the last word in the R. R. question in California. I am going to study the whole thing *on the ground,* and come back here in the winter and make a novel out of it."[1] In *The Octopus,* Norris develops these concerns through a struggle between wheat ranchers in the San Joaquin Valley and the powerful Pacific and Southwestern Railroad, drawing on the practices of the Southern Pacific Railroad Company to depict the institutional forces that shape the perspectives of individuals at all levels of society.[2] While both the company and the growers seek to maximize earnings, the monopoly's control over the transportation network and legislative apparatus of California creates a clear power imbalance with the ranchers, who have no means to redress their grievances within a legal system controlled by railroad. This reality leads the ranchers to more drastic actions that hasten their inevitable defeat. Through Norris's conflict between the ranchers and the railroad, *The Octopus* expresses the dangers of monopoly ownership over essential resources, which enables companies to manipulate market conditions to protect their profit margins heedless of the consequences for the public.

To develop his ranchers' struggle with the Pacific and Southwestern, Norris drew on a gunfight between farmers and representatives of the Southern Pacific on May 11, 1880, known as the Mussel Slough tragedy. This incident originated from the expansion of California's rail network and the broader role of the railroad in the development of the West. Under the Pacific Railroad Act of 1862, the federal government financed the Transcontinental Railroad in part by giving these railroad companies tracts of land as capital incentives for building tracks in specific locations. These lots followed the planned route of the rail line, and each lot alternated with a tract of land owned by the government, which could either be sold or given to homesteaders for settlement. The government took a similar approach to develop the rail network of California, awarding extensive land grants to the Southern Pacific.[3] Notably, Congress authorized the Southern Pacific to build tracks through Tulare County in 1866, granting the railroad company 25,000 acres that were divided into individual lots of 640 acres.[4] The corporation encouraged settlement on these holdings, even before laying the tracks necessary to claim possession, and people began to improve these properties based on the understanding that they could later buy acreage at fixed prices.[5] After the settlers had turned the properties into profitable farmland, Jerome Madden, the land agent for the Southern Pacific, announced that anyone could purchase these tracts for rates from 150 percent to 350 percent higher than the earlier figure.[6] In response, the farmers called a mass meeting and formed the Grand Settlers' League to promote their interests. After a series of legal challenges, including an appeal before the Supreme Court, a U.S. marshal's attempt to evict the inhabitants led to a shootout that killed seven men.[7]

The parameters of the Mussel Slough tragedy provide the structure of the plot, and Norris's handling of this event coheres with the press coverage in San Francisco's two largest newspapers, the *Chronicle* and *Examiner.*[8] To research the struggles between farmers and the Southern Pacific, which reformers had deemed "the Octopus" because its reach extended to every corner of the state, Norris traveled to San Francisco on April 10, 1900, remaining in California until the end of summer. He interviewed participants in the events that he would represent in the novel: Seymour Waterhouse planned luncheons with officers of the Southern Pacific, and John O'Hara Cosgrave, Norris's former editor at the *Wave,* arranged a meeting with railroad magnate Collis P. Huntington.[9] Norris also spent many hours combing through the files of the *Chronicle* and *Examiner,* which provided critical coverage of the company's undertakings during the late nineteenth century.[10] In addition, Norris visited the Santa Anita Rancho near Hollister, where he gleaned details about the production, transportation, and distribution of grain. Robert D. Lundy asserts that this sojourn provided numerous ideas for *The Octopus,* from a neighboring barn dance that supplied the inspiration for Annixter's party to the nearby San Juan Bautista mission, which Norris transported to his fictional Bonneville.[11] After finishing his inquiries in California, he returned to New York and started *The Octopus,* working on the manuscript until December 15, 1900, when he dated his prefatory note. Due to the length of the novel, which totaled 652 pages in the first edition, Norris was unable to secure serial publication. The book first appeared on April 1, 1901, and entered its fourth printing in July; by the end of 1902, *The Octopus* had become Norris's most popular work to date, with sales of 33,420 copies in the United States.[12]

Through his focus on the tactics of the Southern Pacific, Norris was able to engage with a central issue that shaped California and the nation as a whole: the dangers of corporate monopolies. The Southern Pacific was originally formed by Collis P. Huntington, Mark Hopkins, Leland Stanford, and Charles Crocker as a landholding company in 1865, eventually absorbing the Central Pacific Railroad and growing to dominate rail networks throughout the western United States: by 1877, the company controlled 85 percent of railroad mileage in California.[13] The power of the company increased when the federal government carved out significant portions of California as an inducement to develop more transit lines and gave them to the Southern Pacific, which possessed 20 million acres by 1870.[14] This conglomerate was still the chief landowner in 1919, with nearly 2.6 million acres in Southern California and 642,246 in one county alone.[15] The Southern Pacific exacted an additional toll on people who relied on the firm to transport goods by setting exorbitant rates, and the company even forced those who wanted to ship freight to submit their books to the Southern Pacific's accountants so that transportation costs could be increased if a business's profits began to rise.[16] For instance, the lemon industry in Southern California was prospering until the railroad raised the tariff from $1.00 to $1.15 per box, which eradicated the growers' profits and caused them to uproot their orchards.[17] Further, when the Payne-Aldrich Tariff of 1909 went into effect and augmented the revenues of California farmers by fifty cents per ton, the Southern Pacific raised its rates accordingly and pocketed nearly half of these earnings.[18]

The Southern Pacific's monopoly extended from the land and transit of California to control over the state government. George Mowry observes that "California, like so many of her sister commonwealths at the turn of the century, had only the shadow of representative government, while the real substance of power resided largely in the Southern Pacific Railroad Company. To a degree perhaps unparalleled in the nation, the Southern Pacific and a web of associated economic interests ruled the state."[19] The details of this process emerged through the correspondence between Huntington and David D. Colton as these documents contain numerous references to the expected prices for particular legislative measures and politicians. In one, Huntington wrote that it "costs money to fix things. . . . I believe with $200,000 I can pass our bill, but that it is not worth this much to us"; in another dispatch, he observed that "the boys are very hungry, and it will cost us considerably to be saved."[20] Through these means, Huntington and his associates used their power to avoid effective regulation and to protect their interests, which were secured through engineering the elections of three successive governors: Henry T. Gage, George Pardee, and James Gillett.[21] The California Railroad Commission was of special interest to the Southern Pacific since this body had the ability to establish shipping rates, yet the commission was largely controlled by the railroad.[22] Reflecting on the company's power over this regulatory body, a study in 1895 declared that not "a single majority report has ever been issued from the railroad commission of a nature unsatisfactory to the company the commission was established to control."[23] These actions had a destructive effect on the state, diverting resources from the public to serve the interests of the Southern Pacific and providing limited means of redress within the political framework.

The expansion of the Southern Pacific paralleled the growth of corporate monopolies throughout the United States, which created vast disparities of wealth within an economic system that seemed to be outside the average worker's command. At the dawn of the twentieth century, major companies significantly increased the scope of their operations to drive smaller firms out of business and to consolidate power. Between 1894 and 1904, 131 mergers absorbed 1,800 businesses into conglomerates; in the same period, more than half of these acquisitions consumed over 50 percent of their industries, and nearly a third gained control of 70 percent.[24] Major banks had interests in so many of these concerns that they created an interlocking network of corporate directors who also had stakes in other firms. According to a Senate report, John Pierpont Morgan sat on the boards of forty-eight businesses at his peak and John D. Rockefeller on thirty-seven.[25] These institutions fostered immense wealth, yet this material progress primarily benefited those in the upper echelons of society as the number of millionaires increased from 400 before the Civil War to 4,047 by 1892.[26] Andrew Carnegie and Rockefeller provided the most prominent figures of achievement during this period since both men had risen from humble origins to acquire vast fortunes. However, they owed their success to their clever manipulation of economic forces: they amassed their riches through maintaining high prices; assimilating or destroying all competition; and paying low wages, practices that had an adverse impact on the general public.[27]

As with the Southern Pacific in California, these monopolies had extraordinary control over the political process, and they used their vast resources to mold policy in accordance with their interests. Even when popular pressures demanded government action, the resulting laws seldom undermined the interests of the business community. For instance, conglomerates used their influence to shape the Interstate Commerce Act of 1887 and the Sherman Antitrust Act of 1890. The former was implemented to prevent collusion among the major railroads and to regulate their activities on behalf of consumers, yet Richard Olney, a lawyer for the Boston & Maine and soon to be attorney general in the administration of Grover Cleveland, noted that the commission could "be made of great use to the railroads. It satisfies the popular clamor for a government supervision of the railroads, at the same time that supervision is almost entirely nominal. . . . The part of wisdom is not to destroy the Commission, but to utilize it."[28] Since this body was composed of representatives from the very institutions that the act was supposed to govern, the legislation created the semblance of a regulatory apparatus yet failed to change how these firms functioned. The Sherman Antitrust Act, designed to curb the power of business combinations, focused on eliminating practices that undermined competition within industries, and judicial interpretations further weakened this law, employing it to serve the interests of the powerful. In 1895, the Supreme Court applied the Sherman Act in a manner that rendered it largely harmless, arguing that a monopoly of sugar refining was one of manufacturing and not of commerce, which left it outside the parameters of the edict.[29] Further, the Sherman Act had a limited impact in terms of engendering competitive markets. While the Supreme Court utilized this legislation to break up Standard Oil and American Tobacco in 1911, Walter

Licht observes that "the firms were broken into separate new concerns, but these new large-scale entities themselves came to dominate their industries. In effect, anti-monopolism led to oligopoly, or the control of trades by a few firms, not to truly competitive marketplaces."[30] As a result, the people had limited means to protect themselves from institutions of economic power, which continued to expand despite statutes designed to check their growth.

Norris's research into these issues provided the basis for his treatment of how the Pacific and Southwestern dictates the actions of the characters through its control over the infrastructure of California. The narrator highlights this function through S. Behrman, the chief banker of Bonneville and the representative of the monopoly, observing that the "railroad did little business in that part of the country that S. Behrman did not supervise, from the consignment of a shipment of wheat to the management of a damage suit, or even to the repair and maintenance of the right of way.... The ranchers about Bonneville knew whom to look to as a source of trouble. There was no denying that fact that for Ostermann, Broderson, Annixter and Derrick, S. Behrman was the railroad."[31] Behrman is the immediate source of the ranchers' suffering as he manipulates the conditions of production and distribution in Bonneville, evident through his authority over the shipment of wheat. By controlling the resources on which the farmers depend for their livelihoods, Behrman can shape the terms of economic activity, and the growers have no means to oppose his practices. Norris furthers this representation of the conglomerate's influence through Shelgrim, the president of the Pacific and Southwestern, who directs shipping throughout the state and has a significant presence in the fiscal policies of the nation. Annixter notes that this industrialist "owns the courts. He's got men like Ulsteen in his pocket. He's got the Railroad Commission in his pocket. He's got the Governor of the State in his pocket. He keeps a million-dollar lobby at Sacramento every minute of the time the legislature is in session; he's got his own men on the floor of the United States Senate.... He sits in his office in San Francisco and pulls the strings and we've got to dance" (104–5). This control over the political, financial, and legal system of California, especially those legislative bodies created to regulate the company, offers the settlers no alternatives to the imperatives of the railroad and engenders the violent conflict that serves as the pivotal event of *The Octopus*.

The narrator reinforces the company's hegemony through a description of the California railway map, which expresses the detrimental effects of the

Pacific and Southwestern on the laboring population. The narrator observes that the

> whole map was gridironed by a vast, complicated network of red lines marked P. and S. W. R. R. These centralized at San Francisco and thence ramified and spread north, east, and south, to every quarter of the State. ... The map was white, and it seemed as if all the colour which should have gone to vivify the various counties, towns, and cities marked upon it had been absorbed by that huge, sprawling organism, with its ruddy arteries converging to a central point. It was as though the State had been sucked white and colourless, and against this pallid background the red arteries of the monster stood out, swollen with life-blood, reaching out to infinity, gorged to bursting; an excrescence, a gigantic parasite fattening upon the life-blood of an entire commonwealth. (288–89)

Regarding this passage, Clare Virginia Eby asserts that "the P. and S. W. unifies the people of California, bringing them together. Norris' corporealization of the map into a system of arteries underscores how thoroughly the railroad connects and, however insidiously, sustains California."[32] While the tracks integrate the state into a unified whole, the railroad company sustains itself by exploiting the efforts of others and consuming the resources of the region. The narrator further conveys this parasitic function through the references to blood with the implication that this corporation drains the life from local communities through its power over the means of transporting essential commodities. Returning to this metaphor later, the narrator refers to the railroad as "the iron-hearted monster of steel and steam, implacable, insatiable, huge—its entrails gorged with the life blood that it sucked from an entire commonwealth, its ever hungry maw glutted with the harvests that should have fed the famished bellies of the whole world" (322). The consequences that the monopoly fosters for California have broader implications in that they interfere with the distribution of necessary foodstuffs, and Norris's imagery reinforces that the firm embarks on a course that compromises the survival of the populace in order to maximize profits.

To illuminate the consequences that result from a concentration of property ownership, Norris drew on pivotal episodes from the Mussel Slough tragedy. Chapter 3 provides exposition for the struggle between the ranchers and the Pacific and Southwestern, tracing the railroad's refusal to honor the agreements that encouraged people to settle on company land. Norris gleaned the background for this occurrence from the San Francisco newspapers. According to the *Chronicle,* the Southern Pacific distributed circulars stating that "the company invites settlers to go upon their lands before patents are issued or the road is completed, and intends in such cases to sell to them in preference to any other applicants, and at a price based upon the value of the land without the improvements put upon them by the settlers. If the settlers desire to buy, the company gives them the first privilege of purchase, at a fixed price, which in every case shall only be the value of the land, without regard to improvements."[33] Both the document quoted in the *Chronicle* and Norris's reproduction center on improvements to the contested land, which would logically increase its value to prices beyond the means of average farmers. Such references occur four times in the *Chronicle,* presumably to alleviate concerns that the men's industry would ultimately be used against them. Norris made only minor changes to this source, substituting the impersonal *its* for *their,* an alteration that establishes the corporation as an institution rather than a collection of individuals and thereby anticipates Shelgrim's speech (117). Norris also removed the mention of the settlers in the first sentence, and this change minimizes their agency by presenting the improvements to the land in more abstract terms. Norris further omitted the second sentence, a logical revision since this passage merely restates contractual terms reiterated throughout the pamphlet. However, it is important to note that the documents circulated by the railroad were not formal contracts that would stand up in a court of law. As such, the failure of the ranchers to perceive the reality of the situation reveals their inability to negotiate the complexities of the modern economic arena and further suggests the inevitability of their defeat. Based on their misapprehension of these documents, both the characters and their historical antecedents began to cultivate these spaces, which were primarily deserts that would not have been worth the quoted prices.

The labor connected with the farmers expresses their role in transforming barren earth into fertile farmland in contrast to the Pacific and Southwestern, which holds its grants for the purposes of speculation. Norris highlights this point when Presley refers to "Derrick's main irrigating ditch, a vast trench not yet completed, which he and Annixter . . . were jointly constructing" (14). This reference connects *The Octopus* to the Mussel Slough ranchers, who engaged in a similar project that increased land values. According to the *Chronicle,* the "settlers went peacefully to work, and, as shown by the State Engineer's report for 1880, by untiring industry against many discouragements, with no aid but three teams, dug ditches and laid out a system of irrigation that, though not perfect, nevertheless sufficed to increase the value of the lands immensely, and out of an arid desert create a fertile farming country."[34] Such projects were important to the Central Valley, which Kevin Starr refers to "as a semiarid steppe, with soil baked by the sun to such hardness that it frequently had to be broken with dynamite. For California to become inhabitable and productive in its entirety would require a statewide water system of heroic magnitude."[35] The settlers were thereby involved not only in the immediate venture of economic expansion but also the broader undertaking of creating the conditions that would give rise to modern California.[36] Annixter further defines his connection to his property when he responds to statements by Cyrus Blakelee Ruggles, the land agent for the railroad, about price increases by asking: "Who made it worth twenty? ... I've improved it up to that figure.... Do you people think that you can hold that land, untaxed, for speculative purposes until it goes up to thirty dollars and then sell out to someone else—sell it over our heads?" (196). Annixter articulates the labor theory of value, which stipulates that the worth of a commodity stems from the effort necessary to produce it. In *Two Treatises of Government,* John Locke associates possession with such practices, stating that whatever one "removes out of that state that Nature hath provided and left it in, he hath mixed his labor with it, and joined to it something that is his own, and thereby makes it his property."[37] This conception has a slightly different application in the novel since Annixter and his fellow growers employ tenants to work in their fields, yet the capital improvements, including the construction of the waterway and Annixter's barn, operate in the context of Locke's formulation.

The Octopus further demonstrates this engagement with the land through Dyke, a former railroad engineer turned farmer, who hopes to attain mobility through agricultural labor. Dyke articulates this desire by noting: "I'm dead sure of a bonanza crop by now. The rain came *just* right. I actually don't know as I can store the crop in those barns I built, it's going to be so big.... After I've paid off the mortgage ... I'll clear big money, m' son. Yes, sir. I *knew* there was boodle in hops" (343). The bountiful harvest illustrates the promise of the West through a successful interaction with the natural world. The narrator underscores this point by asserting that Dyke "was his own man, a proprietor, an owner of land, furthering a successful enterprise. No one had helped him; he had followed no man's lead. He had struck out unaided for himself, and his success was due solely to his own intelligence, industry, and foresight" (344). For Dyke, the productive act of labor supplies a framework for self-sufficiency, and prosperity has a practical purpose, evident through his desire to pay off his debts, to enroll his daughter in the seminary, and to expand his enterprise. The narrator's invocation of the national success story signifies that these conventional approaches to advancement are not applicable to the era of monopolies as even diligent labor and foresight do not offer the means for advancement because of the institutions that control the economic system.

Dyke reflects attributes of the original Mussel Slough settlers, yet Norris replaces the small farmers who participated in the conflict with large land-owners, an alteration that allows for a more complex treatment of his major themes. The individuals involved in the actual dispute worked farms that averaged about six hundred acres; however, the ranchers in *The Octopus* control vast estates tilled by an itinerant labor force. Norris's growers have little engagement with the soil, which they view not as a means to self-sufficiency but as a source of wealth to be exploited.[38] The narrator develops this point in relation to Magnus Derrick, the owner of the El Rancho de Los Muertos, stating that it "was the true California spirit that found expression through him, the spirit of the West, unwilling to occupy itself with details, refusing to wait, to be patient, to achieve by legitimate plodding; the miner's instinct of wealth acquired in a single night prevailed, in spite of all. It was in this frame of mind that Magnus and the multitude of other ranchers of whom he was a type, farmed their ranches. They had no love for their land. . . . They worked their ranches as a quarter of a century before they had worked their mines. . . . To get all there was out of the land, to squeeze it dry, to exhaust it, seemed their policy" (298). With the earth reduced to a commodity, the destruction of its resource base is of little consequence to Derrick and his associates, who wish to extract every ounce of profit from their holdings like their predecessors had destroyed the mining regions to remove their mineral deposits. As a result of this outlook, these characters operate in the same context as the Pacific and Southwestern, fighting for their right to maximize earnings against the impulses of the company to do the same.[39] Through this process, Norris indicates that capitalism corrupts individuals at all levels of the social order, offering alternatives for development that are similar to the structures they seek to eradicate.

Although the ranchers in *The Octopus* differ from the Mussel Slough settlers, Norris accurately presents developments in California following the gold rush. He draws on this event through Magnus, who came West in search of a fortune and then adapted to changing conditions after the 1850s. The narrator states that Derrick "had been as lucky in his mines as in his gambling, sinking shafts and tunneling in violation of expert theory and finding 'pay' in every case. Without knowing it, he allowed himself to work his ranch much as if he was still working his mine. The old-time spirit of '49, hap-hazard, unscientific, persisted in his mind. Everything was a gamble— who took the greatest chances was most apt to be the greatest winner" (65). The primary attributes of Derrick—the gambling instinct, his selfish pursuit of financial gain, his willingness to exploit resources heedless of long-term effects—evoke the central imperatives of the gold rush. Magnus's movement from miner to farmer followed the trajectory of many who ventured west to find riches and then shifted their focus to cultivating grain, which had replaced gold as the primary source of prosperity in the state by the 1870s. According to John J. Powell, this precious metal, after reaching its peak of $57.3 million in 1853, declined to an annual output of between twenty and thirty million dollars by the 1870s.[40] Agriculture, in fact, had far outstripped gold, increasing from $75 million in 1872 to nearly $100 million in 1873.[41] Although farming in California was quite varied, the principal crop was wheat, with a yield of twenty-five million bushels per year by 1873.[42] The extent of agricultural production and its resulting wealth produced a view of the land that differed from earlier versions of the American Dream.

Norris augments the land dispute between the railroad and the ranchers by combining this struggle with the company's manipulation of freight rates, which presents the activities of the Pacific and Southwestern within a broader pattern of abuses.[43] Judge Ulsteen's decision to side with the Pacific and Southwestern and block the new rate schedule further illustrates the corporation's ability to control the economic framework that governs the central characters. For the details of this episode, Norris incorporated real-life clashes between the Southern Pacific and the California Railroad Commission, which created a rate schedule in 1895 that reduced prices by 8 percent. Joseph McKenna, a district court judge who became attorney general in 1897 and a Supreme Court justice in 1898, granted a temporary injunction against this order, deciding after a protracted hearing that "a tariff of rates is not reasonable which barely omits confiscation.... To be reasonable, it must reimburse charges and expenses and give, besides, an adequate return to investment," and he continued the injunction.[44]

This conflict manifests in *The Octopus* as McKenna's judgment reflects that attributed to Ulsteen. Magnus's son Harran articulates Ulsteen's perspective by observing that "grain rates as low as the new figure would amount to confiscation of property, and that, on such a basis, the railroad could not be operated at a legitimate profit. As he is powerless to legislate in this matter, he can only put the rates back at what they originally were before the commissioners made the cut, and it is so ordered." Norris indicates that the political system does not function impartially for the benefit of both producers and shippers; instead, this legislative apparatus supplies the conglomerate with a means to safeguard its interests at the expense of the farmers. Clarifying this point, Harran Derrick notes that the return to the old figure was the work of Behrman, who was "in the city the whole of the time the new schedule was being drawn, and he and Ulsteen and the Railroad Commission were as thick as thieves. He had been up there all this last week, too, doing the railroad's dirty work, and backing Ulsteen up.... Can we raise wheat at a legitimate profit with a tariff of four dollars a ton for moving it two hundred miles to tide-water, with wheat at eighty-seven cents? Why not hold us up with a gun in our faces, and say, 'hands up,' and be done with it?" (11). The reference to being held up at gunpoint suggests that the actions of the company are based on expropriation, yet these practices are not viewed as theft since they originate within the structure of a legal system that serves the predatory inclinations of the Pacific and Southwestern and therefore provides the ranchers with no means of protection.[45]

Norris further illustrates the power of the railroad and its manipulation of land prices during Annixter's party, which juxtaposes the belligerence of the characters with the aggression of the company to prefigure their final confrontation. The scene initially focuses on the fight between Annixter and Delaney, who works at the former's Quien Sabe Ranch, and Norris employs deterministic imagery in his presentation of the circumstances surrounding this quarrel. Describing the responses to the hostilities, the narrator observes that it "was sand blown off a rock; the throng of guests, carried by an impulse that was not to be resisted, bore back against the sides of the barn, overturning chairs, tripping upon each other, falling down, scrambling to their feet again, stepping over one another, getting behind each other" (256). The tranquility during the earlier stages of the gathering contrasts with this chaos, which developed through Annixter's jealousy in his pursuit of Hilma and the resulting termination of Delaney. This scene is of further importance as it anticipates the climactic gun battle. This episode also relies on a sudden outbreak of violence amid an otherwise festive occasion, the rabbit drive and barbeque, and the account of people fleeing when Annixter and Delaney open fire mirrors the behavior of the animals once they have been caged before their extermination. The connection between the creatures and the party guests, including those who will die in the shootout, highlights the inevitability of the coming conflict and indicates that their actions stem from a desire for self-preservation.

Norris also situates the barn dance within the representation of economic determinism through the arrival of notices that state the new costs for the property the ranchers have occupied. Recounting their reactions, the narrator notes that the "sense of wrongs, the injustices, the oppression, extortion, and pillage of twenty years suddenly culminated and found voice in a raucous howl of execration. For a second there was nothing articulate in that cry of savage exasperation, nothing even intelligent. It was the human animal hounded into its corner, exploited, harried to its last stand, at bay, ferocious, terrible, turning at last with bared teeth and upraised claws to meet the death grapple" (272). The juxtaposition of Annixter and Delaney's fight with the announcement of the new rates conveys a battle with more serious repercussions than the interpersonal conflict that has just transpired. The first merely involves two men and ends with a minor injury; the second constitutes a larger struggle against a corporate monopoly that controls an entire state and exerts significant influence over national affairs. This ensuing clash culminates in the deaths of seven men, the loss of many others' means of subsistence, and the end of the lives they had built. Norris's presentation of this theme expresses the reduction of the farmers to mere beasts hounded by the railroad and suggests that their deeds result from those of the Pacific and Southwestern, with bloodshed as the necessary consequence of these practices.

In portraying these tactics, Norris incorporated the Southern Pacific's deviations from the provisions in its circulars for the sale of the land grants. The corporation began grading these holdings, first under the direction of the aptly named Mr. Crooks, whose quotes were far higher than those initially given by the railroad, and then under the direction of William H. Clark, who arrived at monetary figures that the farmers deemed to be outrageous.[46] In 1878, Jerome Madden announced that the cost per acre would now be from twenty-two to twenty-seven dollars, which is the amount stated in the correspondence to Magnus.[47] As in the novel, the company notified the current inhabitants of the new prices through letters from Madden, who also wrote that the properties would be available for purchase by anyone, with the implication that the ranchers would be evicted if they did not pay the specified rates.[48] In their appeal to the general population, the settlers stated that "many hundreds of our people stood aloof from this trouble and would take no hand in it, but would rather recognize the rights of the company and buy of them, believing that they would live up to their promises and so believed until they had built this branch of their road and received patents for these lands and sent their graders in here to grade them."[49] The Southern Pacific responded to such claims by attributing this increase to the value produced by the laying of tracks, and Charles Crocker asserted that the circulars only said $2.50 and upward, terms that imposed few constraints on what the conglomerate could charge.[50]

In response to Madden's notices, the farmers called a mass meeting in Hanford, then in Tulare County and six miles to the southeast of Mussel Slough, forming the Grand Settlers' League to represent its interests. This organization resolved that "we are not willing, and we look upon it as a case of injustice without parallel in the United States that we should have to pay the enhanced value made by our industry and toil."[51] This group concerned itself primarily with challenging the Southern Pacific in the state legislature, U.S. Congress, and the Supreme Court, contesting the company's claim to these properties and its right to raise land prices from those stated in its handbills.[52] These avenues offered limited chances for success since the Supreme Court in *Schulenberg v. Harriman* (1874) had nullified the provisions in land grants that required companies to meet certain requirements in order to claim title, a decision that applied to all cases involving railroads.[53] The settlers suffered a crucial defeat when Judge Lorenzo Sawyer, who had shares of Southern Pacific stock, ruled in *Southern Pacific v. Orton* (1879) that the corporation still owned the tracts in question, which it could reclaim without compensation.[54] The league also appealed directly to President Rutherford B. Hayes when he visited San Francisco in 1880, presenting him with a petition that read, "Through sheer energy and perseverance by the investment of our means, by excessive toil and privation continued through the best years of our lives, and relying firmly upon the rights we had acquired as American citizens, and upon the pledges of the Southern Pacific Railroad Company, we converted a desert into one of the garden spots of the State."[55] These legal challenges provided no recompense for the ranchers' grievances and affirmed the right of the conglomerate to sell its holdings to any interested party at whatever price the market would bear.

In presenting these concerns, Norris deviated significantly from the particulars of the Grand Settlers' League.[56] While the fictional organization also attempts to address their concerns through the legal system, Norris devotes little attention to these maneuvers and focuses instead on the settlers' attempts to elect a more favorable Railroad Commission. Explaining this plot point in a letter to Marcosson, Norris wrote that the ranchers "despairing of ever getting fair freight rates from the Railroad or of electing a board of Railroad Commissioners by fair means themselves, set about gaining their ends by any means available. What they want to do is to cause the nomination and election of railroad commissioners of their own choosing, with the idea that these commissioners will make proper reductions in freight rates."[57] Norris then asked: "Can you tell me just about how they would go about to get their men in? Do you think it *could* be done at all?"[58] Since he had to inquire about the possibility of such an occurrence, his research presumably did not uncover evidence of a similar scheme. Further, the studies on the Mussel Slough tragedy do not mention the settlers offering bribes, and a survey of periodical accounts about freight rates in the 1890s revealed no discussion of such undertakings. This subplot, however, serves an important function in *The Octopus* by highlighting the consequences of straying from the principles commonly associated with the American experience. This theme emerges through Magnus, a figure of "honesty, rectitude, uncompromising integrity," whose initial refusal to enter the scheme represents a stand against "the devious manœuvring, the evil communications, the rotten expediency of a corrupted institution" (114). The rejection of such practices conveys the fundamental integrity of Magnus, who once resigned from political life to preserve these values, yet he abandons them as a result of economic pressures.

This tension between monetary concerns and ethical behavior governs Magnus's undertakings for the remainder of *The Octopus*. When Magnus considers the bribery plot, the narrator refers to the character's reputation as "the most redoubtable poker player in El Dorado County," a reference that denotes a mining district in California. The perspective fostered through these experiences, one that values "achievement, fame, influence, prestige, possibly great wealth," supersedes his "cherished, lifelong integrity, the unstained purity of his principles" as his position within the League will enable him to potentially attain his objectives but only through the sacrifice of his principles(185). Norris further develops this conflict through deterministic imagery when the narrator observes that Magnus "was entangled, already his foot was caught in the mesh that was being spun" (188). This passage suggests that the rancher is at the mercy of both his earlier ambitions and the Pacific and Southwestern, which have separated his actions from his principles. The narrator extends the meaning of this reference after Magnus acquiesces to the bribery scheme, noting again that he "was hopelessly caught in the mesh. Wrong seemed indissolubly knitted into the texture of Right. He was blinded, dizzied, overwhelmed, caught in the current of events, and hurried along he knew not where" (291–92). This repetition compounds the impact of the agents arrayed against the settlers, indicating that Magnus is animated by these forces to the extent that he no longer operates in accordance with his free will. This process culminates when the crowd at the Opera House confronts him about the scheme to elect the railroad commissioners, and when Magnus attempts to challenge his opponents, he learns that it "was gone—that old-time power of mastery, that faculty of command. The ground crumbled beneath his feet. Long since it had been, by his own hand, undermined. Authority was gone.... His own honour had been prostituted" (559). This connection between integrity and identity articulates Magnus's tragedy, which expresses the need for a return to the values that have been corrupted within a changing social order.

In further explicating the forces aligned against the central characters, Norris returned to the Pacific and Southwestern's manipulation of freight costs. This concern is central to the betrayal of the ranchers by Magnus's son Lyman Derrick, who was supposed to promote the interests of the ranchers after his election to the Railroad Commission. Norris again incorporated the tactics of the Southern Pacific, which employed the California Railroad Commission, an agency that ostensibly regulated the company, to its advantage. An article in Norris's notebook titled "Gold Brick Grain-Rate Reduction" focuses on the formulation of a new rate schedule that offered an apparent price decrease by lowering charges between points with little rail activity yet making no changes in high-traffic destinations. The anonymous writer observed that the "great victory for the Southern Pacific lies in the fact that it has got rid forever of the real reductions made by the old Board, and has in its place a tariff in which no reductions are made between important wheat-shipping points, but a bogus average of 10 per cent reduction is shown on paper by changes in rates from stations where no wheat is ever shipped."[59] By implementing cuts to areas where people did not cultivate wheat and maintaining prices where growers produced and transported grain, the commission provided a semblance of progress within a structure that favored the railroad. Norris bracketed this passage, underlined the phrase about the appearance of lowered rates, and integrated this idea into the narrative through Lyman's proposal, one that relies on superficial reductions that do not address shipping in the San Joaquin Valley. This material highlights the inevitably of violent confrontation since the railroad's infiltration of regulatory bodies has left the settlers without peaceable means to safeguard their interests. Norris heightens this tragedy through Lyman's role in subordinating the farmers, including his father and brother, as the individual elected through the bribery scheme sells out the ranchers to further his political ambitions.

Norris further illustrates the predatory tactics of the company through the fate of Dyke, whose exploitation by the Pacific and Southwestern and his recourse to violence anticipate the bloody denouement of *The Octopus*. After crop failures throughout the nation increase the demand for California hops, the conglomerate raises its shipping charges from two cents a pound, which would have meant a fortune for Dyke, to five, a figure that conditions his ruin. When he protests this increase, the clerk explains that "the freight rate has gone up to meet the price. We're not doing business for our health" (349). This manipulation enables the monopoly to drain the potential profit from others' labor, and the clerk's reply indicates that economic imperatives supersede concern for the consequences of railroad policies. When Dyke asks Behrman to clarify the basis for calculating rates, the agent states, "All—the—traffic—will—bear" (350). This response, outlining a practice of charging the most money that people will spend, presents the dominance of the corporation as its officials can set prices that absorb the value of crops, and because they lack alternative means to sell their produce, farmers are obliged to pay. Reflecting on the character's defeat, the narrator observes that Dyke "had been merely the object of a colossal trick, a sordid injustice, a victim of the insatiate greed of the monster, caught and choked by one of those millions of tentacles suddenly reaching up from below, from out the dark beneath his feet, coiling around his throat, throttling him, strangling him, sucking his blood" (352–53). Dyke's attempt to beat the Pacific and Southwestern through a successful harvest represents his final undoing, and the reference to the tentacles of the octopus suggests that the contest has been rigged against him because of the firm's control of the state, its legal apparatus, and shipping lines.

In this context, the train robbery is the logical result of the procedures employed by the railroad and suggests that violence often serves as a predictable response to exploitation. An article in Norris's scrapbook for *The Octopus* reflects the climax of Dyke's narrative: the anonymous author of "Train Hold-Up in Arizona" stated that a "Wells Fargo express car safe was broken open by dynamite and looted of at least $10,000."[60] This act parallels Dyke's transgression as both incidents center on monetary gain, and the culprits were only interested in the safe rather than the federal mail or any other valuables. Norris, however, deviates from this source, which noted that the deed was "perpetrated by two men and was accomplished without firing a shot."[61] By substituting an individual for the two robbers, Norris expresses Dyke's isolation, coupled with the insignificance of his attempt to combat the conglomerate. In addition to reducing the sum to $5,000, Norris also invented a murder since no one had been injured in the actual crime. This alteration indicates that economic injustice has broader human consequences and locates bloodshed within the context of financial pressures. Annixter advances a similar interpretation, stating that the corporation "drove Dyke from his job because he wouldn't work for starvation wages. Then you raised freight rates on him and robbed him of all he had. . . . He's only taken back what you plundered him of" (423). This attempt to strike back at the monopoly through targeting its wealth reflects the pattern of abuse that he has suffered. Norris develops this point through the use of indirect discourse that represents the public's perception of Dyke's offense when the narrator notes, "He was not so much to blame; the railroad people had brought it on themselves. But he had shot a man to death. Ah, that was a serious business" (424). The killing highlights the detrimental effects of the company's business practices, culminating in the death of an innocent man and anticipating the final confrontation between the ranchers and the railroad.

For the gunfight, Norris used the basic structure of the Mussel Slough tragedy, and these elements again illustrate the power of the railroad. While residents were assembled at a barbeque on May 11, 1880, U.S. marshal Alonzo W. Poole attempted to evict settlers from the disputed land and to install the new owners, former station agent Mills D. Hartt and Walter J. Crow, who were believed to be dummy buyers for the company like Delaney and Christian in *The Octopus*.[62] After dispossessing William Braden, the assemblage traveled to the home of Henry Brewer to remove his partner, John Storer, from property owned by the Southern Pacific, a movement that parallels the seizure of Annixter's Quien Sabe and the attempt to reclaim Magnus's Los Muertos.[63] While negotiating the ownership of crops already in the ground, the men were interrupted by a group led by James N. Patterson that sought to prevent the evictions. Few of these individuals were armed, and they desired a peaceful resolution in line with the positions of Annixter and Magnus.[64] The ranchers asked Poole to surrender his revolver; he refused but pledged to leave his weapon holstered.[65] As Patterson and Poole were speaking, ranchers surrounded the marshal and his associates, which led to a quarrel between Crow and James Harris, and gunfire commenced after one of the horses struck Poole with its hoof and knocked him to the ground.[66] Press reports advanced a range of arguments about who had fired the first shot. A correspondent for the *San Francisco Call* asserted that Harris and Crow had opened fire simultaneously; another in the *Chronicle* advanced the position that "statements point to [the shots] having been discharged by Crow or Hartt, the men in the company of the Marshal"; and a writer for the *Examiner* claimed that it "is not known who commenced the firing."[67] Although these accounts differed, the aftermath was clear: the ensuing fight claimed the lives of five farmers: Harris, Archibald McGregor, John E. Henderson, Daniel Kelly, and Iver Knutson. Hartt was also killed at the scene, and Crow fled, only to be murdered by an unknown assailant.[68] The dead and wounded were taken to Brewer's house, a sight that a reporter for the *Call* termed "a sickening spectacle" with "the bloody and lifeless remains" of the combatants on the porch.[69] The suffering of the injured men inside revealed "a no less ghastly spectacle" intensified by the "piercing shrieks and heart-rending cries" of the victims' families, which Norris incorporated into the beginning of chapter 7.[70]

 The Octopus follows the basic outline of the Mussel Slough tragedy, yet Norris made several deviations from his sources that reinforced the central themes of the work. Norris de-emphasizes the negotiations with the marshal, situating this episode from the perspectives of the other settlers rather than

Magnus, who was involved in the efforts to broker a tentative peace. This obfuscation conveys the inevitability of the gunfight, an incident that serves as the logical culmination of the struggle depicted through the text. In both this skirmish and its historical antecedent, hostilities commence by accident because of the panicked horse that throws Garnett in the novel and the animal that knocked over Marshal Poole. These incidents reflect the operations of chance, which often plays a pivotal role in works of naturalism as a random occurrence facilitates the movement toward an inevitable conclusion.[71] Norris also deviated from newspaper reports in terms of the events preceding the fight. In *The Octopus,* Derrick and the marshal are surrounded by men from the latter's party, yet farmers advanced on Patterson and Poole in actuality.[72] This alteration intensifies the obstacles facing Norris's principals, who are outnumbered by individuals aligned with the most powerful institution in California, conditions that necessitate a violent response. Norris also attributes the first shot to a rancher named Hooven, whereas press accounts of the Mussel Slough tragedy did not claim that a rancher fired first. This change highlights the growers' inability to accurately perceive what has transpired as they misinterpret Garnett's fall as an act of aggression against them. This development seems to engender a broader responsibility for the drastic consequences unleashed by Hooven's deed, but the shooting is the result of circumstances that have been brought about by a confrontation with a stronger force, which could only have been avoided if the men were motivated by concerns other than financial gain. Norris underscores this point after the shootout when the "horror of that dreadful business had driven all other considerations from the mind. The sworn foes of the last hour had no thoughts of anything but to care for those whom, in their fury, they had shot down" (528). This emergence of a collective consciousness, one that allows the survivors to view their fellows in terms of a common humanity, signifies the potential for development when freed from the economic considerations that had governed the actions of the principals. This ironic commentary heightens the tragedy of the narrative since this realization has come too late to prevent bloodshed.

The final chapters of *The Octopus* heighten the social criticism of the work through the perspective of Presley, who advances ideas of progress despite the absence of any evidence to support his view. Critics have construed the conclusion as an illustration of Norris's Transcendentalism, yet such readings confuse Presley's interpretation of events with that of the writer.[73] This conflation of the author and his character does have some merit as Norris assigns some of his attitudes to Presley through the poet's hostility toward aestheticism, which mirrors Norris's position in "An Opening for Novelists," and the fact that both are trying to fashion literature out of the West. However, as McElrath notes, Presley ignores these raw materials to base his work on the models of others, which reflects tendencies that Norris condemned.[74] Further, Presley is separated from the realm of action: while the farmers are involved in a physical struggle for survival, Presley's battle is limited to the composition of verse until his convoluted speech and failed attempt to assassinate Behrman. When Presley is not searching for inspiration for his epic, he is a passive observer who simply listens to the ranchers' discussions, takes a peripheral role in the coming conflict, and even bases his poem on Jean-François Millet's *The Man with the Hoe* rather than the settlers' experiences.[75] Shelgrim makes this point when he states that the painting "leaves nothing more to be said. You might have well kept quiet. There's only one best way to say anything. And what has made the picture of 'The Toilers' great is that the artist said in it the *best* that could be said on the subject" (574). Presley's text is merely a copy of one drawn from life, a facsimile that offers no original contribution to the fight against the railroad. This approach differs from that of Norris, who transforms the Mussel Slough tragedy into a representation of a principal source of injustice, fashioning its participants' struggles into a novel that challenges the imperatives of the economic elite.

The representation of Presley further undermines the plausibility of assertions that he serves as Norris's spokesman as the narrator highlights both the limitations of the poet's perceptions and his tendency to adopt the perspectives of the people around him. Norris stresses these elements in his sketch of Presley, writing that he is "easily impressed—impressionable," possesses "an unbalanced mind," and "could easily go insane."[76] This disordered mind does not seem to be the logical repository for Norris's attitude toward his material, suggesting instead the broader separation between the novelist and his character. The narrator advances the problematic nature of Presley's observations by noting that he "devoured, rather than read, and emerged from the affair, his mind a confused jumble of conflicting notions, sick with over-effort, raging against injustice and oppression, and with not one sane suggestion as to remedy or redress" (307–8). Presley's impressions reflect a superficial engagement with the actual struggles of the narrative, and the fact that his thoughts are shaped by an emotional response rather than a rational framework prevents him from seeing these experiences clearly. Since these ideas emerge within the subjectivity of the aesthete, Presley's interpretations should not be elevated to the status of wisdom. Norris further emphasizes the instability of Presley's point of view through his tendency to take on the beliefs and practices of his stronger counterparts: his decision to bomb Behrman's house comes from his interaction with the bar owner, Caraher, and the poet's final pronouncements are an amalgamation of beliefs espoused by Vanamee, a wandering shepherd, and Shelgrim, which should not be confused with the underlying argument of *The Octopus.*

Instead, Presley's perspective offers a critical commentary on adhering to concepts that are not consistent with experience, which manifests through his interactions with the president of the Pacific and Southwestern.[77] Norris highlights the falsity of Shelgrim's assertions by filtering them through Presley's unreliable point of view, evident through his perceptions of the boss's charitable act. The narrator states that Presley "had been prepared to come upon an ogre, a brute, a terrible man of blood and iron, and instead had discovered a sentimentalist and an art critic. No standards of measurement in his mental equipment would apply to the actual man" (574). The apparent compassion of the railroad magnate does not match Presley's initial interpretation because he perceives life through simplistic oppositions, and he cannot separate the executive's interpersonal conduct from his business undertakings. This context frames Shelgrim's claim to Presley that

> you are dealing with forces, young man, when you speak of Wheat and the Railroads, not with men. There is the Wheat, the supply. It must be carried to feed the People. There is the demand. The Wheat is one force, the Railroad, another, and there is the law that governs them—supply and demand. Men have only little to do in the whole business. Complications may arise, conditions that bear hard on the individual—crush him maybe—*but the Wheat will be carried to feed the people* as inevitably as it will grow. If you want to fasten the blame of the affair at Los Muertos on any one person, you will make a mistake. Blame conditions, not men. (576)

While Shelgrim contends that actions result from abstract laws of exchange divorced from human agency, he obscures the essential truth that the circumstances governing the marketplace stem from men. The analogy of the wheat is appropriate, yet it demonstrates a different position since the grain would not have grown without the ranchers creating a system of irrigation, planting the crops, tending them, and harvesting these commodities. The socioeconomic conditions that determine the fates of the farmers are likewise the products of individuals: company officials have manipulated supply and demand by fixing the price of land and arbitrarily setting freight rates to maximize earnings. This control over the social order engenders broader culpability because these executives orchestrated the practices that have caused such drastic consequences.

Norris casts further doubt on Shelgrim's position when Presley leaves the industrial magnate's office. The narrator remarks that "Presley regained the street stupefied, his brain in a whirl. This new idea, this new conception dumbfounded him. Somehow, he could not deny it. It rang with the clear reverberation of truth" (576–77). The narrator reiterates one of the common motifs associated with Presley's instability, which gains credence through his earlier admission that he has suffered a nervous breakdown. These references undermine Shelgrim's contentions, indicating that they possess "the clear reverberation of truth" only for people whose engagement with reality is based on emotion rather than reason and who search aimlessly for a theory to govern existence rather than attempting to understand the world around them.

The juxtaposition of the opulence at the party of Mr. Gerard, a vice president of the railroad, with the starvation of Mrs. Hooven further undermines Shelgrim's position, illustrating the extremes of wealth and poverty that emerge as a result of the practices employed by the Pacific and Southwestern. This episode also has its basis in Norris's research. One of the articles in his notebook for *The Octopus,* "John Miller / A Suicide," provides a description of a lavish dinner: "The wines were of the rarest vintages. The service was irreproachable, the viands fit for a Roman orgie [sic] in the days of the decadence. The magnates clinked glasses with John Miller. They responded to toasts with flattering allusions to his ability and faithful service. They complimented him on his home, its furnishings, his pictures, statuary, servants, his dinner. None was more fulsome in flattery than old Collis P. Huntington, none more gracious. But all dinners end."[78] The magnificence of the scene, with its fine wine and attentive service, reflects Norris's emphasis in his description of the Gerards' banquet. The party also reflects the Roman "days of decadence" as the guests are so preoccupied with their possessions, amusements, and luxuries, most notable in Mrs. Gerard's refusal to eat asparagus that has not been freshly cut, that they are blissfully unaware of the coming social upheaval when "the Man in the Street, grimed with powder smoke, foul with the gutter," would burn the imposing house to its foundations (609). The use of John Miller as a potential source is even more significant given that he was an executive who stole more than a million dollars from the Southern Pacific Contract and Finance Company. This allusion underscores the duplicity of the railroad officials, indicating that such luxury and ease are the result of fleecing others, which parallels the Pacific and Southwestern's usurpation of the land improved by the settlers.

The fate of Mrs. Hooven conveys the consequences of such practices, and this character's downfall also has its basis in Norris's research. Another piece in his notebook, "Mother Starves to Death," presents a woman's demise on the streets of New York after being refused admittance to an almshouse because she did not meet the requirements for aid.[79] While Norris omitted the poorhouse and substituted Mrs. Hooven's interactions with the police officer who prevents her from sleeping in the park, the author preserves the tenor of the article as Mrs. Hooven finds no relief aside from whatever she is able to beg. Norris augments this material through Mrs. Hooven's failure to negotiate the urban space after her husband's death in the gunfight, an alteration that reinforces the effect of environment on the individual and her inability to adapt to changed circumstances. The juxtaposition between the abundance at the dinner party and the starvation of Mrs. Hooven expresses a fundamental relationship between these episodes: the affluence of those like the party guests stems from the poverty of people like Mrs. Hooven. Presley advances a similar interpretation when he reflects that "years of extortion and oppression had wrung money from all the San Joaquin, money that had made possible this very scene in which he found himself," and concludes that "because the farmers of the valley were poor, these men were rich." The fact that this interpretation is situated within Presley's consciousness denotes its problematic nature. Norris does not draw a literal correlation between the banquet and the deaths of the ranchers; the party guests would still enjoy immense wealth without the exploitation of the San Joaquin Valley as the Pacific and Southwestern operates on such a vast scale that the resources extracted from this conflict represent a largely insignificant fraction of the company's earnings. Norris further destabilizes Presley's conclusion through his overstatement: the guests do not literally "fatten on the blood of the People, on the men who had been killed at the ditch," and the women at the table are not "harpies tearing human flesh" (608). Rather than establishing a connection between the events of the narrative and the present scene, the use of Presley's perspective invites a broader interpretation of the causes of such tragedies, one that locates the killing of the settlers within a broader pattern of abuses. Norris identifies such outcomes as the logical results of an emphasis on capital accumulation over more humane concerns, a point that he illustrates clearly through Mrs. Hooven's death.

This context illuminates Presley's position at the end of the novel, which provides a critique of viewpoints that neglect immediate economic reality and obscure suffering.[80] Norris again uses indirect discourse to reflect Presley's perspective as the narrator prefaces the concluding paragraphs with the statement that "Vanamee's words came back to [Presley's] mind," a reference that attributes the following material to the character rather than to the narrator or author. In the closing section, Presley observes that "men—motes in the sunshine—perished, were shot down in the very noon of life, hearts were broken, little children started in life lamentably handicapped; young girls were brought to a life of shame; old women died in the heart of life for lack of food. In that little, isolated group of human insects, misery, death, and anguish spun like a wheel of fire" (651). Presley echoes Shelgrim through the emphasis on the insignificance of men, evident through the reference to "human insects." The focus on the Hoovens for the principal illustrations of this inexorable fate, however, highlights the fact that these outcomes resulted from policies instituted in the upper echelons of the socioeconomic system rather than the operation of abstract laws.

Nonetheless, Presley continues to evade such concerns through his reflections on the natural world and its power. The narrator, still relying on indirect discourse to reflect Presley's position, notes that "*the* WHEAT *remained. Untouched, unassailable, undefiled, that mighty world-force, that nourisher of nations, wrapped in Nirvanic calm, indifferent to the human swarm, gigantic, resistless, moved onward in its appointed groves*" (651). As these meditations occur aboard a vessel transporting grain to relieve a famine, Presley focuses on the potential benefits to emerge out of the tragedy, viewing the wheat as an elemental force that operates in line with Shelgrim's earlier assertions, while the broader argument has its origins in Vanamee's claims about the ultimate triumph of good. This Machiavellian argument contradicts the majority of *The Octopus* with its emphasis on the process of labor necessary to generate this commodity as it moves only in the "appointed grooves" made by the people who control the networks of distribution, which thereby suggests that need for men and women to remedy the injustices presented throughout the book. Presley further develops his contention that everything trends inevitably toward the good, positing that "falseness dies; injustice and oppression in the end of everything fade and vanish away. Greed, cruelty, selfishness, and inhumanity are short-lived; the individual suffers, but the race goes on. Annixter dies, but in a far distant corner of the world a thousand lives are saved. The larger view always and through all shams, all wickedness, discovers the Truth that will, in the end, prevail, and all things, surely, inevitably, resistlessly work together for the good" (651–52). While this logic appeals to Presley after his nervous breakdown, the ideas are the product of Vanamee, who is even more mentally unstable than Presley, and this connection further undermines his outlook with a demonstration of how his opinions are formed by others. The narrative does not advance a philosophy that justifies widespread suffering; instead, the conclusion provides a critical framework for examining positions that trivialize the fates of individuals, and Norris indicates that Presley's viewpoint should not be taken seriously since it is completely divorced from the central events of the work.

The representation of the natural world also challenges Presley's position, conveying the need to change the practices that govern the economic system as they have engendered a broader conflict between people and their surroundings in the desire for acquisition. Early in *The Octopus,* the narrator describes the land through imagery associated with birth and notes that "the earth, after its period of reproduction, its pains of labor, had been delivered of the fruit of its loins, and now slept the sleep of exhaustion" (14). The personification of the environment highlights its potential role in shaping conditions to propagate the species; however, the majority of *The Octopus* illustrates that financial concerns interfere with the ability of the earth to perform this function. Norris dramatizes these consequences early in the novel, when Harran sees a sidecar carrying the plows necessary to plant wheat at Los Muertos, yet while the devices are already in Bonneville, they must be sent to San Francisco and then back. The Pacific and Southwestern, despite providing the essential service of transporting goods, impedes the process of cultivation and production in order to charge an increased rate of eleven cents per ton. This scene parallels the broader monetary struggle in *The Octopus,* expressing the forces that undermine the potential of the soil: the ranchers are principally concerned that such actions will jeopardize their earnings, and these men focus solely on the high prices for grain. Likewise, the railroad executives are not concerned with what a bumper crop portends for the hungry, viewing the harvest as a means to raise rates and to maximize earnings. Since such perspectives dominate the market and influence human interactions, the benevolence of nature will not magically emerge to alleviate suffering but instead must stem from the work of men and women to foster such outcomes.

Norris also destabilizes this potential beneficence through human efforts to master the natural world, which further undermines the optimistic perspective that Presley adopts at the end of the novel. Annie Derrick, the wife of Magnus, observes that the hospitality of the earth manifests only when "the human ant-swarm was submissive to it, working with it," yet when people "strive to make head against the power of this nature, and at once it becomes relentless, a gigantic engine, a vast power, huge, terrible; a leviathan with a heart of steel, knowing no compunction, no forgiveness, no tolerance; crushing out the human atom with soundless calm, the agony of destruction never sending a jar" (180). This hostility results from attempts to bend the environment to the interests of men and a general failure to act in harmony with their surroundings, which would provide for the continuation of the species and an alleviation of suffering. Although the narrative seems to corroborate Presley's view through the representations of Mrs. Cedarquist's relief organization and the death of S. Behrman, these episodes actually further challenge the poet's position. Despite the promise offered by the shipment of grain, Norris gives few details about this act of charity and focuses primarily on how it enables Behrman to maximize profits as he will sell the committee crops that he now owns through the dispossession of Magnus, controlling all aspects of the process of distribution. Further, Behrman's subsequent demise as a result of drowning in an avalanche of wheat is not a form of divine justice and instead emanates from the processes he has created. To maximize profitability, Behrman devised the idea of using a chute to load the vessel, which allows for fewer laborers and indirectly seals Behrman's fate since no one will be able to help him escape from the cargo hold. The narrator's statement that "the grain seemed impelled by a force of its own" is contextualized by a reference to Behrman's labor-saving techniques, and this information reinforces the idea that his fate stems from his greed (641). The tension between the practices of man and the potential of the land reinforces that this promise cannot be realized without concrete actions taken by individuals.

Norris offers an alternate course of action through Annixter, who expresses the "larger view" that Presley cannot attain and indicates the potential for growth when people deviate from pursuits based on self-interest.[81] Annixter progresses from an exclusive focus on his requirements to an outlook that situates these impulses within a clear social context, one that does not reduce suffering to a necessary step toward a better future. Initially, Annixter is a misanthrope whose interactions are characterized by cruelty, yet his attitude changes through his love for Hilma Tree, which enables him to broaden his perspective. After she flees instead of becoming Annixter's mistress, the narrator observes that "the idea of the self dwindled. Annixter no longer considered himself; no longer considered the notion of marriage from the point of view of his own comfort, his own wishes, his own advantage. He realised that in his new-found desire to make her happy, he was sincere. There was something in that idea, after all. To make some one happy—how about that now? It was worth thinking of" (367). This relationship contrasts the operation of the main plot and provides further commentary on the undertakings of the ranchers and railroad officials, who have allowed the desire for financial gain to dictate their activities.

Eventually, Annixter's consciousness expands from Hilma to embrace humanity as he realizes that the conditions confronting one person reflect those facing others. Contemplating this development, Annixter asserts: "I began to see that a fellow can't live *for* himself any more than he can live *by* himself. He's got to think of others. . . . I've got a whole lot of ideas since I began to love Hilma, and just as soon as I can, I'm going to get in and *help* people, and I'm going to keep that idea for the rest of my natural life. That ain't much of a religion, but it's the best I've got" (467–68). Annixter parallels Stephen Council from Hamlin Garland's "Under the Lion's Paw" and Jim Casy from Steinbeck's *The Grapes of Wrath,* who emphasize collective interests in relation to those of the individual, who should realize their place within the broader human family and act accordingly. Despite the fact that Annixter does not develop this philosophy to the extent of Council and Casy, he does engage in comparable acts of charity through his support of Mrs. Dyke and Sidney. The narrator also reveals the potential for further development, stating that Annixter's perceptions "had broadened to enfold another child and another mother bound to him by no other ties than those of humanity and pity. In time, starting from this point it would reach out more and more till it should take in all men and women" (498). This conception of social justice provides a framework to examine the financial imperatives of American life and posits the need for a set of values more conducive to the majority. Annixter's death prevents the complete realization of this point of view, which heightens the tragedy of the narrative through the demise of the only character who attempted to transform himself based on such insight.

Annixter's development supplies a more logical response to the institutional forces that facilitate such drastic consequences than Presley's grandiose pronouncements. The rancher's shift to a perspective that incorporates the needs of the collective highlights the necessity of a change in consciousness as a prelude to transforming society. Although Norris refrained from proposing specific remedies for social ills, claiming that the "novelist—by nature—can hardly be a political economist; and it is to the latter rather than to the former that one must look for a way out of the 'present discontents,'" *The Octopus* offers avenues for the critical reflection necessary to address the causes of suffering within the current economic system.[82] In portraying the tragedies that emerge from privileging financial gain over the common good, Norris articulates the need for an alternate set of values to govern the human enterprise, which could prevent the outcomes represented in this novel and more efficiently promote the greater good.

3

AN INJURY TO ONE

Class Conflict in "The Apostate" and Martin Eden

Jack London's social writings play an important role in the development of American naturalism as he provided more nuanced portrayals of working-class life and allowed his characters greater agency than his predecessors in this tradition. Philip S. Foner asserts that "it was Jack London more than any other writer of his day, who broke the ice that was congealing American letters and brought life and literature into a meaningful relation to each other."[1] This engagement between fiction and lived experience manifests through London's representations of the constraints that impact his characters' actions and their attempts to shape the conditions of their lives. Reflecting on London's role in the development of naturalist fiction, Jeanne Campbell Reesman and Leonard Cassuto observe that "London's work provides a rich ground for the probing examination naturalism has undergone as its boundaries have become more permeable, and the study of London's writing enriches both humanistic and deterministic reevaluations of naturalism."[2] Rather than stressing his protagonists' inevitable deterioration due to elements rooted within their surroundings, London endows his characters with a measure of agency that helps to sharpen the social themes of his works. This development is readily apparent in "The Apostate" and *Martin Eden.* Through their engagement with the American Dream, these works illustrate the dangers of capitalism through its impact on the protagonists, tracing how the present economic order thwarts human progress and offering a critique of attempts at amelioration that place the elevation of the individual above the needs of the collective.

The American Dream appears throughout London's fiction, and this thematic concern suggests elements of his own advancement. London, the illegitimate son of astrologer William Chaney and spiritualist Flora Wellman, was born into poverty, and his family's financial prospects only marginally improved through his mother's marriage to John London. Accordingly, Jack began working at an early age to supplement his parents' income, laboring first at the R. Hickmott Canning Company before becoming an oyster pirate; a deputy of the Fish Patrol; a sailor; and an employee of the Oakland, San Leandro, and Haywards Electric Railway. Regarding these experiences, London wrote: "I still believed in the old myths which were the heritage of the American boy when I was a boy. . . . A canal boy could become a president. Any boy, who took employment with any firm, could, by thrift, energy, and sobriety, learn the business and rise from position to position until he was taken in as a junior partner. After that the senior partnership was only a matter of time."[3] London ironically presents the conventional belief that one can rise in the ranks through initiative and diligence since America is an open society governed by fair rules applicable to all. London had already demonstrated these traits at the cannery and aboard the *Sophia Sutherland* without any commensurate increase in his earnings, and his job for the streetcar company reduced him to "a proper work-beast. I worked, and ate, and slept while my mind slept all the time," a motif that he developed in "The Apostate" and *Martin Eden*.[4] As James L. Haley observes, London objected not to strenuous labor but to "the idea of slaving at a pittance of a wage for a class of owners and investors who lived like lords and took their sense of entitlement for granted."[5] This realization illustrated the nature of an economic system that offered the potential for material progress and yet imposed significant barriers to such advancement for many workers.

London responded to his exploitation by embarking on a period as a tramp, and his experiences further illuminated the harsh reality of capitalism. In 1894, London rode the rails with a group organized by Charles T. Kelly that was planning to meet Jacob Coxey's Army of the Unemployed in Washington, DC, to protest at the U.S. Capitol. While London did not participate in the culminating demonstration, his time on the road brought him into contact with those who had been cast aside by their employers.[6] Reflecting on this period, London observed: "I found there all sorts of men, many of whom had once been as good as myself and just as *blond-beastly;* sailor-men, soldier-men, labor-men, all wrenched and distorted and twisted out of shape by toil and hardship and accident, and cast adrift by their masters like so many old horses. I battered on the drag and slammed back gates, or shivered with them in box cars and city parks, listening the while to life-histories which began under auspices as fair as mine, with digestions and bodies equal to and better than mine, and which ended there before my eyes in the shambles at the bottom of the Social Pit."[7] London realized that his reliance on physical strength would reduce him to the same status of degradation that he noted in his companions as he would be unable to sustain his existence after outliving his productivity.

When he returned to California, London determined that he would keep himself out of the social pit. He asserted that "my new concept was that manual labor was undignified, and that it didn't pay. . . . Brains paid, not brawn, and I resolved never again to offer my muscles in the brawn market. Brain, and brain only, would I sell."[8] Toward this end, London began a course of intellectual improvement, striving first to escape poverty through education and then through fiction after arriving home from the Yukon in 1898 with $4.50 in gold dust in his pockets.[9] London published his first collection of short stories, *The Son of the Wolf,* in 1900; cemented his fame with *The Call of the Wild* in 1903, for which he received $750 from the *Saturday Evening Post* and $2,000 from Macmillan; and became one of the highest-paid writers in America after the success of *The Sea Wolf* (1904).[10] At his commercial peak, London purchased a ranch in Glen Ellen, financed the construction of a yacht to sail around the world, and attained a standard of living that most individuals would envy.

While London was able to improve his financial position, the circumstances of his early life convinced him that such development was atypical in the United States, which is buttressed by analyses of conditions in fin de siècle America. Stephan Thernstrom observes that there

> were definite rigidities in the occupational structure, a series of barriers that impeded mobility and perpetuated inequality. The level at which a young man entered the labor market strongly influenced the course of his subsequent career. His point of entry into the occupational competition was in turn significantly related to the social-class position of the family in which he was reared. Thus it was that sons of professionals and substantial businessmen were four times as likely as children from low white-collar homes to attain upper white-collar status themselves,

6 ½ times as likely as the sons of skilled workers, and no less than 12 times as likely as the youths from households headed by an unskilled or semiskilled laborer.[11]

This inability to rise in the ranks did not necessarily stem from the attributes of the individual but from wage rates and the extent to which they shaped opportunities for future generations. As a result of compensation that was insufficient to meet physical requirements, parents often had to augment their pay by sending their progeny into the factories, mines, and mills. In a study of Philadelphia, Michael R. Haines found that 77.2 percent of families in the bottom economic quartile had to rely partly on the earnings of their offspring, which prevented them from obtaining the education and training necessary to prosper.[12] Examining the prospects for mobility between generations, Thernstrom found that only one in ten children born into the working class succeeded in becoming substantial businessmen or professionals and that only three in ten secured positions as salesman, clerks, or proprietors of small shops.[13] Thus, most people found that they had a limited ability to improve their material circumstances.

London dramatizes these ideas in "The Apostate," which first appeared in the *Woman's Home Companion* (September 1906) and was republished in *When God Laughs and Other Stories* (1911). The narrative chronicles the experiences of a young factory worker who struggles against the monotonous routine of industrial production, and most critics view the story in the context of reform movements at the turn of the century. For instance, James I. McClintock argues that the work is simply "a muck-raking story attacking the inadequacy of child-labor legislation and an irreverent social commentary that it is preferable to be a tramp than a work beast," and Jeanne Campbell Reesman observes that the text provides "a depressing portrait of the life-numbing reality of child labor as well as a romantic American escape from such slavery."[14] This injustice of child labor is central to "The Apostate," yet the representation of this particular subject possesses broader ramifications. The depiction of Johnny's experiences in the workforce advances a trenchant critique of capitalism, highlighting the human consequences that result when society prioritizes industrial profits over human need, and the central character's flight signifies that his development is not possible within the existing economic framework.

The immediate impetus for "The Apostate" came from London's inability to accept an invitation to visit southern textile mills.[15] Instead, he created a narrative that dramatized similar injustices through the fate of the protagonist, whose experiences have their origins in the author's employment as a factory worker beginning in 1891. Discussing his job at the R. Hickmott Canning Company, London wrote: "I was up and at work at six in the morning. I took half an hour for dinner. I took half an hour for supper. I worked every night till ten, eleven, twelve o'clock. My wages were small, but I worked such long hours that I sometimes made as high as fifty dollars a month."[16] The time spent at the factory prevented London from exploring the Oakland Estuary and reading the books set before him by Ina Coolbrith, a librarian at the Oakland Free Library and later the poet laureate of California. Reflecting on this period, London observed: "I asked myself if this were to be the meaning of life—to be a work-beast? I knew of no horse in the city of Oakland that worked the hours I worked. If this were living, I was entirely unenamored of it. . . . There was only one way to escape my deadening toil. I must get out and away on the water."[17] This contrast between the "deadening" routine of industrial production and the restorative power of nature suggests the thematic contours of "The Apostate." London augmented these autobiographical elements with evidence drawn from contemporary accounts of child labor, and his files at the Huntington Library feature numerous articles on the issue that anticipate the central ideas and concrete details of the story.[18]

These sources and experiences provide the empirical foundation of "The Apostate," which develops its social themes by providing a narrative that counters the national success story as Johnny's attempts to improve his prospects do not engender mobility but instead intensify his exploitation. This emphasis on the American Dream emerges in the opening of the narrative. The first line, "If you don't git up Johnny, I won't give you a bite to eat," alludes to Horatio Alger Jr.'s *Ragged Dick* (1868), which begins with "Wake up there, youngster. . . . I suppose you'd lay there all day, if I hadn't called you."[19] This connection positions "The Apostate" against the ideas of economic progress associated with Alger, whose novels emphasize the potential for financial security or even affluence as a result of hard work, luck, and the intervention of a wealthy gentleman. London develops this formulation when the narrator notes that Johnny's "earlier years had been full of dreaming. Once he had been in love. It was when he first began guiding the cloth over the hot roller, and it was with the daughter of the superintendent. . . . On the surface of the cloth stream that poured past him, he pictured radiant futures wherein he performed prodigies of toil, invented miraculous machines, won to the mastership of the mills, and in the end took her in his arms and kissed her soberly on the brow" (231–32). The process by which the young worker wins the love of the superintendent's daughter evokes the narrative arc of Alger's fiction through the protagonist's mental picture of ascending to the ownership of the mill through his "prodigies of toil." London, however, inverts the Alger archetype as Johnny cannot attain advancement through his exertions. "The Apostate" omits the other components of Alger's formula from Johnny's dream since they find no outlet in his world: chance does not result in positive change in the factory, and benevolence seldom governs relations between labor and capital. London underscores Johnny's plight through the representation of his imagined future on the cloth that winds endlessly through the machine, ironically presenting the central character's toil as a means of realizing prosperity when it confines him to the socioeconomic position of his birth.

Within these parameters, "The Apostate" advances a condemnation of the economic system of London's era, indicating that the conditions governing Johnny's life circumscribe his progress with his apparent fate as a predictable outcome for one of his station. This theme manifests through the protagonist's employment history: at seven, he started at a jute mill, began weaving cloth the following year, and proceeded to a glass plant as a teenager before returning to the first factory. The circularity of the central character's experiences reveals his limited options as even his most diligent exertions prevent him from moving past his initial point for a significant period of time, and each slight progression results in a swift descent because of his substandard living and working conditions. The narrator develops these elements in the description of the youth's daily routine, emphasizing the squalid environment that results from the family's poverty. The narrator conveys the nature of these surroundings when he refers to Johnny's attempts to clean himself and observes, "That a sink should smell was to him part of the natural order, just as it was part of the natural order that the soap should be grimy with the dishwater and hard to lather" (223). This description would have been particularly jarring to the readership of the *Woman's Home Companion*, a monthly magazine that focused on the domestic concerns of the middle class. Accordingly, London's depiction of these unsanitary conditions emphasizes Johnny's necessary deviation from the conventions of polite society as a result of his economic position. The narrator accentuates this idea through the child's meager breakfast of cold pork, thin slices of bread, and a "hot and muddy liquid" that he confuses with good coffee, which intensifies the representation of the family's impecunious state since they cannot obtain sufficient nourishment (224). Further, the compression of time in the opening section, with the implication that this scene plays out every morning without variation, illustrates the monotony of Johnny's days in addition to his confinement within a system that he cannot alter.

Johnny's opportunities for development are further diminished by the nature of his labor and its adverse impact on his health. This portrayal seems to originate from an article in London's files titled "The Modern Slaughter of the Innocents," by Owen R. Lovejoy, the general-secretary of the National Child Labor Committee. London circled a passage: "The little boy who can sit for ten hours a day on a low stool bent over his work and with lightning fingers tie three hundred dozen glass stoppers into their bottles in the ten hours, is a marvel of mechanical efficiency. But the nervous twitch of the muscles at rest, the sunken chest and feeble lungs, the bent back and drooping shoulders, the sallow face and expressionless eyes foretell the curse which outraged Nature is already writing with his life blood against the race."[20] These maladies emerge in "The Apostate" as the chronic illnesses that cost Johnny each of his jobs, and London also incorporates the precise quota for production into the story. These elements ground the narrative in its immediate historical context through the representation of maladies common to the working class during this era. The inspector who examines the child articulates these consequences by noting that the "boy's got the rickets—incipient, but he's got them. If epilepsy doesn't get him in the end, it will be because tuberculosis gets him first" (227). These diseases stem from not any inherent infirmity but the unhealthy conditions of the central character's labor, the absence of sunlight, and the lack of adequate nutrients. These issues leave him with no apparent avenue toward prosperity.

"The Apostate" further highlights the consequences of Johnny's exertions through the physical effects of his repetitive movements. This point becomes apparent when the central character ties weaver's knots in his sleep, a representation that London gleaned from an article in his files. In "Child Labor Legislation," the anonymous writer quotes Lovejoy referring to a young worker and noting that "as the precursor of a healthy man he is a failure. He has been reduced to a bundle of quivering nerves and can doubtless tie knots at lightning speed easier than he can sit still."[21] This material reinforces the relationship between such practices and detrimental results for laborers through the physical stresses on the operative. London conveys his debt to this article when the narrator states that there "was nothing difficult about the weaver's knots. He once boasted that he could tie them in his sleep. And for that matter, he sometimes did, toiling centuries long in a single night at tying an endless succession of weaver's knots" (225). The connections to this article are evident through the final reference and Johnny's inability to sit still even at rest, which illustrate how the boy's occupation shapes all aspects of life as he receives no reprieve from his toil. London extends these implications through the protagonist's deterioration, a portrayal that originates from another piece in the author's possession titled "To Protect Childhood." The journalist states that the boy's "working power, however, was about exhausted and, at 16, the time when the normal laborer might just begin his task, he was broken down in health, impoverished in mind and possessed of the bitterness of an old man."[22] In "The Apostate," the unsustainable nature of such labor emerges through the central character's aged appearance, with the suggestion that he has given his most productive years to his employers at the expense of attributes that could have facilitated a brighter future.

The emphasis on Johnny's mechanization further buttresses the social themes of "The Apostate," connecting his fate to the requirements of his labor and the limited progress that such arrangements make possible for the poor. The impetus for this representation also seems to be "Child Labor Legislation," in which London circled a passage: "The proprietor of a successful glass house recently with pride brought me to a small boy who sat on a low stool tying glass stoppers into small bottles. He sat bent over his work, the bottles held between his knees and the bundle of string at his hip, his body thrown forward and his chest contracted, HIS THIN ARMS FLYING WITH THE SWIFT AND ACCURATE MOTION OF A PERFECT MACHINE, AS HE HUMMED IN HIS LABOR FOR TEN HOURS A DAY. Three knots were made for each and the daily task was 300 dozen bottles."[23] From this source, London obtained the details of Johnny's occupation performing piecework at the glass plant. The story employs a similar description of his daily tasks, stresses the resulting physical consequences because of the posture he must adopt, and incorporates the precise quota for production. Further, the designation of the unnamed operative as a "PERFECT MACHINE" anticipates London's focus on the shaping role of the protagonist's labor, and the narrator clarifies this idea when he states that Johnny "excelled, because the clay of him had been moulded by the mills into the perfect machine" (234). The reference to the central character as "clay" formed by his milieu reinforces the deterministic basis of the narrative, with its implication that environmental pressures ultimately dictate individual outcomes.

"The Apostate" offers a powerful illustration of this concept through Johnny's mechanization, which extends the social criticism of the work to register the loss of his humanity resulting from modern industrial processes. The narrator introduces the boy's occupation at the jute mill by noting that he "worked mechanically" (225). At this stage, the speaker focuses on Johnny, with the modifier reflecting the nature of his tasks and introducing their detrimental effects. These concerns gain clear expression through the subsequent references to machines. The narrator observes that from "the perfect worker [Johnny] had evolved into the perfect machine. When his work went wrong, it was with him as with the machine, due to faulty material. It would have been as possible for a perfect nail-die to cut imperfect nails as for him to make a mistake" (226). The similes establish a fundamental connection between the central character and the equipment he operates, denoting that the former has gradually been absorbed into the latter. As a result, the boy exists as an automaton defined by his labor, which the narrator conveys through the shift from the child to his mechanized state in the first sentence, while the comparison of Johnny to the nail die reinforces that he exists only in relation to the value he produces for the company. The narrator locates this transformation within the economic framework that governs the factory and states that the "superintendent was very proud of [Johnny], and brought visitors to look at him. In ten hours three hundred dozen bottles passed through his hands. This meant he had attained machine-like perfection. All waste movements were eliminated. Every motion of his thin arms, every movement of a muscle in the thin fingers, was swift and accurate" (231). The narrator's emphasis on the young man's efficiency demonstrates the qualities that make him a model worker: his accuracy and the absence of excess movement enable him to generate higher profits for ownership, which prompts the superintendent's approval. This diligence, however, accelerates Johnny's decline, diminishing his humanity and turning him into another component in the process of production.

Johnny's dehumanization manifests further through the deterioration of his intellect, which occurs in direct relation to his increased efficiency. For this aspect of the story, London drew on another source to depict the consequences of such labor for both the protagonist and those individuals employed under similar conditions. In "Turning Children into Dollars," Juliet Wilbor Tompkins described a young worker who sat "in a closet lighted by a gas jet, with a little stick in his hand, watching a great stream of cloth that poured down from above and passed over a hot roller that ironed its surface, his business being to guide the cloth if it showed a tendency to swerve to the right or to the left from the roller. It was easy work—horribly, wickedly easy. Not a muscle of his body was getting proper development; his mind slept undisturbed as his eyes dully watched the cloth stream."[24] London bracketed this passage, incorporating the first sentence into the description of the central character's occupation at the mill while also stressing the weakening of his cognitive faculties due to the absence of any stimulation. The narrator develops these detrimental effects through the contrast between Johnny's current state and his earlier perspective, noting that he "was very happy at that job, in spite of the moist heat, for he was still young and in possession of dreams and illusions. And wonderful dreams he dreamed as he watched the steaming cloth streaming endlessly by. But there was no exercise about the work, no call upon his mind, and he dreamed less and less, while his mind grew torpid and drowsy." This lack of intellectual challenges turns the youth into "part of the mechanism" (231), and London alludes to Tompkins's article through the reference to Johnny's brain becoming "torpid and drowsy," which evokes the statement that the young operative's "mind slept undisturbed."

"The Apostate" extends this idea through the loss of the protagonist's capacity to dream. The narrator observes that the "machinery ran faster than when [Johnny] had first gone to work, and his mind ran slower. He no longer dreamed at all" (231). This alteration reflects Johnny's inability to attain his desires within the confines of his employment as increases in his productivity have come at the expense of the traits that might have allowed for a different outcome. The narrator reinforces this development by stating that the "rest of the time he worked, and his consciousness was machine consciousness. Outside this his mind was a blank. He had no ideals, and but one illusion; namely, that he drank excellent coffee. He was a work-beast. He had no mental life whatever" (234). Through the decay of his capability to think and dream, Johnny has lost what separates humans from lower life forms. However, this regression does not reduce him to status of an animal, which still exists within nature, but a "work-beast," an abnormal creature that violates the patterns of the natural world.

The references to food throughout "The Apostate" also illustrate these consequences by supplying additional indications of Johnny's deterioration. In the opening scene, he states that he does not mind living farther away from the factory since the dollar saved on rent "means more grub" and that "I'd sooner do the walkin' and git the grub" (224). Expressing the role that this desire for sustenance plays in shaping the child's actions, the narrator observes that "two dollars represented the difference between acute starvation and chronic underfeeding" (231). Despite his diligent efforts, Johnny cannot earn enough money to satisfy his physical requirements, apparent through the distinction between two forms of insufficient caloric energy, which alludes to the meager meal that he consumes at the beginning of the narrative. The narrator accentuates the prominent position that eating occupies in the boy's consciousness by noting that there "had been several great events in [Johnny's] life. One of these had been when his mother bought some California prunes. Two others had been the two times when she cooked custard" (232). This passage reflects the extent of the protagonist's deprivation, which is so acute that he connects the most noteworthy events in his life to consumption since these are the only instances when he has experienced what amount to luxuries. This context clarifies the thematic significance of the floating island, a French confection consisting of meringue in crème anglaise, as a representation of Johnny's decline. When his mother finally makes this treat, one that he had relegated "to the limbo of unattainable ideals," he takes no apparent interest in it as he is engaged in the task of "mechanically eating what was before him" (232, 234). The modifier reiterates that the central character's labor has produced his current state, preventing him from obtaining any enjoyment from his existence as evident through his disinterest in his dessert. Further, this episode provides the initial manifestation of the illness that causes Johnny's flight and establishes the foundation for his relative transformation at the end of "The Apostate."

London's social criticism extends to the representation of Johnny's domestic life, which highlights how economic pressures can destabilize the natural bonds of affection between individuals as apparent through the boy's estrangement from his family. London highlights these elements when the youth watches his siblings playing outside. The narrator states that Johnny lacked "patience with their excessive and amazing juvenility. He did not understand it. His own childhood was too far behind him. He was like an old and irritable man, annoyed by the turbulence of their young spirits that was to him errant silliness" (228). The protagonist's inability to understand the actions of his siblings results from the fact that he has not shared any similar experiences since he adopted an adult role when he first went to work at age seven. Further, Johnny's hostility emerges from the reality that his labor has afforded his brother Will the potential for a brighter future. Clarifying this point through a contrast between the physical appearances of the boys, the narrator observes that "Will seemed to show the benefit of this giving over and the giving away. He was well-built, fairly rugged, as tall as his elder brother and even heavier. It was as though the lifeblood of the one had been diverted into the other's veins. And in spirits it was the same. Johnny was jaded, worn out, without resilience, while his younger brother seemed bursting and spilling over with exuberance" (229). This comparison reflects the causative role of each character's environment. The factory has turned Johnny into a sickly automaton whose fate has been sealed by his exertions; Will, on the other hand, has the opportunities afforded by education and good health that will seemingly enable him to attain prosperity. This relationship indicates that while mobility might be possible for some, such advancement comes at the expense of another who produces the conditions that contribute to such successes.

This sense of alienation also governs Johnny's relationship with his mother, whom critics have identified as the villain in the story; however, such readings ignore how her acts are prefigured by the same forces that dictate the opportunities available to her eldest child. Joan Hedrick asserts that Johnny's mother "is also the immediate agent of Johnny's oppression, in that it is she who wakes him up and insists he hurry or else 'be docked.'"[25] In a related vein, Stephen T. Dhondt contends that the "degenerate condition of the working class is not entirely the result of injustices on the part of the ruling class. Some of the blame must fall on the ignorance of the uneducated, inept people of the proletariat."[26] While the boy's mother plays a role in his plight, she is not the agent of his oppression. Instead, she merely reflects the fiscal reality that victimizes both the woman and her offspring, causing her to send Johnny into the factory so that the family can survive and his siblings might experience more positive outcomes. Within these confines, Johnny's mother attempts to mitigate the severity of her actions by giving the protagonist part of her meager breakfast, and this undertaking exhibits a maternal concern for his well-being. Further, the mother's repeated statements that "it wasn't my fault. I do the best I can" reveal the limitations imposed by her class position, lack of an education, and the absence of the children's father, elements that have required her to sacrifice Johnny for the prospects of his siblings (230). This impact on the natural bonds within families further informs London's indictment of an economic system that often necessitates greater hardships for some individuals so that others may eventually prosper.

These consequences for Johnny suggest more than an exposé of child labor in the United States, and "The Apostate" instead advances a critique of the fiscal context that conditions such abuses. Even though federal legislation prohibiting such employment was not upheld until the Fair Labor Standards Act in 1938, many states had imposed restrictions on underage employees, beginning with Massachusetts in 1836.[27] London indicates that the story is set in one of these regions through the episode with the one-legged boy since the superintendent refers to the passage of a measure to keep children out of the factories. Further, the presence of the inspector who discharges Johnny's colleague signifies that this regulation is being enforced. This incident has its origins in Tompkins's article, from which London incorporated the one-legged boy's statement that "please, inspector, two babies died on us, and we're awful poor," adding only the formal designation "Mr.," and the fact that the inspector has discharged the child from three factories in the past year (228).[28] Reflecting on the conditions that forced this young man to get a job, Tompkins writes that the "boy, with the helpless loyalty of downtrodden childhood, is paying the rent and has been paying it for two years; all he asks is to go on paying it until the rest of him follows his lost leg into uncomplaining dust. That is all his parents ask of him."[29] London's borrowings from this source contextualize the plight of people like Johnny, denoting that their labor stems from the inadequate options for survival available to many working-class families during this period. As such, the experiences of the children in "The Apostate" convey a criticism of reformist measures, expressing that such legislative actions are ineffective because they fail to address the financial need that compels parents to end their progeny's education, to send them into the workforce so early in life, and to limit their future prospects.

The conclusion of "The Apostate" reinforces the need for systemic change by heightening the power of Johnny's milieu yet also signifying that a new environment can engender a different outcome for the protagonist. This representation correlates to the theory of determinism that London expressed in a letter to George Wharton James. Writing about *White Fang*

(1906), London asserted: "I am an evolutionist and therefore a broad optimist, hence my love for the human (in the slime though he be) comes from my knowing him as he is and seeing the divine possibilities ahead of him. . . . Every atom of life is plastic. The finest specimens now in existence were once all pulpy infants capable of being moulded this way or that. Let the pressure be one way and we have atavism—the reversion to the wild; the other domestication, civilization. I have always been impressed with the awful plasticity of life and I feel that I can never lay enough stress upon the marvelous power and influence of environment."[30] The reference to creatures being molded by their surroundings anticipates "The Apostate," in which London employs similar descriptions of his protagonist, whose experiences reflect "the marvelous power and influence of environment." Further, this emphasis on "the awful plasticity of life" conveys the nature of London's determinism. By endowing his characters with a range of potentialities and connecting the emergence of certain elements to environmental causes, London indicates that an alteration of the conditions that have engendered these effects will allow other aspects of the individual to emerge. As a corollary, London places the blame for his principals' fates on the social order that has produced them and that must be altered to prevent such tragedies.

This theme manifests in "The Apostate" through Johnny's removal from the factory as the change in his surroundings from the industrial arena to the natural world allows dormant aspects of his character to reassert themselves. In the early stages of the story, the boy's engagement with the outdoors is regulated by the temporal scheme of his workplace. The narrator observes that when Johnny "entered the factory gate the whistle blew again. He glanced at the east. Across a ragged sky-line of housetops a pale light was beginning to creep. This much he saw of the day as he turned his back upon it and joined his work-gang" (225). Man-made structures, evident through the whistle that standardizes employment, have displaced the natural cycle of life, and this development expresses Johnny's estrangement from the normal patterns of existence, which he can only recapture outside the limitations of the factory. The additional references to the natural world as a sustaining, hospitable environment indicate the potential for awakening the higher elements of Johnny's character. The narrator observes that while the protagonist labored, "the sun had made a golden ladder of the sky, flooded the world with its gracious warmth, and dropped down and disappeared in the west behind a ragged sky-line of housetops" (228). London's language offers a departure from the stark prose of the work, a rhetorical move that distinguishes this passage from the rest of the narrative and further establishes the significance of what the youth lacks. Further, the "golden ladder" and "gracious warmth" signify the possibilities for change outside the factory and the economic relations it embodies.

Johnny's convalescence reinforces this theme by contrasting his current state with his condition earlier in the narrative, which provides a clear illustration of the youth's transformation. The narrator notes that while the protagonist recuperated, he "was greatly absorbed in the one tree that grew across the street. He studied it for hours at a time, and was unusually interested when the wind swayed its branches and fluttered its leaves. Throughout the week he seemed lost in a great communion with himself. On Sunday, sitting on the stoop, he laughed aloud, several times, to the perturbation of his mother, who had not heard him laugh in years" (236). This examination of the tree evokes the earlier episode when he sat on the front stoop and "did no thinking. He was just resting. So far as his mind was concerned, it was asleep" (229). The outdoors, once unnoticed by the young man, supply the framework for his deeper awareness of the constraints that have governed his existence, and the "communion with himself" conveys the reemergence of the humanity that industrial processes had displaced. Johnny's laughter provides another important counterpoint to the earlier scene as his mirth differs from his former taciturn demeanor and his violent response to the exuberance of his siblings. "The Apostate" further expresses Johnny's transformation when he calculates the number of movements that he made during his employment. This process allows Johnny to recognize the problematic nature of the labor that has shaped his life, and his subsequent flight reflects his capacity for growth when removed from the framework that has previously dictated both his perspective and his actions.

Johnny's escape from the factory seems to express a possibility for his eventual progress, yet the ending of the story indicates that his transformation may have occurred too late to make any difference, which heightens the tragedy of the work. The narrator conveys the limited nature of Johnny's development through the uncertainty of his future: "The Apostate" concludes with him smiling as he leaves his immediate environment aboard a freight train without any discussion of his fate. The protagonist has neither a destination in mind nor any clear objectives to shape his actions, and his lack of any skills that would qualify him for a different occupation suggests that his future will not vary dramatically from his past. The context preceding his departure further undermines his prospects as the narrator asserts that Johnny "did not walk like a man. He did not look like a man. He was a travesty of the human. It was a twisted and stunted and nameless piece of life that shambled like a sickly ape, arms loose-hanging, stoop-shouldered, narrow-chested, grotesque and terrible" (238–39). This description highlights the wasted life of one who has seen his potential blunted by seemingly insuperable forces that have restricted his opportunities regardless of where he travels. Despite Johnny's attempts to alter the conditions of his existence, he has been marked by his labor to the extent that it has effaced his humanity, evident through London's use of animal imagery coupled with the shift in sentence subjects. Further, the reduction of Johnny to "a travesty of the human" provides a powerful indictment of the economic system of London's era and indicates the necessity of social change to minimize such outcomes.

The periodical accounts of child labor that London incorporated into "The Apostate" provide an effective foundation for the author to represent the consequences of economic exploitation. London's emphasis on the national success story locates Johnny's experiences within a broader context, portraying the waste of human potential as a result of the inequitable social order of the period. Through this depiction of consequences produced by unbridled capitalism, "The Apostate" indicates that the plight of the poor stems from not the actions of individual agents but the nature of the socioeconomic system itself, which highlights the need to address the underlying causes of injustice.

Martin Eden also centers on the American Dream, shifting to an illustration of an individual who attains advancement. This novel focuses on a working-class sailor who falls in love with a wealthy young woman, Ruth Morse, and her intellectual milieu, and he embarks on a routine of furious labor to become a successful writer in order to win her hand. *Martin Eden,* initially titled *Success* and based partially on London's early struggles to become an author, has long produced mixed reactions among critics: Franklin Walker presents both extremes when he asserts that the narrative is "uneven in structure, sometimes clumsy in expression, at times mawkish in tone. Yet it possesses great lasting power, having more vitality today than it did the day it issued from the press."[31] Contrary to the first half of this assessment, *Martin Eden* is a complex and tightly patterned work, and its continuing significance stems from its engagement with a fundamental concept of American life that manifests through Martin's movement from the lower class to the bourgeoisie. Although Martin is able to achieve mobility, his romantic, intellectual, and aesthetic ambitions find no true outlet among the elite.[32] Through this portrayal, London advances a powerful indictment of dominant society through representing the emptiness of its values within an economic framework that reduces all aspects of life to commodities, revealing the problematic nature of progress even for the rare person who improves their class position.

London's papers contain several sketches that reflect the main currents of *Martin Eden*. In "Novel on Literary Struggles," London describes a man who experiences "the gradual loss of his art and prostitution of his talent to meet present literary demands, insensibly this works on his ideals and he... becomes cynical, pessimistical."[33] This outline provides the earliest version of the ideas that would coalesce in the book, and London stresses the conflict between the commercial concerns of dominant society and the protagonist's artistic aspirations. London developed similar ideas in "Sociological Study," writing that the hero was an "efficient, rising from the dregs—with all the bitterness. And after all, is it worth the candle? Show the rectitude of purpose of the young man—the bitter, bitter struggle—the empty success."[34] This source is also significant in that it refers to the young writer's suicide, yet he kills himself after realizing that the woman he loves is serving a life sentence for murder. London returned to these ideas in "PLOT FOR PLAY / TRAGEDY." He detailed a first act that would focus on a young novelist's attempts to enter the literary marketplace, portraying him in "the noblest throes of creation" and laboring under the assumption that everything of value resided in the "upper strata of society to which he intends fighting his way."[35] The second act would center on the writer's "complete success. Culmination of success, in love, in everything," with the conclusion involving his disillusionment and subsequent suicide.[36]

London also developed the central themes that would appear in *Martin Eden* in "What Life Means to Me," which establishes clear distinctions between the author and Martin Eden. London presents his initial view of the bourgeoisie as exalted beings characterized by "unselfishness of the spirit, clean and noble thinking, keen intellectual living" instead of the "sordidness and wretchedness" of his lower-class existence, and this perspective reflects Martin's impressions of the Morses' environment and his own.[37] London's experiences among the privileged undermined these perceptions. Instead of people guided by lofty principles, he found individuals "who invoked the name of the Prince of Peace in their diatribes against war, and who put rifles in the hands of Pinkertons with which to shoot down workers in their own factories," and a man who funded foreign missions yet "worked his shop girls ten hours a day on a starvation wage and thereby directly encouraged prostitution."[38] These illustrations reveal the hypocrisy of the affluent as their rhetoric masks the practices that have engendered their wealth, yet Martin's critique of this group centers on a belief that they had squandered their opportunities and wasted their educations rather than on the human consequences of their business dealings. "What Life Means to Me" further juxtaposes the elite with other men and women "who exalted flesh and spirit over dollars and cents," applying the ideals that the rich only invoke in theory, which reflects Martin's encounters with Kreis and the other working-class intellectuals.[39] This element, however, deviates from London's life in that he found a sense of fellowship with these radicals motivated by their faith in social change, whereas Martin has a limited engagement with his fellows. London began drafting *Martin Eden* during the summer of 1907, composing the first half in Honolulu and the remainder aboard the *Snark*. Ninetta Eames, Charmian Kittredge London's aunt, arranged for the serialization of *Martin Eden* in the *Pacific Monthly* from September 1908 to September 1909, when Macmillan published the book.[40]

The early chapters of *Martin Eden* establish the protagonist's desire to transcend the working class through his introduction to the realm of the privileged, which appeals to his finer aptitudes and demonstrates the role of milieu in shaping the individual. In developing these concerns, the narrator initially describes the protagonist through nautical imagery.[41] This point emerges when Martin first visits the Morses for dinner after saving their son Arthur from a beating. The narrator notes that Martin "wore rough clothes that smacked of the sea," and he feels that the "level floors were tilting up and sinking down to the heave and lunge of the sea."[42] These descriptions refer to his previous experiences as a sailor and his uncertain position among the affluent, which the narrator reinforces by observing that the "wide rooms seemed too narrow for his rolling gait, and to himself he was in terror lest his broad shoulders should collide with the doorways or sweep the bric-a-brac from the low mantel" (31). While the central character's "rolling gait" and "broad shoulders" have been created by his earlier life at sea, they are not suited to his current setting as evident through the juxtaposition of these attributes with the restrictive space of the Morses' parlor and his fear of damaging the beauty he sees around him. The strength and vitality that have allowed him to survive aboard ship are antithetical to his present circumstances, yet he looks about him for some tangible link between these worlds, a connection that he finds in an oil painting of a schooner.[43] The narrator states that there "was beauty, and it drew him irresistibly. He forgot his awkward walk and came closer to the painting, very close. The beauty faded out of the canvas" (33). Martin's response displays his aesthetic sensibilities; however, his impression of the image as an illusion further exhibits the impact of his surroundings in that his perceptions stem from his limited exposure to art. Further, this view suggests that his latest environment, despite its appeal to his higher nature, is also deceptive since he is not familiar with its codes and lacks the means, at this stage of his development, to interpret it accurately.

These concerns manifest in Martin's first encounter with Ruth Morse, which complicates the ideal that she represents. Reflecting the protagonist's perspective, the narrator states that this woman "was a spirit, a divinity, a goddess; such sublimated beauty was not of the earth. Or perhaps the books were right, and there were many such as she in the upper walks of life. She might well be sung by that chap Swinburne. Perhaps he had had somebody like her in mind when he painted that girl, Iseult, in that book there on the table" (35). The connection between Ruth and the depiction of the ship, with their illustrations of Martin's responses to beauty, implies that she bears as little resemblance to the image she represents as the picture, when scrutinized up close, exhibits a vessel amid stormy seas. The allusion to Algernon Charles Swinburne's "Tristram of Lyoness" reinforces this impression while establishing a contrast between Iseult and the heroine, who lacks the emotional depth of her mythic counterpart.[44] Further, Ruth's subsequent discussion of the poem as "indelicate" with "many lines that could be spared" expresses the restrictive moral standards of her milieu that will destabilize their union (41). This initial conversation also illustrates the limitations of Martin's perceptions since he views this young lady as an exalted being based on her supposed possession of culture, whereas she merely parrots the conventional positions of others. At this point, Martin cannot perceive her intellectual limitations. Instead, the narrator states that she "lent wings to his imagination, and great luminous canvases spread themselves before him, whereon loomed vague, gigantic figures of love and romance, and of heroic deeds for woman's sake" (40). This grandeur makes her an unattainable ideal divorced from Martin's range of experience, evident through his recollections of the other women he has known. As a result, this desire for the traits seemingly embodied by Ruth sparks Martin's attraction to her and frames his attempts to improve his social position so that he might be worthy of such a creature.

London heightens these concerns in the next chapter, stressing Martin's insecurity in an unfamiliar environment, and the qualities associated with these surroundings engender his desire for advancement. The narrator notes that when the protagonist sits down to dinner with the Morses, he "realized that eating was something more than a utilitarian function. . . . He was feasting his love of beauty at this table where eating was an aesthetic function. It was an intellectual function, too" (48). These efforts to acclimate himself convey his mental aptitudes through his deft attempts to examine the constructs of the bourgeoisie. Martin's emphasis on observing these proprieties also reflects his broader desire for knowledge, which the narrator initially describes through language of hunger and thirst: when the young man enters the house, he "drank in the beauty," and when he sees a book of poetry, he is like "a starving man at the sight of food" (33–34). This focus suggests that his interest in improving himself is predicated on intellectual and aesthetic grounds, yet the narrator indicates the potential limitations to Martin's development when he tries to converse with the Morses. The narrator states that the hero "was oppressed by the consciousness that his carefulness of diction was making a booby of him, preventing him from expressing what he had in him" (49). This tension between the desire to articulate his thoughts and the need to do so within the discourse of polite society highlights the strictures of the bourgeois world, which create a conflict between his actual identity and the facade he wishes to present for the affluent.

The protagonist's difficulty in speaking further conveys the restrictive nature of his new environment, representing his struggle to master the outward forms of decorum necessary within these surroundings. These constructs, which have a parallel in Martin's constrictive collar, indicate the gulf that he must cross in order to realize his ambitions while also revealing the facility for storytelling and the ability to respond to sensory impressions that will make this progress possible. When the young man attempts to mediate the niceties of proper syntax and relays his adventures to the Morses, the narrator states that Martin "selected from the vast mass of detail with an artist's touch, drawing pictures of life that glowed and burned with light and color, injecting movement so that his listeners surged along with him on the flood of rough eloquence, enthusiasm, and power" (52). This control of narrative enables the aspiring individual to fight through conventional grammatical strictures with a grace unbefitting his vulgar language. While Ruth perceives his words as "an insult to her ear" and his experience as "an insult to her soul," she is able to observe "a great soul looking forth, inarticulate and dumb because of those feeble lips that would not give it speech" (53, 56). This realization expresses a primary tension in the work: the extent to which Martin's training in the structures of polite society will develop his higher self or whether such attempts to elevate his station will compromise the integrity of his finer attributes.

London reinforces the difficulty of Martin's progression through portraying the restrictions within his present environment and its contrast with the exalted realm of the Morses. For instance, when returning home after dinner with the Morses, Martin encounters a policeman, who assumes that the protagonist is intoxicated, and this encounter reaffirms his place in the social hierarchy. The officer views Martin's behavior in accordance with conventional expectations for the poor; denies his individuality; and cannot understand the forces that animate his actions, all of which anticipate the Morses' perspectives toward him for the remainder of the narrative. The young man's perceptions of the college students on the streetcar reinforce his alienation from Ruth's mode of existence as they have access to the life of the mind; they "could know her, could see her every day if they wanted to" (60). Martin, however, views these individuals through his experiences, speculating how they would operate as sailors. These reflections produce a sense of superiority since the youths "have been studying about life from the books, while he had been busy living life" (61). The realization that he could acquire the students' knowledge, while they could not obtain his, strengthens the central character's resolve to improve his social standing as these men who would seem to be his superiors owed their attainments to their class positions rather than to specific intellectual endowments.

London continues these contrasts when Martin arrives at the home of Bernard Higginbotham, his brother-in-law, who reflects the trajectory of the self-made man since he has progressed from humble origins to a position of economic security. The narrator reinforces this point during Higginbotham's Sunday dinner by noting that "such a dinner was advertisement of his

worldly achievement and prosperity, and he honored it by delivering plati-
tudinous sermonettes upon American institutions and the opportunity said
institutions gave to any hard-working man to rise" (125–26). This advancement frames his outlook to the extent that he thinks others can experience
similar outcomes just because he did. This ascension, however, has negative
effects for those brought into his sphere. The narrator observes that Higginbotham "effaced himself in the store, reserving for the evening, with his
family, the privilege of being himself," a shift that entails abusing his family
as a means of redress for his subservience, and this burden falls chiefly on his
wife, who "was always tired from the burdens of her flesh, her work, and her
husband" (63). The restrictions of this environment, with its emphasis on
monetary rewards over other concerns, appear to contrast with the milieu of
the Morses, whose affluence enables them to pursue the finer aspects of life.
Martin reflects that "the whole thing, the very air he breathed, was repulsive
and mean. How different, he thought, from the atmosphere of beauty and
repose of the house wherein Ruth dwelt. Here it was all material, and meanly
material" (72). This emphasis on wealth runs contrary to the impulses that
govern the protagonist's desire for mobility, which involves an attempt to
distance himself from his milieu in an effort to reach the Morses' realm.

This economic context further complicates Martin's ability to realize his
ambitions, which London reinforces through his depiction of the class divisions that shape the protagonist's experiences. London develops this idea
through Martin's reflections about Ruth's hands, which were "cool and soft
as a snowflake," and the young man "saw the aristocracy of the people who
did not labor. It towered before him on the wall, a figure in brass, arrogant
and powerful. He had worked himself; his first memories seemed connected
with work, and all his family had worked.... But [Ruth's] hands were soft, and
her mother's hands, and her brothers'. This last came to him as a surprise; it
was tremendously indicative of the highness of their caste, of the enormous
distance that stretched between her and him" (70). This contrast highlights
the altered circumstances that shape the lives of the affluent and the poor,
who must sell their labor in order to survive. These observations convey the
nature of the gulf that he must face in order to win Ruth's affections while
also explaining Ruth's inability to comprehend the impulses that animate
Martin's existence. The narrator indicates that this divide is exacerbated by
forces within the protagonist's environment. Martin "was appalled by the
problem confronting him, weighed down by the incubus of his working-class

station. Everything reached out to hold him down—his sister, his sister's house and family, Jim the apprentice, everybody he knew, every tie of life" (76–77). Martin's desires to acquire knowledge and to become a writer are foreign to those around him, who are preoccupied with monetary needs plus the gratification of their animal impulses, and the central character's deviation from these concerns fosters his growing alienation from individuals within his community.

London links Martin's quest for advancement to acquiring an education, a development that would permit him to operate within Ruth's world while also making him worthy of her love. The narrator, however, indicates the monumental nature of this quest when Martin enters the public library, finding that from "every side the books seemed to press upon him and crush him. He had never dreamed that the fund of human knowledge bulked so big. . . . How could his brain ever master it all?" (77–78). Since he was compelled to join the workforce at an early age and had little formal schooling, the protagonist has had limited access to the avenues of culture, which take on oppressive attributes because of their unfamiliarity, yet he has the necessary aptitudes to meet this challenge. The burgeoning of his intellect correlates to an inner life of sensations that have found few outlets in his previous environment as the narrator notes that the young man "remembered that he had led always a secret life in his thoughts. These thoughts he had tried to share, but never had he found a woman capable of understanding—nor a man. He had tried, at times, but had only puzzled his listeners" (87). The attainment of knowledge enables Martin to situate his experiences within the grand sweep of intellectual history, a progression that will allow him to approach Ruth as an equal rather than as a subordinate.

Martin connects this desire for knowledge to his broader goal of mobility. He states that "I want to make my way to the kind of life you have in this house. . . . I'm willin' to work my passage, you know, an' I can make most men sick when it comes to hard work. Once I get started, I'll work night an' day" (97). Martin invokes the language of the national success story through his emphasis on diligence as the means of progress. Further, the declaration that he will "work his passage" locates this new pursuit in the context of his earlier existence since this phrase has its origins in sailing, and it reinforces the lengths that he must traverse to realize his objectives. The narrator further establishes the contrast between Martin's squalid origins and his aspirations by observing that down "below where he lived was the ignoble, and he wanted to purge himself of the ignoble that had soiled all his days, and to rise to that sublimated realm where dwelt the upper classes" (103). This language of degradation reflects conventional assumptions about the poor, which are strengthened by the fact that these constructs emanate from a member of the proletariat, who has internalized the belief that erudition is the property of the bourgeoisie and that he will only find the kinship he seeks among members of Ruth's class.

While Martin views Ruth as the embodiment of culture and refinement, London represents her interest in the protagonist through ideas of sexual determinism, which influences her conduct contrary to conventional models of propriety.[45] The narrator states that the young man's "fire warmed her. . . . She wanted to lean toward this burning, blazing man that was like a volcano spouting forth strength, robustness, and health. She felt that she must lean toward him, and resisted by an effort" (53). London contrasts physical desire as denoted by the references to fire with the restrictions of the bourgeois world, evident through Ruth's attempts to resist her attraction to Martin. The conflict shapes her perspective for the remainder of the novel, and the narrator continues to emphasize the impulses that animate human behavior beyond the governance of the will. He observes that Ruth "was drawn by some force outside herself and much stronger than gravitation, strong as destiny. . . . But she had become an automaton. Her actions had passed beyond the control of her will—she never thought of control or will in the delicious madness that was upon her" (225). This emphasis on basic drives common to all humanity illustrates the arbitrary nature of social hierarchies through establishing a commonality of experience irrespective of class boundaries. The narrator notes that the "same pressures and caresses, unaccompanied by speech, that were efficacious with the girls of the working class, were equally efficacious with the girls above the working class. They were all of the same flesh, after all, sisters under their skins" (229). This realization complicates Martin's impression of the heroine as an exalted being since her actions reflect the same forces that affect her working-class counterparts, with Ruth's refinement and culture as outward forms to mask these urges. This tension manifests through the fact that she is both repulsed by and yet attracted to the central character's vitality despite her prior training.

Ruth's perceptions further originate within her milieu, and these constructs become evident through her endeavors to shape Martin in accordance with middle-class values regardless of his interests, which develops

London's criticism of the bourgeoisie.[46] Discussing these efforts, the narrator asserts that "it was the first time [Ruth] had ever had a human soul to play with, and the plastic clay of him was a delight to mold; for she thought she was molding it, and her intentions were good" (107). The reference to Martin as "clay" reinforces his adaptability to the dictates of his surroundings, yet this passage further underscores the couple's inequitable relationship. While playing with a human soul implies a measure of agency, Ruth's actions have their basis within her environment. The narrator develops this point when he posits that the heroine's "own limits were the limits of her horizon; but limited minds can recognize limitations only in others" (111). Ruth thinks that she is superior to Martin and thereby is eligible to mold him in accordance with her wishes; however, this resulting model reflects her previous training, which causes her to perceive her partner in line with archetypes that betray a fundamental ignorance of his inclinations. The narrator notes that "Ruth measured his thoughts by comparison of externals and in accordance with her belief in the established. . . . She was too firmly intrenched in the established to have any sympathy with revolutionary ideas" (257). These impressions stem from her reliance on other people's ideas, a practice that emerges when she repeats a former professor's lecture in response to Martin's arguments about the opera. This exchange conveys her general condescension toward the central character. She clarifies the nature of these attempts to reformulate the protagonist when she tells her mother that "it seems that he is a bulldog I have taken for a plaything, like some of the 'frat' girls, and he is tugging hard, and showing his teeth, and threatening to break loose" (211). Ruth's use of animal imagery expresses her view that Martin is a brute who must learn obedience, apparent through her choice of a dog struggling against his confinement as the young man will soon rebel against the vision imposed on him.

London reinforces the effects of Ruth's prior training through the figure of Charles Butler, her father's lawyer, who exemplifies the self-made man. While Ruth invokes Butler as a model for advancement, this character further highlights the restrictions of the bourgeois milieu. Recounting Butler's experiences to guide Martin's pursuit of mobility, Ruth states that the lawyer "went to work in a printing-office,—I have heard him tell of it many times,—and he got three dollars a week, at first. His income today is at least thirty thousand a year. How did he do it? He was honest, and faithful, and industrious, and economical. He denied himself the enjoyments that most boys indulge in" (108). The circumstances that enabled Butler's ascension exhibit conventional features of the American Dream. London reinforces this vision through an allusion to Benjamin Franklin, who also began his rise from humble origins in a printing office. Franklin's later life also manifests in the arc of Butler's progress: each man emphasized the value of education, evident through Butler's having attended night school and earning his law degree, to facilitate their elevation to positions of prominence. London reinforces Butler's pivotal role in Ruth's conception of attainment when she urges Martin to practice "sacrifice, patience, industry, and high endeavor," with the narrator observing that "such abstractions being objectified in her mind by her father, and Mr. Butler, and by Andrew Carnegie" (209). The connection to Carnegie, another potent figure of individual progress, and the attributes traditionally associated with advancement reflect the gains possible for those who operate in a comparable manner.

Butler serves another important function by providing a counterpoint to Martin's quest for advancement. The narrator states that the protagonist "could not find an adequate motive in Mr. Butler's life of pinching and privation. Had he done it for the love of a woman, or for attainment of beauty, Martin would have understood. God's own mad lover should do anything for the kiss, but not for thirty thousand dollars a year" (112). Martin's impulses are not limited to his predecessor's economic objectives; instead, the young man's aspirations express values that have been displaced by the monetary conception of the national success story. The narrator connects these meditations to the juxtaposition with Butler through the central character's urge to write, observing that the "men of literature were the world's giants, and he conceived them to be far finer than the Mr. Butlers who earned thirty thousand a year and could be Supreme Court justices if they wanted to" (115). Martin's emphasis on mobility centers on intellectual and romantic qualities that he feels should be the focus of the human enterprise rather than the material concerns that often animate people's actions. This perspective further illustrates the gulf separating Martin and Ruth since his ambitions conflict with her adherence to the constructs of the marketplace, a tension that conditions the dissolution of their relationship.

This tension manifests through Ruth's hostility toward her partner's art, which causes him to deviate from Mr. Butler's idea of progress. When Martin reads one of his stories aloud, Ruth states that it is "degrading! It is not nice! It is nasty" and later asks: "Why don't you select a nice subject? . . . We know there are nasty things in the world, but that is no reason—" (167–68). The first response echoes her initial remarks on Swinburne in chapter 2, with her emphasis on restrictive moral standards that separate life from literature, and she prioritizes surface-level elements of form as opposed to the broader ideas conveyed by his work. The heroine's second comment alludes to the reaction of Martin's sister to his writing when she declares that there are "too many sad things in the world anyway. It makes me happy to think about happy things" (135). The connection of these positions further undermines Ruth's perspective by associating comparable sentiments with one who has not possessed her advantages yet makes a statement that conveys a similar lack of understanding. This correlation indicates that the protagonist's aspirations will find a limited outlet among the bourgeoisie as Ruth utilizes the constructs of her class to perceive his ambitions. Her chief objection to Martin's vocation stems from the fact that his creative output, by not adhering to established structures and themes, will not enable him to attain mobility or make him eligible to marry. As such, the central character's actions do not adhere to his intended's definition of success since she assumes that literary expression is beyond the means of the common people, and her focus on "the more serious affairs of life" through a respectable career demonstrates her inability to recognize the impulses that govern Martin's desire for advancement (173).

While the protagonist rejects the impulses behind Butler's development, Martin sacrifices all pleasures to attain his objectives as the lawyer once did to engender his rise. Reflecting on Martin's efforts, the narrator states that there "were twenty-four hours in each day. He was invincible. He knew how to work, and the citadels would go down before him. He would not have to go to sea again—as a sailor; and for the instant he caught a vision of a steam yacht. There were other writers who possessed steam yachts" (115). This emphasis on diligent effort reinforces the conventional arc of the American Dream and situates Martin's quest within the context of his previous experiences, contrasting his time as a sailor with the prosperity that awaits him. However, the reference to the yacht portends a different future in that it anticipates the central character's eventual suicide as a result of his disillusionment with the world of the bourgeoisie coupled with his estrangement from his former environment. The narrator devotes considerable attention to Martin's toil as he attempts to become a successful writer. He completes in one day "the equivalent to a week's work of the average successful writer" and lives on less than five hours of sleep per night, which keeps him in a perpetual state of nervous exhaustion that culminates in his illness (137). To sustain himself, he pawns nearly all of his possessions, including his bicycle and best suit. These acts of self-denial further separate him from his fiancée as the conveyance played an important role in their courtship, while the loss of his good clothing prevents Martin from seeing his intended since he no longer has the proper attire to enter her world. He further implements Butler's tactics through the acquisition of an oil-burning stove, which parallels the kerosene one that featured prominently in Ruth's version of the lawyer's rise, a purchase that "especially pleased her" and "won her admiration" (235, 277). This routine, however, creates further distance from the heroine, who is horrified by his squalid dwelling, a habitation that, despite its necessity for a person who hopes to win his place in the world, is unbefitting her future husband.

Chapter 15 provides a further illustration of the attributes necessary for Martin's advancement, revealing the lengths he has already come while also exhibiting his ability to adapt to environmental pressures. After his initial efforts to become a writer yield only a pile of rejection slips, the protagonist remembers fights with an antagonist of his youth named Cheese-Face, which offers a parallel to Martin's present struggles to make a living with his pen. Remembering how his defeats at the hands of his adversary intensified his desire to best his opponent, Martin tells himself: "You licked Cheese-face, and you'll lick the editors if it takes thrice eleven years to do it in. You can't stop here. You've got to go on. It's to a finish, you know" (183). The connection between these altercations and his attempts to support himself through his fiction reflects the central character's desire to put this new pursuit in the context of his previous experiences. Further, he later establishes a precise correlation between these events when he obtains payment from one editor through physical intimidation, and he relinquishes control of another story after a beating from the staff of the *Hornet*. The memory of the fights with Cheese-Face gives Martin the determination to continue his endeavors to become an author, revealing that the aptitudes gleaned from these incidents of his youth have helped him to develop the resolve necessary to win the current conflict. However, the description of the brawl also supplies a glimpse of the young man's earlier life with a representation of his ability to transform himself in accordance with his surroundings. The narrator states that "the painful, thousand years' gains of man in his upward climb through creation were lost. Only the electric light remained, a milestone on the path of the great human adventure. Martin and Cheese-Face were two savages, of the stone age, of the squatting place and the tree refuge. They sank lower and lower into the muddy abyss, back into the dregs of the raw beginnings of life" (179). This emphasis on reversion further demonstrates the influence of milieu amid the plasticity of existence while also indicating Martin's ability to survive in both savage and exalted realms.

Martin's experiences at Shelly Hot Springs also illustrate attributes that seem to promise advancement, yet his endeavors in this setting undermine his ability to realize his larger objectives. In order to earn the money necessary to subsidize his writing, Martin takes a job at a laundry in Shelly Hot Springs, where he must perform long shifts of "nerve-racking, body-destroying toil" (195). His capacity for work parallels his efforts to become a writer; however, his industry at washing clothes differs from his exertions at his desk, which stem from his highest aspirations rather than financial need. In describing the effects of the protagonist's current job, London returns to the motifs of mechanization from "The Apostate" and the resulting intellectual decline of the protagonist. The narrator notes that "Martin's consciousness was concentrated in the work. Ceaselessly active, head and hand, an intelligent machine, all that constituted him a man was devoted to furnishing that intelligence. There was no room in his brain for the universe and its mighty problems. All the broad and spacious corridors of his mind were closed and hermetically sealed" (194). Like Johnny in "The Apostate," Martin is shaped by the nature of this production to the extent that he gradually adopts the attributes of the mechanism. This development comes at the expense of his cognitive capabilities since his repetitive tasks prevent the further cultivation of his finer attributes until he is nothing more than a "machine that thought of itself as once having been one Martin Eden, a man" (202). The protagonist's deterioration is significant because his existence centers on the attainment of knowledge as a means of individual progress, and his degeneration produces a dramatic demonstration of the shaping role of his environment. Further, this episode widens the gulf between Martin and Ruth, reflecting the elements of life that she cannot incorporate into her worldview coupled with her inability to understand his quest for advancement.

This discrepancy between Martin's ambitions and Ruth's perceptions highlights his growing disillusionment with his intended and her milieu, which does not cohere with the ideals he once thought that it embodied.

The protagonist clarifies this point when he states that "up here I thought all men and women were brilliant and radiant. But now, from what little I've seen of them, they strike me as a pack of ninnies, most of them, and ninety per cent of the remainder as bores" (297). Martin's exposure to the privileged has eroded his earlier impressions of these individuals, who mouth platitudes that reflect great cognitive limitations, have a mastery of surface forms that denote erudition, and cannot delve past these externals to perceive the broader forces that animate existence. While these people have clear advantages, they merely repeat the opinions of established thinkers, lacking any meaningful engagement with outward reality. The narrator observes that for Martin, "culture and collars had gone together" and that "he had been deceived into believing that college educations and mastery were the same things" (310). The reference to collars indicates the restrictions of the bourgeois world, one predicated on the appearances of higher qualities, yet the people in the Morses' circle betray a dearth of knowledge unbefitting their exalted rank. Contrasting this group with his previous companions, the central character asserts that "the difference between these lawyers, officers, business men, and bank cashiers he had met and the members of the working class he had known was on a par with the difference in the food they ate, clothes they wore, neighborhoods in which they lived" (311). This distinction between the rich and the poor through opportunities and exterior attributes illustrates that the Morses and their peers have done little to merit their positions. They have not added to the body of human wisdom; instead, they rest on the achievements of others, which causes them to live in a comparable state of ignorance to those whom they deem inferior. Martin's recognition of this intellectual bankruptcy heightens his disenchantment, and the realization that he exchanged his former environment for one that is ultimately without value suggests that he has separated himself from the potential for a meaningful life. This realization prefigures the conclusion of the work.

London heightens Martin's growing disillusionment through juxtaposing dominant society against an alternate framework provided by Russ Brissenden, an affluent poet who does not succumb to the intellectual restrictions of the upper class. Instead, he further develops the critique of this group. Unlike the affluent characters, he exhibits a broader understanding of the protagonist, recognizing the aesthetic merits of his writing while supplying the financial assistance necessary to sustain him through his struggles. While Brissenden realizes the fiscal necessity of the young man's actions, the former notes that the attainment of success would come at the cost of the latter's talent, a sacrifice that would be too great for the monetary rewards he would earn. This point emerges in the reaction to Brissenden's "Ephemera," which anticipates Martin's demise through the bourgeois appropriation of his art. When the poem is published, the narrator describes its reception by observing that Brissenden "had hated the crowd so, and here all that was finest and most sacred of him had been thrown to the crowd. Daily the vivisection of Beauty went on. Every nincompoop in the land rushed into free print, floating their wizened little egos into the public eye on the surge of Brissenden's greatness" (414). This response illustrates the commodification of literature and the cheapening of beauty to mere economic calculations, which parallels the response to Martin's output to signify the emptiness of his aspirations.

The chapters with Brissenden also involve Martin's introduction to working-class intellectuals who contrast with the bourgeoisie to further reflect his growing sense of alienation. Describing the people gathered at the apartment of Kreis, a former professor turned working-class intellectual, in San Francisco, the narrator asserts that nobody "manufactured their opinions for them; they were all rebels of one variety or another, and their lips were strangers to platitudes. Never had Martin, at the Morses', heard so amazing a range of topics discussed" (373). The reference to platitudes establishes Kreis's group as a counterpoint to the scholars and upwardly mobile professionals at the Morses' dinner parties who speak only in such terms as their opinions have been manufactured by polite society. Kreis and his associates, however, are not enthralled by these constructs, instead striving to delve past surface forms to perceive the elements that animate existence. The narrator states that Martin did not hear "the philosophy of the dry, printed word, written by half-mythical demigods like Kant and Spencer. It was living philosophy, with warm, red blood, incarnated in these two men till its very features worked with excitement" (374). For these individuals, knowledge is a vital force in dialogue with human experience, a progression displayed through the narrator's personification of philosophy.

These men present Martin with the intellectual companionship that he had been unable to find among the affluent, and the narrator reinforces this point through juxtaposing this scene with the restrictive environment at the Morse home. These constraints manifest through Judge Blount, an acquaintance of the Morses. He merely repeats conventional judgments that demonstrate a fundamental ignorance of Martin's belief system and reveal the "intellectual pretense and fraud of those who sat in high places" (386). While the exchanges at Kreis's residence offer the potential for an alternate course of development, the young writer does not initially participate in the discussions, which exhibits his alienation from a community that could have provided the stimulation he required. Further, when Martin does speak at a meeting in chapter 38, the subsequent press account causes the end of his relationship with Ruth. This occurrence intensifies his disenchantment as he has become disconnected from both the exalted realm he attempted to enter and the world of the working class. London underscores this idea when the protagonist declines an offer to return to Kreis's group later in the narrative.

Although critics have asserted that Martin's disillusionment and self-destruction are incompatible with his representation through the novel, London establishes the context for these developments through unifying the motifs that he has introduced throughout the work and illustrating the emptiness of the hero's objectives.[47] These elements emerge when Ruth ends her union with the protagonist after a newspaper article identifies him as a revolutionary Socialist, which is inconsistent with his actual ideological stance. The heroine's failure to recognize Martin's belief system provides the culmination of their fundamental incompatibility. Further, London presents the rationale for the breakup through a discussion of economic and hereditary determinism. Ruth writes her former fiancé: "I can understand that you are not to be blamed. You could only act according to your nature and your early training. So I do not blame you, Martin.... As father and mother have contended, we were not made for each other" (400). This position reflects the central tenets of American naturalism, yet Ruth's handling of these ideas overlooks the fact that Martin has transcended the constraints of his early training to adapt to new surroundings with an alternate set of societal pressures. While she de-emphasizes the causative agents in her environment that have framed their relationship, London suggests these components through references to her parents, who have trained their daughter to share their limited standards of value. London parallels this scene with the first instances of Martin's success as a writer, yet his financial advancement is separated from his emphasis on love and the attainment of knowledge, which produces an intellectual malaise that robs his achievements of any importance. The narrator states that money "had no meaning to him now except what it would immediately buy. He was chartless and rudderless, and he had no port to make, while drifting involved the least living, and it was living that hurt"

(412). The use of nautical imagery both underscores the nature of Martin's progress from the ranks of the working class and anticipates his suicide at sea due to this absence of direction.

This growing sense of detachment manifests most profoundly through Martin's realization that he had traded an environment in which others valued him as an individual for one in which people only hold him in high regard due to his wealth and fame. When he attends a picnic in his old neighborhood, the protagonist realizes that he "was a fool to ever have left them ... and he was very certain that his sum of happiness would have been greater had he remained with them and let alone the books and the people who sat in the high places" (421–22). Since his efforts at self-improvement have separated him from the working class, Martin feels only a momentary sense of recognition when he goes through the motions of his former life but cannot recapture the enjoyment he once derived from these pursuits. This estrangement is most discernible when he interacts with Lizzie Connolly, a young woman from the working class who has fallen in love with him. Although Martin recognizes the sincerity of her passion, he tries to remake her in a manner that reflects Ruth's earlier position toward him. Rather than accepting Lizzie on her own terms, Martin persuades her "to go to night school and business college and to have herself gowned by a wonderful dressmaker who charged outrageous prices," and she complies in order "to make herself of worth in his eyes—of the sort of worth he seemed to value" (436). He has reservations about these attempts to mold Lizzie into his ideal female, which exhibits a self-awareness that Ruth did not possess as she attempted to shape Martin, yet his actions result from a similar inability to see the beauty and value of the working class because these attributes take different forms among the privileged. Through these actions, Martin has signaled the gulf that now separates him from his previous companions, a development that the narrator underscores when the protagonist encounters former acquaintances after he becomes successful.

The portrayal of Martin's fame exposes the emptiness of dominant society, and the crystallization of this vision and the recognition that he can no longer return to his former life provide the impetus for his suicide. The narrator states that it "was the bourgeoisie that bought his books and poured its gold into his money-sack, and from what little he knew of the bourgeoisie it was not clear to him how it could possibly appreciate or comprehend what he had written. His intrinsic beauty and power meant nothing to the hundreds of thousands that were acclaiming him and buying his books. He was the fad of the hour, the adventurer who stormed Parnassus while the gods nodded" (441–42). Though the young man's fortunes have turned, his success is merely a monetary one since those who read his books are interested in them because they have been judged as valuable in relation to the dictates of the marketplace, the same standards that led to Ruth's rejection of his writing in addition to the Morses forcing her to break the engagement.

The narrator illustrates the hypocritical nature of this logic through the efforts of those who once rejected Martin to cultivate his favor once he has become successful. The characters who once ridiculed his ambitions, from Bernard Higginbotham to Mr. Morse, now seek to extract whatever they can from his celebrity by inviting him to dinners, invitations that they had withheld during his desperate poverty. The narrator observes that these individuals did not want Martin "for himself or for his work, but for the fame that was his, because he was somebody amongst men, and—why not?—because he had a hundred thousand dollars or so. That was the way bourgeois society valued a man, and who was he to expect it otherwise?" (444). These scenes parallel the attempts of various publishers to secure Martin's output, which they had rejected earlier since his writing failed to conform to middle-class proprieties. These editors are not concerned with the artistic or intellectual merits of his poetry and prose. Instead, these men only want to procure the protagonist's works because of his popularity and potential to generate revenue, concerns that override their convictions to the extent that they are willing to pay lavishly for stories from his apprenticeship period that he regards as inferior products.

The culmination of Martin's disillusionment comes through his reunion with Ruth, which heightens the emptiness of his accomplishments. When Ruth attempts to resume her relationship with the protagonist, he connects her impulses to his celebrity, asserting that the people who desire his company "don't want me for myself, for myself is the same old self they did not want. Then they must want me for something else, for something that is outside of me, for something that is not I . . . . It is for the recognition I have received. That recognition is not I. It resides in the mind of others. Then again for the money I have earned and am earning. But that money is not I" (460). This passage reflects Martin's preoccupation with the distinction between his external self, the famous writer whom everyone values, and the actual Martin Eden, who is more than the name attached to best-selling books or the sum of his bank balance. The encounter with Ruth provides the most powerful illustration of this theme as the Morses, who once opposed their daughter's marriage to an impoverished sailor, now impose no obstacles to their coupling due to the young author's improved class position, despite the fact that he is same person as before his success. When he walks Ruth home after rejecting her advances, he observes her brother Norman, who once threatened to call the police if Martin came near his sister, and states: "These bourgeois! When I was broke, I was not fit to be seen with his sister. When I have a bank account, he brings her to me" (467). This irony conveys the reduction of natural bonds of affection to the valuation of the marketplace, which reveals that the moral strictures of the elite are merely justifications for the actions they choose to embrace and which can quickly be discarded to promote their interests. These events reinforce that Martin has exchanged his earlier environment for one that denies his identity in accordance with market forces, and this development completes his alienation from both worlds, setting in motion the events that end in his suicide.

London further contextualizes Martin's suicide through emphasizing the broader malaise that diminishes his will to live. These elements manifest through the weakening of his intellectual abilities, which heightens the consequences of his success. The protagonist has become disconnected from his inner life, ceasing to think, read, or write to the extent that his "mind was a blank, save for the intervals when unsummoned memory pictures took form and color and radiance just under his eyelids" (456), and his brain eventually becomes "dead to impressions." This decline of his cognitive capabilities reflects the broader results of his disenchantment since he abandons the constructs that have governed his existence, isolating himself from any engagement with the outside world or the life of the mind. London juxtaposes these descriptions with Martin's craving for sleep, which "had become to him oblivion, and each day that he awoke, he awoke with regret" (468). The narrator also notes that Martin "realized how much he had slept, and how much he desired to sleep. Of old, he had hated sleep. It had robbed him of precious moments of living" (472). The contrast between the central character's earlier self and his current state expresses the extent of his deterioration, while his longing for oblivion anticipates his suicide.

London clarifies the impetus for Martin's demise when he boards the *Mariposa* to sail for Tahiti, and his experiences on the ship reinforce his estrangement from his previous way of life to reveal that he has nowhere else to go after abandoning the bourgeois world. When the protagonist tries to befriend the sailors, he "could find no kinship with these stolid-featured, ox-minded bestial creatures. He was in despair. Up above nobody had wanted Martin Eden for his own sake, and he could not go back to those of his class who had wanted him in the past. He did not want them" (477). His attempts to recapture aspects of his time at sea indicate that his intellectual transformation prevents him from ever returning to this earlier mode of existence. This passage evokes his alienation from Lizzie and Joe Dawson, his former colleague at the laundry, earlier in the chapter, and London suggests that an escape to Tahiti would not result in the peace Martin craved since he "found no delight in the old familiar things of life" (478). London brings these elements together when Martin reads Swinburne's "The Garden of Proserpine." This reference evokes his first encounter with Ruth when they discuss the poet, a scene that offers the initial presentation of her limited perspective, yet the work does not appeal to the central character's aesthetic sensibilities or reflect his desire for knowledge. Instead, the poem points to the solution for his disillusionment. The narrator notes that "Swinburne had furnished the key. Life was ill, or, rather, it had become ill—an unbearable thing. 'That dead men rise up never!' That line stirred him with a profound feeling of gratitude. . . . When life became an aching weariness, death was ready to soothe away to everlasting sleep" (480). The use of Swinburne unifies the ideas that London has developed throughout *Martin Eden,* providing the culmination of his disenchantment while suggesting a way forward. In this context, his suicide, with its tension between his body's struggle for survival and his mind's refusal to acquiesce to these instincts, represents his ultimate rejection of dominant society.

Martin Eden highlights the dangers of prioritizing individual success over the concerns of the majority as this process disconnects him from his environment and engenders his demise. Reflecting on his central conception in this novel, London wrote that "Martin Eden died because he was so made. He was an individualist. He was unaware of the needs of others. He worked for himself, for fame, for love, for all self-satisfactions."[48] London, however, recognized the value of the working-class milieu that Martin rejected. In "What Life Means to Me," London wrote that the "imposing edifice of society above my head holds no delights for me. It is the foundation of the edifice that interests me. There I am content to labor, crowbar in hand, shoulder to shoulder with intellectuals, idealists, and class-conscious workingmen, getting a solid pry now and again and setting the whole edifice rocking. Some day, when we get a few more hands and crowbars to work, we'll topple it over, along with its rotten life and unburied dead, its monstrous selfishness and sodden materialism."[49] London's emphasis on the foundation of society signifies the importance of those who perform the requisite labor to support those at the higher levels while expressing the need to renovate the structure of American life to create greater opportunities for all men and women.

4

WAR OF THE CLASSES

Collective Action in "The Dream of Debs" and The Iron Heel

London's social criticism clearly emerges in *The Iron Heel* and "The Dream of Debs," which further express London's indictment of capitalism and his desire for an economic system that is more responsive to human need. Cecelia Tichi observes that London was concerned with using his forum as a public intellectual to enlighten his audience about the injustices of his era so that people could take action to address these issues. As Tichi observes, London thought that the process of social transformation "could be initiated only when the dire social facts of the present were laid bare before the public. In turn, he believed that public opinion could—and surely would—be swayed by and solidified in support of social change."[1] *The Iron Heel* and "The Dream of Debs" not only marshaled the "dire social facts" of London's contemporary world to elucidate the need for systemic change but also modeled the process by which existing conditions ultimately could be altered. Both works emphasize the role of collective action in the transformation of society, and London's workers demonstrate greater control over their lives since they can confront their adversaries from a position of relative strength, options that are not available to Martin Eden or Johnny as they focus on individualistic concerns. *The Iron Heel* and "The Dream of Debs" further develop London's social criticism by illustrating the need to connect the aspirations of the individual to those of the collective, expressing that if working people fight alongside their fellows for the rights of all, then they can effectively challenge the seemingly insurmountable barriers to social progress.

London's fiction engages with the major developments of a transformative period in American history, illuminating the obstacles to economic progress for members of the working class, who seldom earned enough to share in the general prosperity of London's era. For instance, Paul Douglas observes that wage rates stagnated between 1890 and 1926 despite advances for some following the recovery of 1897. These gains accrued to highly skilled employees, while their unskilled counterparts saw their pay decrease until World War I.[2] In the early decades of the twentieth century, the average worker continued to earn wages that were seldom sufficient to cover basic needs. For instance, social workers investigated living standards among the poor in New York City and estimated the compensation necessary to support an average family with some measure of health and decency. These figures ranged from a total of $800 to $876 for a family of three or four to $505 for a single man and $446 for a working woman, yet numerous federal, state, and private studies found that the majority of the population existed beneath this threshold.[3] In a sample of 10,000 male laborers in 1909, the United States Commission of Immigration determined that the average compensation amounted to $413 and that nearly half of those who were questioned received less than $400 annually.[4] From 1911 to 1915, the New York State Factory Investigating Commission revealed equally troubling evidence of hardship. After surveying 109,481 wage earners, the commission discovered that most were paid less than $10 a week and that 15 to 30 percent received only $3 to $6.[5] As a result of these conditions, individuals did not appear to be masters of their fates, and the possibility of rising within American society seemed to be the product of economic forces that shaped outcomes regardless of any attempts to alter these circumstances.

The possibilities for material progress were hindered further by an unstable economic system characterized by frequent depressions and panics, the consequences of which disproportionately affected the working class. The first fiscal catastrophe of the late nineteenth century, the panic of 1873, caused banks across the country to fail as people rushed to withdraw their deposits, and five thousand businesses shut their doors over the next few years.[6] As a result, unemployment reached three million by 1877–78, with two-fifths of the labor force working only seven months out of the year.[7] Although the panic of 1873 wiped out small firms and intensified the hardships for poor families, the robber barons took advantage of market conditions to increase their fortunes and power. During the crisis, Andrew Carnegie captured the steel industry, and John D. Rockefeller eliminated his competitors in oil.[8] The nation experienced another significant downturn from March 1882 to May 1885, which occurred because of a decline in rail construction and related industries, and suffered another serious depression from 1893 to 1898 as a result of rampant speculation and overproduction. The insolvency of the Philadelphia and Reading Railroad inaugurated this calamity, and more than 150 enterprises in this industry were bankrupt by the middle of 1894, including the Northern Pacific; the Union Pacific; and the Atchison, Topeka & Santa Fe.[9] Following the stock market collapse on May 3, 1893, 360 banks and 8,000 companies failed, two to three million American workers were unemployed, and those who kept their jobs experienced drastic wage reductions.[10] As with the panic of 1873, the poor suffered disproportionately during the 1890s, with 11 million families earning an average of $380 annually, while the richest 1 percent collected more income than the poorest 50 percent and possessed more wealth than the bottom 99 percent.[11] Reflecting on the depression of 1893, Lichtenstein observes that drawn "ever more tightly into a national economy, Americans were increasingly vulnerable to economic forces they could not control. What happened on Wall Street now affected the lives of Massachusetts railroad workers and Mississippi sharecroppers who would never own stocks or bonds."[12] These determinants were not isolated to the 1890s as the recurrent downturns were disastrous for the impoverished, who lacked the means to insulate themselves from the vicissitudes of the financial system.

In response to their economic subordination during this period, workers organized themselves into trade unions to promote their interests against the violent opposition of the owners, with strikes as the principal means of increasing wages and improving conditions. After the Great Upheaval of 1877, these practices intensified, with an average of 500 work stoppages annually from 1881 to 1885, and peaked with 1,411 in 1886 involving 499,489 people.[13] Many of these disputes pertained to demands for an eight-hour day, and 340,000 laborers participated in various actions toward this objective, with 190,000 striking on May Day.[14] The industrial conflicts of the 1890s offer a parallel illustration of attempts by the working class to gain control over the economic forces that shaped the nation, most notably during the Homestead strike of 1892 and the Pullman boycott of 1894. In the former, steelworkers fought off the importation of strikebreakers by Pinkerton detectives and gained control of Carnegie's Homestead plant. In the latter, the American Railway Union (ARU) organized a boycott of all trains hauling Pullman cars, and the resulting actions paralyzed shipping and transit throughout the country.[15] However, these early successes only supplied the impetus for what became the standard pattern of managerial response as executives secured court injunctions against their employees, which were enforced by federal troops and state militias; local police forces arrested the leaders; and those who walked off their jobs were blacklisted. These practices led to the weakening of the Amalgamated Association of Iron and Steel Workers and the ARU, ultimately culminating in victories for Carnegie and Pullman. Although both struggles ended in defeat, they demonstrated the potential of collective action and paved the way for the labor militancy that characterized the early twentieth century.

Based on his experiences in the workforce during this period, London embraced socialism as a means to address the iniquity of capitalism. He joined the Socialist Labor Party in April 1896 and in 1901 became a member of the Socialist Party of America, in which he would remain until early 1916. During these years, London served as the first president of the Intercollegiate Socialist Society, lectured throughout the country advocating the necessity of revolutionary change, and published widely on the class struggle. Defining his ideology in 1895, London asserted: "Socialism means a reconstruction of society with a more just application of labor and distribution of the returns thereof. It cries out, 'Every one according to his deeds!' Its logical foundation is economic; its moral foundation, 'All men are born free and equal,' and its ultimate aim is pure democracy."[16] Expanding on these ideas in 1913, London stated, "Socialism should strive to eliminate the capitalist class and wipe away the private ownership of mines, mills, factories, railroads and other social needs" and that the workers "should take upon themselves the task of doing away with the robbing capitalist system, do away with the profit system and place the workers in possession of the industries."[17] London's belief in socialism centered on a conviction that the collective control of industry could better suit the interests of the general population than capitalism, which prioritized the profitability of the minority over the requirements of the majority.

London's indictment of capitalism resulted from what he deemed to be the owners' irrational administration of society and the ensuing consequences for labor. He asserted that the "capitalist class, blind and greedy, grasping madly, has not only not made the best of its management, but made the worst of it. . . . In face of the facts that modern man lives more wretchedly than the caveman, and that modern man's food- and shelter-getting efficiency is a thousandfold greater than the caveman's, no other solution is possible than that the management is prodigiously wasteful."[18] London returns to this point from *The People of the Abyss* (1903) to "The Dream of Debs," critiquing the owners' inability to arrange production in a manner that would benefit the industrial workforce. London, however, did not object to fortunes gained through honest effort since he owed his rise to such exertions. Instead, he opposed the consolidation of wealth that limited such progress for the majority as he noted that "gateway of opportunity after opportunity has been closed, and closed for all time.... These doors will not open again, and before them pause thousands of ambitious young men to read the placard: NO THOROUGHFARE."[19]

Although London's most active period as a Socialist had largely ended by 1908, he remained a militant revolutionary until the end of his life, when he resigned from the party because of its emphasis on achieving reform through legislative means and its abandonment of the class struggle.[20] Explaining his decision, London wrote that "the working class, by fighting, by never fusing, by never making terms with the enemy, could emancipate itself," yet he claimed that "the whole trend of Socialism in the United States of recent years had been one of peaceableness and compromise."[21] Throughout his life, the fundamental concerns of London's ideology remained consistent, rooted in the need for militant action to gain control of the means of production, which workers would democratically manage to create a just division of the fruits of labor and to enable individuals to develop in accordance with their potential.

London develops these ideas in *The Iron Heel,* a dystopian novel that chronicles the rise of a capitalist oligarchy that subjugates labor for centuries until the successful revolution ushers in a Socialist state.[22] The narrative takes the form of a manuscript written by Avis Everhard, a woman of privilege who becomes a dedicated revolutionary; the manuscript was discovered by the inhabitants of a future postrevolutionary society, and London employs a narrative frame consisting of an introduction and footnotes written by Anthony Meredith, a scholar who explains the peculiarities of twentieth-century America to the citizens of the future. Reflecting conventional views of the book, Earle Labor and Jeanne Campbell Reesman refer to *The Iron Heel* as "little more than an ideological treatise cast in narrative form" and opine that Avis Everhard's sentimental narration makes the novel seem like "*1984* as it might have been penned by a Harlequin romance writer."[23] Other critics, however, have perceived the political nature of the narrative as a source of strength. Nathaniel Teich praises London's "successful synthesis of his socialistic ideology and novelistic form," and Paul Stein asserts that the text "provides a synthesis in most concrete and coherent terms of London's grasp of Marxist ideology and demonstrates the extent of his ability to use literary devices for programmatic purpose."[24] In its representation of these concerns, *The Iron Heel* incorporates elements from London's society into a dystopian future, expressing the need for the transformation of the socioeconomic system to address the internal contradictions and human consequences of capitalism, which are intensified through the Iron Heel to illuminate the dangers if conditions are allowed to develop along their present course.

After London had cemented his popularity with *The Sea Wolf* and *White Fang,* he returned to an idea that he had contemplated for years. In his post-Klondike notebook, London described plans for "a novel, a la Wells, out of idea of wage-slaves ruled by industrial oligarchs, finally ceasing to reproduce. And either figure out new ways of penetrating the future, or begin far ahead of the actual time of the story, by having the writing dug up by the people of a new and very immature civilization."[25] The reference to H. G. Wells suggests a debt to *When the Sleeper Wakes* (1899), a utopian novel in which the hero is transported to a world afflicted by a class war. Further, the statement about having the manuscript uncovered by the inhabitants of a future society anticipates London's approach in *The Iron Heel,* although his "immature" civilization is replaced by a highly advanced Socialist state that came into existence hundreds of years after the events depicted in the central narrative. In his notes for the novel, London locates the book's themes within the language of dialectical materialism, the Marxian conception that society moves through stages when the dominant class is displaced by an emerging one and when existing relations of production no longer correspond to new industrial forces. London wrote that the "hero bases his faith, on the generalization that every system contains itself the germs of its own decay. Develop this point of his—+ have a footnote showing that he was right—only it took longer to decay than he thought."[26] This emphasis conveys London's complex representation of economic determinism: on one hand, the central narrative of the Everhard manuscript presents the ruling class as the causative force that shapes the characters' actions; on the other, the foreword and footnotes that comprise Meredith's narrative frame situate these occurrences within a broader historical perspective, one that demonstrates the inevitable victory of labor despite the efforts of the privileged to maintain their rule, which highlights the growing agency of the working class. London began drafting *The Iron Heel* in the spring of 1906 and sent the completed manuscript to his editor, George P. Brett, that December. Despite London's optimism regarding the commercial potential of the narrative, he was unable to secure serial publication, and Macmillan published *The Iron Heel* in February 1908 to a lukewarm reception.[27]

London's conception of the novel was informed by both the electoral gains that the Socialist Party made in 1904, which seemed to portend a peaceful transfer of authority to the working class, and the aborted Russian Revolution of 1905, which complicated the belief that the rulers would willingly cede their power. In the case of the election, Eugene Victor Debs received 402,810 votes for president in 1904, a dramatic increase over the 255,903 cast for Socialist candidates in 1902, 98,424 in 1900, 36,275 in 1896, and 21,512 in 1892.[28] Explaining this phenomenon in the *San Francisco Examiner,* London asserted that these developments were part of a movement that "has fastened upon every civilized country in the world, and in no country has it subsided. Not only that, but in every country it is stronger to-day than ever before, is constantly adding to its strength and constantly gaining a footing in new countries."[29] For London, the inequality and exploitation under capitalism necessitated the complete transformation of society, and the 1904 election seemed to demonstrate that this result could emerge through "a peaceable and orderly revolt at the ballot box, under democratic conditions, where the majority rules."[30]

However, London's position, one that reflected the sentiments of many Socialists during this period, changed after Bloody Sunday on January 22, 1905. In response to the assembly of peaceful protesters in St. Petersburg, the Imperial Guard of Czar Nicholas II opened fire, killing 130 people and wounding 299 more.[31] In response, 414,000 workers went on strike, university students staged a walkout to protest the lack of civil liberties, and peasants seized large tracts of land throughout the countryside.[32] These incidents caused Nicholas II to issue the October Manifesto, a document that established broader participation in the parliamentary system, civil liberties, and freedom of the press, yet the political system was still controlled by the czar, who maintained his authority through imprisoning and executing radicals.[33] Expressing the relevance of these events to America, London noted that there "is a mighty ruling class that intends to hold fast to its possessions. I see years and years of bloodshed. I see the master class hiring armies of murderers to keep the workers in subjection, to beat them back should they attempt to dispossess the capitalists," and that history "shows that no master class is ever willing to let go without a quarrel. The capitalists own the governments, the armies and the militia. Don't you think the capitalists will use these institutions to keep themselves in power? I do."[34] This vision of a predatory owning class animates *The Iron Heel,* with the violent suppression of labor serving as a cautionary tale of what might transpire if the population attempts to gain control of the economic system through the ballot box.

This novel further has its origins in W. J. Ghent's *Our Benevolent Feudalism* (1902), a work that London reviewed in 1903. Ghent asserts that the "new Feudalism will be but an orderly outgrowth of present tendencies and conditions. All societies evolve naturally out of their predecessors. . . . The society of each generation develops a multitude of spontaneous and acquired variations, and out of these, by a blending process of natural and conscious selection, the succeeding society is evolved. The new order will differ in no important respects from the present, except in the completer development of its more salient features."[35] Both Ghent and London present the rise of a capitalist oligarchy as the logical outcome of prevalent social conditions through the accumulation of wealth by a few individuals and companies that dictate national affairs. As a result of these developments, Ghent posits that labor would become a dependent class similar to serfs during the Middle Ages, but the bondage to the land would be replaced with servitude to the machine. While this work reflects the dominant characteristics of the rulers in *The Iron Heel,* London's review of *Our Benevolent Feudalism* was lukewarm at best, and criticisms of Ghent also manifest in the novel. In discussing the rise of the Iron Heel, Ernest Everhard asserts that "Ghent has taught the oligarchs how to do it" and states that "I'll wager they've made a text-book out of his 'Benevolent Feudalism.'"[36] Anthony Meredith reinforces the prevalence of this position in a footnote, yet he also asserts that this belief is not accurate, observing that Ghent "is the most abused innocent man in all history" (464). The action of *The Iron Heel,* however, further expresses a challenge to Ghent's formulations in that the book focuses on an intensification of the brutality that he insists will be replaced by order and unity, which do not manifest in the Everhard manuscript.

In developing these themes, London extends elements of his contemporary society into a dystopian future to highlight the need for revolution in the United States. In London's version of America, a capitalist oligarchy controls the institutional structure of the nation, manipulating the financial system to promote their interests and attempting to provoke a response by the Socialists that will allow the rich to respond with force. Tracing the conditions that gave rise to the abuses represented in *The Iron Heel*, Avis states that "they alone knew how to reap the whirlwind and make a profit out of it. And such profits! Colossal profits! Strong enough themselves to weather the storm that was largely their own brewing, they turned loose and plundered the wrecks that floated about them. Values were pitifully and inconceivably shrunken, and the trusts added hugely to their holdings, even extending their enterprises into many new fields" (435). This power over the economic order enables the ruling class to dictate the basic terms of existence, while the references to the "storm," "whirlwind," and "wrecks" illustrate the adverse effects of their practices to express the necessity of a reaction from labor. However, this broader control provides the populace with no means of redress and guides dissent into channels that are advantageous to the powerful. This point manifests through the economic elite's influence over the media, apparent through the press accounts that precipitate the First Revolt and the suppression of the article about a workman named Jackson who loses an arm in an industrial accident; the courts through the cases of Jackson and Dr. Cunningham, a college professor whose property is seized when he no longer serves the interests of the economic elite; and the military through its role in the suppression of the working class. As a result, the Iron Heel can maintain its authority in the face of widespread popular opposition. Further, the absence of any alternatives to the dictates of the bourgeoisie engenders the violent conflict throughout *The Iron Heel*, which is intensified when the rulers form a paramilitary order that adopts the counterrevolutionary measures necessary to perpetuate their rule.[37]

Meredith's foreword reinforces these elements by contextualizing the occurrences in the Everhard manuscript yet challenging the central preoccupations of the revolutionaries. Reflecting on the Iron Heel, Meredith states that other "great historical events have their place in social evolution. They were inevitable. Their coming could have been predicted with the same certitude that astronomers to-day predict the outcome of the movements of the stars. . . . Primitive communism, chattel slavery, serf slavery, and wage slavery were necessary stepping-stones in the evolution of society. But it were ridiculous to assert that the Iron Heel was a necessary stepping-stone. Rather, to-day, is it adjudged a step aside, or a step backward, to the social tyrannies that made the early world a hell, but were as necessary as the Iron Heel was unnecessary" (320–21). This framework echoes that of dialectical materialism, which Karl Marx viewed as a predictable movement with each stage as a necessary component that would create an egalitarian world. London complicates this concept through the Iron Heel, which interrupts the predicted shift from capitalism to socialism. This development results from the emergence of a brutal state apparatus that serves as a warning to "those rash political theorists of to-day who speak with certitude of social processes" (321). This vision of inevitable change despite prevalent signs to the contrary reflects the perspectives of the Socialists in Avis's narrative, who insist "that victory could be gained through the elections. . . . Ernest could not get them seriously to fear the coming of the Oligarchy. . . . There was no room in their theoretical revolution for an oligarchy, therefore the Oligarchy could not be" (435–36). The rise of this regime suggests that the desired change will emanate from neither a peaceful transfer of power nor preordained laws since the privileged can adapt their practices to the necessities of the moment.[38] This argument is even bound up with the structure of the work. Paul Lauter notes that "London's novel is directed toward forestalling the imposition of the Iron Heel on twentieth-century America. . . . The argument of the book is that preventing the horrors narrated in the final sixteen chapters depends on learning the lessons laid out in the first nine."[39] Toward this end, London suggests that the reorganization of the social order depends on committed men and women willing to confront institutions of economic power despite immense personal sacrifice.

Meredith's footnotes serve an important function as the perspective of a distant observer enables London to present structural features of twentieth-century America for critical contemplation, stripped of the rhetorical justifications that have obscured their operations. This point is evident when Meredith explains a transit strike by remarking that "groups of predatory individuals controlled all the means of transportation, and for the use of same levied toll upon the public" (342). The reference to "predatory individuals" expresses the impulses underlying the practices of the powerful, which are conducive to the formation of the Iron Heel, and London also indicates the problems that emerge when necessary services are operated solely to maximize profit. Meredith emphasizes these ideas when he refers to the recurrent financial calamities during the nineteenth century by noting that under "the capitalist régime these periods of hard times were as inevitable as they are absurd. Prosperity always brought calamity. This, of course, was due to the excess of unconsumed profits that was piled up" (432). Meredith's explanation bolsters Ernest's formulation of surplus value in chapters 8 and 9 while further accentuating the volatility of an economic system characterized by an extreme concentration of wealth. The narrator reinforces this idea through his definition of Wall Street, observing that it was "named from a street in ancient New York, where was situated the stock exchange, and where the irrational organization of society permitted underhanded manipulation of all the industries of the country" (434). The ability of the bourgeoisie to manipulate the basic terms of exchange further signifies the instability of the social order, which anticipates the financial calamity in chapter 12 that the oligarchs engineer to solidify their control over the nation.

The narrative frame develops these ideas by juxtaposing Avis's tendency to romanticize Ernest's contributions to the revolutionary struggle with Meredith's commentary, a strategy that establishes a tension between individual and collective action and provides a more nuanced view of the protagonist. Discussing Avis's idyllic view of her husband, Meredith posits that she "lacked perspective. She was too close to the events she writes about. Nay, she was merged in the events she has described," and that Ernest "was, after all, but one of a large number of heroes who, throughout the world, devoted their lives to the Revolution" (319). The frame situates such efforts within the scope of social evolution, in which the deeds of one person attain significance in relation to the activities of others motivated by the same purpose. This opposition continues throughout the novel as Avis claims that her spouse devoted his life to the revolution as manifested through the Second Revolt—"and for it he gave his life. It was his handiwork. He made it"—while Meredith asserts that "it must be pointed out that Everhard was but one of many able leaders who carried out the Second Revolt, and we, to-day, looking back across the centuries, can safely say that even had he lived, the Second Revolt would not have been less calamitous in its outcome" (324). The defeat of the uprising highlights the insufficiency of individual initiative, and the hero's greatest contribution to the movement reflects his powerlessness against the agents of capital. Meredith, however, complicates *The Iron Heel* through his comments on the central character's analysis of economic injustice and its intensification under the Oligarchy, stating that "Everhard's social foresight was remarkable" and later observing, "We cannot but marvel at Everhard's foresight" (468, 469). The tension between the failure of his immediate objectives and the eventual success of his vision conveys that while one man cannot bring about meaningful change, these exertions, along with those of others animated by the same ideals, can contribute to the positive transformation of society.

Avis's narrative serves another important function in *The Iron Heel* by mirroring the process by which the reader should be brought to political consciousness. Despite its ostensible focus on Ernest, the Everhard manuscript centers on Avis's conversion to socialism from her privileged background, which blinded her to the plight of the working class, coupled with her recognition of the need for systemic change to address circumstances that cannot be ameliorated within the present socioeconomic framework. In this context, the excesses of her language, most notable in the first two chapters when she recalls her introduction to Ernest, reflect the vestiges of her previous class position and rely on the discourse of sentimental fiction. This language correlates to the literary expectations of a middle-class spectator, providing a frame to engage the reader with issues of economic injustice. Jude Davies observes that through Avis, "London provides an exemplary narrative of a shift from middle-class to working-class political outlook, while her middle-class sensibility, refracted especially through the novel's diction, is aimed at satisfying readers' literary preferences."[40] The portrayal of Avis suggests that this novel was not necessarily directed at the laboring masses, who were already familiar with the practices of capital, and London did not serialize *The Iron Heel* in the *Appeal to Reason* or any of the other radical periodicals that published his political writings. Instead, the book seems directed at people like Avis prior to her awakening, who have not confronted the nature of capitalism and profit from the inequitable social order that London assails throughout the work. As Kathy Knapp observes, Avis is the character "who learns, grows, and changes. In other words, while the novel may borrow from dystopian and science fiction as well as leftist lectures and essays, at its heart, *The Iron Heel* is a bourgeois bildungsroman that has much to say to a generation coming of age in an era of dramatically rising economic inequality."[41] By depicting the transformation of someone who parallels the privileged audience into a committed revolutionist and presenting the narrative from her point of view, London highlights the necessary evolution that individuals must undergo in order to participate in social change.

The Iron Heel demonstrates the necessity of this development when Avis investigates Jackson's case in chapters 3 and 4, an episode that provides her introduction to the human consequences of capitalism and illustrates how the actions of individuals are dictated by those who preside over the economy.[42] This incident has its origins in a piece published in the *Outlook* that detailed the case of a man whose arm had been mangled when he tried to save a piece of machinery from destruction, and the perjured testimony, the reporter's questioning, and the silence of the press closely correspond to Avis's account.[43] These raw materials highlight the nature of the forces aligned against labor, further signifying the complicity of the professional class in the plight of the working class since the individuals in the former maintain their positions and financial security through their service to the wealthy. London develops this point through the foreman, Peter Donnelly, who offers false testimony to protect the company from damages "because it wouldn't a-ben healthy" for him to tell the truth (354); the superintendent who parrots the same line since it "means hundreds of thousands a year to the stockholders" (355); the corporation lawyers who manipulate the legal framework in accordance with the dictates of the elite; and the journalist who refuses to print the article as the paper is "all solid with the corporations" (363). Everyone is implicated in the fate of this lone individual, including Avis and her father because they own stock in the company that has caused this course of events. While these characters play their parts in Jackson's fate, Ernest attributes primary responsibility to those who direct the economic system by noting that no "man in the industrial machine is a free-will agent, except the large capitalist, and he isn't. . . . You see, the masters are quite sure that they are right in what they are doing. That is the crowning absurdity of the whole situation" (365). All individuals within the framework of production must play a certain role to guarantee the smooth operation of society, and London indicates that their perspectives are framed by a desire for economic gain, which often necessitates the use of questionable practices.

London buttresses this theme through the representation of the oligarchs, who do not acquiesce to the demands of labor and instead fight to protect their wealth. This point emerges when Ernest gives a speech before a gathering of the owning class at the Philomath Club, articulating a desire for the transfer of economic control to the proletariat. The narrator observes "the token of the brute in man, the earnest of his primitive passions. . . . It was the growl of the pack, mouthed by the pack. . . . I realized that not easily would they let their lordship of the world be wrested from them" (376). After Ernest delivers his indictment of capitalism, an analysis that has its origins in London's "Revolution" and "What Life Means to Me," those endowed with social prominence and the surface forms of culture become violent, and London's use of animal imagery accentuates the predatory nature of these individuals. Avis reinforces this idea when she notes that these men "were cool captains of industry and lords of society, these snarling, growling savages in evening clothes" (379). Their reserve, their politeness, and their erudition vanish in the face of this threat to their authority, which Wickson displays in his final statement to Ernest: "When you reach out your vaunted strong hands for our palaces and purpled ease, we will show you what strength is. In roar of shell and shrapnel and in whine of machine-guns will our answer be couched" (384). Rather than consenting to the expropriation of their resources, the rulers employ the means at their disposal to destroy any challenges to their interests. The remainder of the narrative traces out this process, dramatizing the consequences that might emerge from the consolidation of financial and political power.

The strength of the Oligarchy gains clear expression through the narratives of Bishop Morehouse and Dr. Cunningham. While these men once served the interests of capital from the pulpit and the university classroom, their fates after their radicalization reveal the costs for those who challenge the imperatives of capital. Regarding the opportunities for individuals who promote the interests of the ruling class, Ernest asserts that "the professors, the preachers, and the editors, hold their jobs by serving the Plutocracy, and their service consists of propagating only such ideas as are either harmless to or commendatory of the Plutocracy. When they propagate ideas that menace the Plutocracy, they lose their jobs, in which case, if they have not provided for the rainy day, they descend into the proletariat and either perish or become working-class agitators" (423). This passage encapsulates the experiences of Bishop Morehouse and Dr. Cunningham. Insofar as the former preaches a version of Christianity amenable to the privileged and the latter devotes himself to scientific study divorced from any consideration of social issues, these characters are rewarded with wealth and influence. However, after Ernest introduces the minister to the plight of the poor, which causes him to advance an interpretation of Christ's teachings that emphasized social justice before his affluent congregation, he is institutionalized because his "views were perilous to society, and society could not conceive that such perilous views could be the product of a sane mind" (444). When Cunningham shifts his research to examining how the capitalists control education, he is stripped of his academic position, his book is suppressed, his holdings in the Sierra Mills are erased from the company records, and a nonexistent mortgage provides a pretext for seizing his home. He has no means of redress through legal avenues since the corporation controls the courts, and the "machinery of society was in the hands of those who were bent on breaking him" (439). London prefaces this episode with an offer from Wickson, one of the oligarchs, to make Cunningham the president of a college the capitalists are planning if he repudiates his radicalism, which reinforces the rewards for obedience and illustrates the methods that the economic elite employ to perpetuate their authority.

The fates of Cunningham and Morehouse operate within the Oligarchy's further efforts to strengthen its power, and these representations highlight the perils facing even the relatively privileged under capitalism. London first worked out these ideas in "Disappearing Class," notes for a planned series of essays about the forces that would be responsible for the destruction of the middle class. London presented this group as being the most vulnerable since they depended on both workers and owners for survival, yet this prospect seemed tenuous as capital aggregated into fewer hands and produced greater social strife. Placing this movement in a broader historical context, London observes that as "the worker passed from the comparative freedom of domestic production to the slavery of factory production, so the small capitalist to-day is passing from the comparative freedom of pre-trust competitive industry to slavery of post-trust industry (better)—incidentally point out, that there is a class struggle even within the capitalist class, between small and large capitalists."[44] For his primary illustration of this thesis, London invokes the conditions facing small producers, who find themselves squeezed out of production by the "Beef Trust," a monopoly formation that controlled the price and distribution of livestock. London compares the earlier status of a cattleman, when he "was prosperous, was somebody, had something to say about the things that went to the making of his own welfare, was himself an economic force, empowered with initiative," with his present state, when he can either accept the offer of the Beef Trust or perish, a development that reduces him to the status of a slave in service to the established order.[45]

These ideas are relevant to *The Iron Heel* as London emphasizes the demise of the middle class and the agrarian population during the Oligarchy's rise. To eliminate the first group, the Iron Heel manufactures a fiscal crisis, turning "the stock market into a maelstrom where the values of all the land crumbled away almost to nothingness. And out of all the rack and ruin rose the form of the nascent Oligarchy, imperturbable, indifferent and sure. . . . Not only did it use its own vast power, but it used all the power of the United States Treasury" (434–35). The ability to control the marketplace reinforces the power of the oligarchs. London further dramatizes this point through the destruction of the class that symbolizes the economic progress possible in America, while their demise results from the manipulation of a financial system often associated with prosperity. London reinforces this point through the destruction of the farmers. Avis observes that as a result of the wealthy dictating prices and freight rates in addition to commencing widespread foreclosures, the growers "simply surrendered the land to the farm trust" and became "managers, superintendents, foreman, and common laborers. They worked for wages. They became villeins, in short—serfs bound to the soil by a living wage. They could not leave their masters, for their masters composed the Plutocracy" (456). This occurrence inverts traditional narratives of progress through engagement with the soil, providing instead further subordination to landowners, to whom the farmers must sell their labor in order to live. This process highlights the forces that limit the opportunities for small producers when resources are held by a minority of the population.

London further develops the rise of the Iron Heel and the resulting consequences for the population through the labor castes that divide the workers from one another, enabling one group to attain prosperity while reducing others to poverty and desperation. After a general strike that paralyzes commerce throughout the country, the plutocracy subsidizes unions in the most vital industries to form an aristocracy of labor divorced from employees in other fields. This tactic has two primary advantages. By paying these individuals higher wages, granting them access to superior schools, and building them nicer homes in better neighborhoods, the Oligarchy has created a privileged faction that would be unlikely to jeopardize the smooth operation of society since they now have a stake in it. Regarding the second benefit, Ernest notes that every "fit workman in the United States will be possessed by the ambition to become a member of the favored unions. . . . Thus will the strong men, who might else be revolutionists, be won away and their strength used to bolster the Oligarchy" (467–68). Accordingly, the Oligarchy can weaken challenges to their authority by not only co-opting potential leaders but also focusing hostility on the members of these trade associations, who "were branded as traitors, and in saloons and brothels, on the streets and at work, and, in fact, everywhere, they were assaulted by the comrades they had so treacherously deserted" (472). These perceptions and subsequent acts of retribution undermine the potential power of the common people since such undertakings divert attention from the men responsible for inequitable conditions, a development that diminishes the workers' ability to challenge existing social relations.

The representation of the favored unions has its origins in American labor history. This connection is evident through a footnote that refers to Peter M. Arthur, the grand chief of the Brotherhood of Locomotive Engineers, who made their own terms with the railroads following the Great Upheaval of 1877 to separate one segment of the workforce from the majority (472). Further, Arthur engaged in strikebreaking during the Pullman boycott and announced to his membership that "it is the duty of the engineers to run their engines. Any member refusing to do so lays himself liable to dismissal, and will not receive support from the union."[46] These attempts to accommodate capital by dividing the working class have a precursor in the tactics of Samuel L. Gompers, who served as president of the American Federation of Labor (AFL) from 1886 to 1894 and again from 1895 to 1924. This trade association only organized skilled craftsmen, ignoring the conditions facing the unskilled in exchange for recognition from industry. Gompers also collaborated with employers to form the National Civic Federation. This organization consisted primarily of representatives from anti-union firms, such as the presidents of the Federal Steel Company, McCormick Harvesting Machine Company, and Swift & Company in addition to a number of conservative leaders, including Gompers and Arthur.[47] As Philip S. Foner observes, the purpose of the National Civic Federation was to channel "the labor movement into conservative avenues and to rob it of any semblance of radicalism and militancy. The craft unions would win recognition from the leaders of the trustified industries for a small minority of the workers on the condition they would 'not make trouble' for the corporations by organizing the mass of workers in their plants and factories."[48] In essence, Gompers abandoned the majority of the workforce for the advancement of those who belonged to the AFL, placing the concerns of a group over the needs of the population to create a situation comparable to what London represents in the novel.

London also incorporates prominent episodes from American history in the oligarchs' use of organized violence to eradicate labor militancy. This development manifests through the rise of the Black Hundreds, a paramilitary branch of the Iron Heel that takes its name from the forces loyal to the czar during the 1905 Russian Revolution. Meredith conveys the importance of this reference when he observes that the "name only, and not the idea, was imported from Russia. The Black Hundreds were a development out of the secret agents of the capitalists, and their use arose in the labor struggles of the nineteenth century" (434). This passage indicates the extent to which the novel is informed by the major work stoppages prior to its composition, and London integrates these conflicts into the representation of the Iron Heel. Ernest's statement that instead "of habeas corpus you will get post mortems" echoes a declaration from Adjutant General Sherman Bell of the Colorado National Guard during the Colorado labor wars, which was characterized by violent behavior from vigilantes and federal troops (410).[49] Further, a footnote that describes the practice of confining protesters in bullpens alludes to the Coeur d'Alene strike in 1892, when such practices were first employed (433). Another note discusses James Farley, "a notorious strikebreaker of the period," who organized bands of mercenaries to intervene in labor disputes, most notably on the side of the San Francisco United Railroad in 1903 and again in 1907, when his men opened fire on a crowd of strikers, killing two and wounding twenty (467).[50] The suppression of the Peasant Revolt in chapter 16 also operates in this context as London alludes to the Homestead strike, the Pullman boycott, and the Colorado labor wars as state militias and private security companies employed increasingly forceful means to quell each disturbance.[51] Through these incidents, London connects his dystopian future to tendencies rooted within his contemporary society, with the text thereby providing a frame for the critical contemplation of tensions within twentieth-century America.

The removal of the Socialists from Congress in chapter 17 also illustrates the Oligarchy's use of violence to shape social conditions, and London again draws on contemporary events in portraying the forces aligned against labor. In developing this incident, Avis discusses a bombing that provides the justification for imprisoning Ernest and his associates, which Meredith explains in a lengthy footnote that refers to two episodes when such tactics offered a pretext for the suppression of dissidents: the Haymarket massacre of 1886 and the Independence Train Depot explosion in 1904 (492). In the Haymarket episode, after 180 policemen stormed a peaceful demonstration and ordered protesters to disperse, an explosive device detonated in their midst, killing seven officers; in response, the surviving officers fired into the crowd, murdering several people and wounding two hundred.[52] As a result of this occurrence, nine prominent radicals were charged with conspiracy to commit murder, tried, convicted, and sentenced to death without evidence connecting them to this affair, which was later suspected to have been committed by Rudolph Schnaubelt, a supposed Anarchist who was allegedly an agent of the police.[53] Meredith further develops the context for the rulers' actions through mentioning an explosion at the Independence Depot during the Colorado labor wars that took the lives of thirteen nonunion workers and injured sixteen others. This event supplied the rationale for launching a renewed offensive against the Western Federation of Miners (WFM), whose leaders were indicted in a case that was later dismissed for lack of evidence.[54] Further, the Mine Owners' Association and the Victor Citizens' Alliance replaced elected officials with men who assumed that the strikers were guilty, and these groups organized mobs that opened fire on miners, destroyed the union hall, herded individuals affiliated with the WFM into bullpens, and eventually deported them from the district.[55] However, testimony from A. C. Cole, the secretary of the Victor Citizen's Alliance, and J. M. Huff, a member of the Victor Militia, indicated that the Mine Owners' Association was responsible for planting the bomb.[56] The references to these events suggest that the practices of the Oligarchy are the outgrowths of tactics prevalent prior to the composition of the novel, which expresses the need to alter such conditions before they facilitate the even more extreme forms that London presents in *The Iron Heel*.

The brutality of the Oligarchy necessitates the further development of revolutionary organizations, which accentuates the central theme that social change stems not from historical laws but from popular struggles to create a more equitable world. Describing the formation of the Fighting Groups and the initial attempts to weed out agents provocateurs, Avis observes that it "was bitter, bloody work, but we were fighting for life and for the Revolution, and we had to fight the enemy with its own weapons. Yet we were fair. No agent of the Iron Heel was ever executed without a trial." Avis conveys that the radicals' violent tactics are the logical response to a continued pattern of abuses and provide the only means to promote their objectives. However, the emphasis on fair trials for the agents of the Iron Heel contrasts with the summary killings committed on behalf of the ruling class, highlighting the values that have been superseded within the legal system of the oligarchs. Meredith emphasizes the just nature of the insurgents' proceedings through references to their "passionless and judicial procedure" with "a fair trial and opportunity for defence" for the accused (483). He extends these ideas when he states that members of the Fighting Groups "gave up their lives for humanity, no sacrifice was too great for them to accomplish, while inexorable necessity compelled them to bloody expression in an age of blood" (484). The connection between the oligarchs' actions and the revolutionaries' reactions supports the causative role of the former in dictating the undertakings of the latter and necessitating deeds that "violated their own natures" since they were "opposed to the taking of life" (483).

While many of these individuals give their lives to build an egalitarian society, London also traces their interpersonal contributions. This aspect manifests through Anna Roylston, a fearsome operative of the revolutionaries who adores children yet refuses to have any of her own as they would prevent her from being of service to the workers, and John Carlson, who, at great risk, maintains the refuge where the militants hide in order to evade execution. Reflecting on the perspectives underlying such practices, Avis notes that the Socialists "worshipped at the shrine of the Revolution, which was the shrine of liberty. It was the divine flashing through us. Men and women had devoted their lives to the Cause, and newborn babes were sealed to it as of old they had been sealed to the service of God" (485). This religious imagery expresses the impulses that frame the sacrifices made by these men and women, whose exploits contribute to the eventual realization of the Brotherhood of Man.

Chapter 19 highlights the need for revolution by reintroducing the cast of characters from the first half of the narrative and tracing their destinies at the hands of the Oligarchy. After his maiming at the Sierra Mills and his inability to rectify his grievances through the legal system, Jackson, "embittered by his fate, brooding over his wrongs ... became an anarchist—not a philosophical anarchist, but a mere animal, mad with hate and lust for revenge," blowing up the palace of the primary stockholder in the firm (505). The reference to Jackson as a "mere animal" suggests that his deed stems from the forces arrayed against him, which have closed all other avenues of redress and have left bloodshed as his only possible means of retaliation. Avis reiterates this point through the transformation of Peter Donnelly, who testified on behalf of the company at Jackson's trial, into a member of a fighting organization composed of "fanatics, madmen," and he explains his current course by noting that "'tis revenge for my blasted manhood I'm after" as a result of the death of his wife in addition to the defection of his youngest son into the mercenaries of the Iron Heel (506). Jackson's and Donnelly's experiences signify that the violence of the working class results inevitably from the nature of the social order and that these men merely replicate on a small scale the tactics that have been employed against them. London supplies contrasting examples through the trajectories of Dr. Hammerfield and Dr. Ballingford, the ministers who advanced views favorable to the powerful in chapter 1 and "have been correspondingly rewarded with ecclesiastical palaces wherein they dwell at peace with the world" for adapting their metaphysics to the requirements of the Oligarchy (505). These positive outcomes stress the incentives for those aligned with the powerful, reinforcing the ability of the Iron Heel to shape conditions in accordance with their interests and offering a counterpoint to the earlier fates of Cunningham and Morehouse.

The chapters devoted to the Chicago Commune and the First Revolt unify the central themes of *The Iron Heel* by demonstrating the effects of the Oligarchy on the most vulnerable sectors of the population. Describing the unskilled, Avis notes that they "lived like beasts in great squalid labor-ghettoes, festering in misery and degradation. All their old liberties were gone. They were labor-slaves. Choice of work was denied them. Likewise was denied them the right to move from place to place, or the right to bear or possess arms. . . . They were machine-serfs and labor-serfs" (520). London underscores the impact of milieu through the reference to the workers as "beasts," a development that stems from their confinement within urban slums and the denial of their basic rights. London extends this idea through the reference to the workers as "labor-serfs," which denotes the state of peasants under feudalism and suggests a regression to an earlier stage of human development. This connotation further undermines an optimistic view of history inexorably leading toward a just society as institutions of economic power have the ability to thwart progress as evident during the suppression of the First Revolt. Through their control over the press, the oligarchs print a series of reports that prematurely trigger the insurrection, which supplies the pretext for indiscriminate slaughter and guarantees the failure of its immediate objectives. Reflecting on the people who participate in the rebellion, Avis refers to men and women "with all the godlike blotted from their features and all the fiendlike stamped in, apes and tigers, anæmic consumptives and great hairy beasts of burden, wan faces from which vampire society had sucked the juice of life," who signify "the refuse and scum of life, a raging, screaming, screeching, demoniacal horde" (535). While this passage provides another illustration of the effect of environment on the individual, London accentuates the fates of those deemed inessential to the operation of the social order, who are consigned to a perpetual poverty that strips them of their humanity.

London posits the need for a fundamental reorganization of society, yet he provides little information about the end of the Iron Heel or the particulars of the Brotherhood of Man. Rather than developing the events that facilitated a more just world, the Everhard Manuscript ends in the middle of a sentence as Avis discusses the magnitude of Ernest and the other leaders' attempts to rebuild their organization after the First Revolt. London only offers generalized commentary on the process that culminated in the Socialist victory. Ernest observes that the Oligarchy and the labor castes, which by their nature would be separated from the rest of the working class, would gradually weaken without the influx of new blood from the proletariat, and "through it all the inevitable caste-weakening will go on, so that in the end the common people will come into their own." In response, Meredith praises Ernest's foresight and states that "he saw the defection of the favored unions, the rise and the slow decay of the labor castes, and the struggle between the decaying oligarchs and labor castes for control of the great governmental machine" (468). By omitting the concrete details of the successful revolution, London accentuates the importance of the immediate political problems represented throughout the narrative, and he draws attention to these ills in the context of a warning about the structures that could materialize if people do not work to ameliorate these conditions. Through this method, *The Iron Heel* suggests that the parameters of an egalitarian society and the process responsible for its emergence should not be the product of the individual. Instead, these decisions should emanate from the collective in accordance with their interests, which London expresses through Meredith's endeavors to situate Ernest's actions in a broader historical context.

London illustrates this collective action in "The Dream of Debs," originally published in the *International Socialist Review* (January–February 1909) and included in *The Strength of the Strong* (1914), through a successful general strike that reveals the power of labor to shape living and working conditions.[57] According to Stephen Naft, the purpose of such a work stoppage is "to completely interrupt production in the whole country, and stop communication and consumption for the ruling classes, and that for a time long enough to totally disorganize the capitalistic society; so that after the complete annihilation of the old system, the working people can take possession through its labor unions of all the means of production."[58] This focus on transforming the socioeconomic system differs from conventional labor disputes, which have often emphasized the concerns of one group of employees rather than the conditions facing the majority. The dramatization of this concept in "The Dream of Debs" represents a noteworthy development in American naturalism, indicating that while individuals cannot effectively challenge dominant social institutions, workers have the ability to engender meaningful change when operating as a unit. Through this portrayal of collective strength, the narrative highlights both the arbitrary economic arrangements that often dictate the circumstances facing labor and the necessity of a framework that is more receptive to the needs of the majority.

London aligns "The Dream of Debs" with significant developments in American labor history, connections that present his fictional strike as the logical outcome of measures the affluent have taken to safeguard their resources. The choice of a title unites the text with a particular notion of progress through the reference to the militant radical who formed the ARU, cofounded the Industrial Workers of the World (IWW), and ran for president five times as the Socialist candidate.[59] Eugene V. Debs argued that "the labor movement means more, infinitely more, than a paltry increase in wages and the strike necessary to secure it; that while it engages to do all that possibly can be done to better the working conditions of its members, its higher object is to overthrow the capitalist system of private ownership of the tools of labor, abolish wage-slavery and achieve the freedom of the whole working class."[60] The actual dream of Debs, the revolutionary action of a class-conscious proletariat to create a Socialist state, finds clear expression in the IWW, which London identified in his notes as the model for his fictional labor organization, the ILW.[61] In contrast to the craft unionism prevalent during this era, the IWW sought to organize entire industries, involved both skilled and unskilled employees, and advocated the elimination of the existing economic order. At the founding conference, Big Bill Haywood, who appears in "The Dream of Debs" through an allusion to the persecution of the WFM leadership, stated that the "aims and objects of [the IWW] should be to put the working-class in possession of the economic power, the means of life, in control of the machinery of production and distribution without regard to capitalist masters."[62] To accomplish these objectives, the IWW supported direct action from boycotts to sabotage with the general strike as a means to establish the framework of a new society within the shell of the old.

"The Dream of Debs" advances a similar conception of the general strike as a vehicle to remedy the workers' grievances and to level existing economic hierarchies. London conveys this disruption of conventional relations when the narrator cites a proclamation from the ILW, which asserts that the dispute will cease "when our demands are satisfied, and our demands will be satisfied when we have starved our employers into submission, as we ourselves in the past have often been starved into submission."[63] This connection between the current strike and past ones emphasizes the growing power of labor, a development made possible through destabilizing the institutions that have enabled the capitalists to dictate the operations of the social order. As a result, the ILW is able to undermine usual managerial responses to such clashes. The owners cannot starve their employees since they have stocked the supplies necessary to sustain themselves, the bosses cannot secure injunctions because they cannot contact government officials because the laborers cut the telegraph wires, and the employers cannot utilize violence against the strikers as they have provided no pretext for the use of force. Through these methods, the workers have insulated themselves from the practices that contributed to the defeats of the principal labor struggles of this era, most notably the Great Upheaval, the Homestead strike, the Pullman boycott, and the Colorado labor wars, among many others. As a result of the ILW's tactics, the wealthy are incapable of controlling the situation, and they are at the mercy of those they once dominated.

London registers the severity of this change through employing a first-person retrospective narration from Mr. Cerf, a member of the owning class whose perspective is informed by the nature of his economic position. He initially views the dispute in dispassionate terms, recalling that he had once "written an article on the subject for one of the magazines and that I had entitled it, 'The Dream of Debs.' And I must confess that I had treated the idea very carefully and academically as a dream and nothing more" (241). Cerf's statement reveals his failure to accurately apprehend the nature of the conflict, one that seems divorced from his lived experience as suggested by his reference to the general strike as a mere "dream." While Cerf implies that such occurrences only exist in the realm of fantasy, the industrial action in the text presents Debs's vision as the model that will enable the free development of labor, and the protagonist's inability to consider this possibility conveys the irony of using the same title for both his article and the story. London reiterates the flaws in the narrator's perceptions when he begins to witness the effects of the work stoppage. After leaving his home, Cerf states that it "would certainly be interesting to be out in the streets of San Francisco when . . . the whole city was taking an enforced vacation" and later finds that his "nerves were tinkling with mild excitement" (241, 242). This reaction anticipates the views of other members of his class. One acquaintance "was enjoying it hugely," and Cerf remarks that "no one really apprehended anything serious" (243). For the affluent, this particular disturbance does not pose a threat to those in power; instead, it merely provides a source of amusement, a respite from their daily routines, evident through the references to the strike as "interesting," as a "vacation," as nothing "serious." These descriptions reflect the conceptions of one who is so closely aligned with the established order that he cannot perceive any possible challenges to its authority, which conditions his belief that this clash is merely a passing fancy that will be quickly overcome.

London extends this critique to encompass the structures of power that the affluent characters represent since they profit from the inequitable conditions that have caused the general strike. The narrator clarifies this point through the description of Bertie Messener, a younger member of Cerf's club who was "worth twenty millions, all of it in safe investments, and he had never done a tap of productive work in his life—inherited it all from his father and two uncles" (244). As this example attests, this particular group owes its position to the efforts of other people, a development that complicates the conventional structure of the national success story because some enjoy the benefits of fortunes accrued through no labor of their own. This representation stresses the corruption of the ideals central to American society, which allows for vast concentrations of wealth that have undesirable consequences for both owners and workers. Regarding the former, the narrator observes that Bertie "didn't care about anything, had no ambitions, no passions, no desire to do the very things he did so much better than other men" (244–45). This detachment from any meaningful engagement with life illustrates the consequences of the present economic order for the privileged, whose reliance on the accomplishments of previous generations facilitates a pervasive sense of ennui. The narrator, however, distinguishes between Bertie and the other members of his class as he has not orchestrated the conditions that allow for the stability of his assets, but he does benefit from the actions undertaken by his peers to safeguard their interests.

London develops these practices through incorporating notable labor disputes into "The Dream of Debs," and this connection to economic reality sharpens the social criticism of the story. Discussing the causes of the general strike, Bertie mentions an earlier episode, observing that the "Employers' Association precipitated that strike.... First you precipitated the strike, then you bought the Mayor and the Chief of Police and broke the strike. A pretty spectacle, you philanthropists getting the teamsters down and then gouging them" (246). This passage refers to a 1901 waterfront strike that paralyzed commerce throughout the San Francisco Bay Area as the Employers' Association played an important role in this conflict. This organization was composed of executives from prominent local businesses—such as Cahn & Nickelburg, W. and J. Sloane & Company, and Levi Strauss—who contributed one thousand dollars apiece, and often more, to impose open-shop policies that would diminish the power of unions.[64] Regarding the aims of this organization, a reporter for the *Examiner* noted that "The Employers' Association of San Francisco has undertaken to destroy unionism in this city, on the ground that it has a right to conduct its business as it pleases, and will not submit to the dictation of unions."[65]

The principal events of this conflict largely correspond to London's depiction in "The Dream of Debs." The Employers' Association escalated unrest by locking out Teamsters in San Francisco and refused to negotiate with their representatives. These actions caused the City Front Federation—formed by the Teamsters, the Sailors' Union of the Pacific, and the Longshoreman's Union—to strike on July 30.[66] As in London's version, Mayor James D. Phelan played a significant role in this struggle, taking steps to help companies maintain operations. He enlisted police officers to protect replacement workers and deputized guards hired by the Employers' Association to patrol the waterfront, which caused violence to intensify for the remainder of the work stoppage.[67] The resolution of this industrial action, however, differs from London's treatment. The actual strike ended through the intervention of Governor Henry T. Gage, who threatened to declare martial law if the disturbance did not cease immediately, and owners reached a deal with the unions. While this development contributed to the demise of the Employers' Association, the position of organized labor was significantly weakened by the settlement: employees returned to their jobs at pre-strike wages; had to work alongside strikebreakers; and received no guarantees of a closed shop, which was the principal grievance of both the City Front Federation and the ILW in "The Dream of Debs."

London further bases the causes underlying the general strike in labor history by referring to an attempt to destabilize the WFM. In developing the context for London's dispute, Bertie states that his associates "kept the President of the Southwestern Amalgamated Association of Miners in jail for three years on trumped up murder charges, and with him out of the way you broke up the Association" (246). This passage denotes the persecution of the WFM, which had waged bitter and violent industrial actions in Coeur d'Alene, Idaho, in 1899 and in the Cripple Creek region of Colorado between 1903 and 1904. The union president, Charles Moyer, was arrested along with Big Bill Haywood and William Pettibone for the murder of Frank Steunenberg, the former governor of Idaho. London became involved in this cause, contributing money to a defense fund for these WFM officials and writing "Something Rotten in Idaho," an article that appeared in the *Daily Socialist* on November 4, 1906. London observed that the desire to imprison these individuals resulted from the fact that they stood "between the mine owner and a pot of money. These men are leaders of organized labor. They plan and direct the efforts of the workingmen to get better wages and shorter hours. The operation of their mines will be more expensive. The higher the running expenses, the smaller the profits. If the mine owners could disrupt the Western Federation of Miners, they would increase the hours of labor, lower wages, and thereby gain millions of dollars."[68] In this view, the trial, which relied on coerced testimony and fraudulent evidence, represented the lengths to which the employers would go in order to protect their interests against the increasing militancy of their workers. This interpretation gains credence from the estimated $75,000 to $100,000 raised by industrialists and the Colorado Mine Owners' Association in their endeavor to eradicate the WFM.[69] Discussing the implications of the accusations against Moyer, Haywood, and Pettibone, one newspaper editorialized that it "is not merely that Haywood and Moyer are on trial at Boise. A great labor organization is on trial. If Moyer and Haywood are found guilty . . . then organized labor will receive its bitterest blow."[70] While the case did not destroy the WFM, and the men served one year of jail time rather than three, the allusion to this litigation reinforces the power of those who preside over the economy and expresses the rationale of the conflict represented in "The Dream of Debs."

London presents the ability of the general strike to fundamentally trans-form conditions through his emphasis on the destabilization of economic hierarchies, an alteration that initially manifests through the powerlessness of the rich to cope with the pressures brought about by the work stoppage. As a result of this dispute, the elite can no longer deal with practical concerns from securing the safety of loved ones to obtaining provisions. For instance, one of Cerf's wealthy acquaintances, Atkinson, cannot locate his wife since the ferries have stopped running, and the striking longshoremen would not load his automobile on a private yacht. The cessation of all trade and industry as a result of the strike prevents the affluent from living in their accustomed manner, an outcome that stems from their inability to perform the work that they once entrusted to others. Cerf reinforces this idea when the cars of the bourgeoisie begin to break down, and he notes that the "repair shops and ga-rages were closed, and whenever a machine broke down it went out of circu-lation. The clutch on mine broke and love nor money could not get it repaired. Like the rest, I was now walking" (249). The vehicles that once illustrated these individuals' prosperity now express the consequences of their socio-economic status, which has left them incapable of sustaining their former mode of existence. Once their control has been stripped away, this lack of practical knowledge gives the common people authority over their former employers, who find that they must fend for themselves in an environment where their money has lost its value. These episodes further highlight the significant role of the working class in American life since they perform the tasks necessary for the operation of society, and the story suggests that these benefits might abruptly cease when employees recognize their power and withhold their labor.

London reiterates the inversion of social hierarchies through the in-ability of the bourgeoisie to secure the necessaries of existence, and this development reduces them to the state of misery that they once forced on the masses. In the early stages of the narrative, Mr. Cerf comments on the absence of the cream for his coffee, the fancy rolls for his breakfast, and the olives for his martinis. However, as the story progresses, his focus changes from these luxuries to staple foodstuffs. Referring to his initial attempts to acquire provisions, Cerf observes, "I filled the car with sacks of flour, baking powder, tinned goods, and all the necessities of life suggested by Harmmed" (243). The fact that Cerf's butler has to recommend the purchase of these items is significant in that he has served as a buffer between the narrator and the outside world, tending to his physical requirements so that he was not bothered by such concerns. After the flight of his servants, Cerf must now take on these responsibilities, and his hardships are intensified by the careful planning of the ILW, whose members have stockpiled supplies to last throughout the strike. This development causes the necessity of creating breadlines for the rich, which places them in the same position as the destitute and further erodes the foundation of their exalted status as they now exist alongside those who have been cast aside by industry after ceasing to generate sufficient profits. After this distribution network ceases, the wealthy must adopt alternate strategies that emerge in a primitive system of exchange. The narrator notes that residents of the working-class districts offer the owners meals in exchange for the silver that once signified their affluence and now accentuates the extent of their deprivation. These shifts emphasize the growing power of labor while also indicating that the economic elite, despite their sense of superiority over the common people, are subject to the same pressures as their subordinates.

London underscores this development through patterns of imagery that reflect the upper-class characters' devolution amid their struggles to obtain the necessaries of existence. London contextualizes this design when Garfield rails against the strikers, and the narrator describes "a very excited gentleman with rumpled, iron-gray hair, a flushed face, mouth sullen and vindictive, and eyes wildly gleaming" (245). This passage indicates the club patrons' predatory nature, evident through the "gleaming" eyes that connote a beast tracking its prey. London reinforces this conception through references to the affluent "squealing" about the practices of the ILW and going on "a hunt for more food" (247, 248). These images intensify when the rations of the rich have been exhausted, which causes them to undertake more drastic measures that manifest in their efforts to slaughter a cow. Cerf states, "I omit the details, for they are not nice—we were unaccustomed to such work, and we bungled it" (250). Through their ignorance of the labor necessary to kill and to butcher the creature, Cerf and his companions are stripped of their former refinement and reduced to the level of animals as a member of his group, Brentwood, approaches a calf "like a wolf or a tiger" (251). These actions become more pronounced when the men fight another group that attempts to commandeer the meat. The narrator observes that the "scene that follows beggars description. We fought and squabbled over the division like savages. Brentwood, I remember, was a perfect brute, snarling and snapping and threatening that murder would be done if we did not get our proper share" (250). This regression from civilized beings to "snarling and snapping" brutes expresses the reawakening of their primal instincts for survival, indicating that even the wealthy are not immune to the impact of environment.

London reinforces these themes during the flight of the bourgeoisie and underclass from San Francisco, which further traces the consequences that emerge as a result of economic deprivation. The narrator emphasizes this development through connecting the affluent with the destitute, noting that "all of the destruction and violence had been done by the slumdwellers and the upper classes" and that "millionaires and paupers had fought side by side for food, and then fought with one another after they got it" (254, 255). This correlation between those who were once at the top of the social order and those at the bottom signifies the eradication of economic hierarchies since the actions of the formerly well-to-do are indistinguishable from the deeds of the poor, who are governed by the same motives. Surveying the damage caused by these groups, Cerf declares that "the country had been turned over to anarchy. Two hundred thousand people had fled south from San Francisco, and we had countless evidences that their flight had been like that of an army of locusts" (253). The reference to the "army of locusts" suggests Exodus, when God warns Pharaoh that if he refuses to free the Israelites, then "I will bring locusts into your country tomorrow. They will cover the face of the ground so that it cannot be seen. They will devour what little you have left after the hail, including every tree that is growing in your fields."[71] This description anticipates the carnage to follow in the narrative. Cerf finds that "all the vegetable patches had been rooted up by the famished hordes," and he observes that the area is "a desolate wasted land" in which not "a living thing remained. The calves, the colts, and all the fancy poultry and thoroughbred stock, everything was gone" (254, 255). The apocalyptic resonance of Cerf's statement offers a warning to those who preside over the economy, indicating that the events depicted in "The Dream of Debs" might transpire if the powerful fail to address the grievances of labor.

The juxtaposition between the savagery of the affluent and the order produced by the strikers illustrates the workers' capacity to shape dominant society coupled with the bourgeoisie's resulting failure to function without the essential labor provided by their subordinates. While the wealthy try to secure provisions, the members of the ILW are "out taking the air and observing the effects of the strike. It was all so unusual, and withal so peaceful," and Cerf refers to "the crowded but orderly streets" (242, 248). This sense of calm is what causes him to conclude that this dispute is not serious. He cannot perceive that this tranquility results from the alteration of normal conditions and the power of ordinary people when they begin to operate as a group. London continues to juxtapose the devolution of the upper class with the disciplined undertakings of organized labor: when Cerf and his companions attempt to butcher the calf and fight other men for the meat, an ILW patrol restores order. Further, when Cerf and his cohorts flee the city in search of food, they observe that among the working class, "well-fed children were playing games, and stout housewives sat on the front steps gossiping" (253). Through the effective organization of the general strike, these individuals are able to attain drastic improvements over their usual conditions as evident through the well-fed children—as opposed to emaciated, sickly wretches like Johnny in "The Apostate"—and the women engaged in small talk rather than silently tending machines in the factories. These elements highlight the ability of the common people to manage their own affairs and their resulting ability to alter the constraints of the deterministic world through acting in concert with their fellows.

The conclusion of "The Dream of Debs" reinforces these themes, suggesting the workers' ability to transform society coupled with the owners' resistance to such developments. After the Employers' Association grants the ILW's demand for the closed shop, the narrator states,

> that was the end of the general strike. I never want to see another one. It was worse than a war. A general strike is a cruel and immoral thing, and the brain of man should be capable of running industry in a more rational way. . . . It was part of the conditions of the I. L. W. that all of its members should be reinstated in their old positions. Brown never came back, but the rest of the servants are with me. I hadn't the heart to discharge them—poor creatures, they were pretty hard pressed when they deserted with the food and silver. And now I can't discharge them. They have all been unionized by the I. L. W. The tyranny of organized labor is getting beyond all human endurance. Something must be done. (257)

On one level, Cerf's perspective has changed in that he acknowledges the source of his employees' actions, evident through his awareness of the deprivation that caused them to abscond with his food and silver. However, the reference to "war" and his presentation of the industrial action as "a cruel and immoral thing" indicate Cerf's position: the circumstances responsible for the general strike must be addressed in order to prevent a similar occurrence, which would result in additional hardships for the owners and further cement the influence of labor. This reading gains further credence through the narrator's objections to the gains produced by the conflict. He cannot dictate terms to his servants, who now have a say in the conditions of their employment because they have implemented the union shop, a concession that Cerf views as an illustration of "the tyranny of organized labor." This phrase coupled with the final sentence reveal that the narrator has learned little from these events, and his desire to restore the previous balance of power demonstrates that his outlook continues to be governed by economic self-interest. This position contradicts an overly optimistic reading of "The Dream of Debs," presenting this victory as one component in a much larger struggle, one that the powerful will not abandon until all of their resources have been exhausted.

Cerf's perspective denotes that meaningful change will ultimately require the transformation of the existing socioeconomic order, a development that the story suggests can only emerge through the concerted action of labor. In this representation, London echoes the sentiments of Eugene V. Debs, who asserted that the "unity of labor, economic and political, upon the basis of the class struggle, is at this time the supreme need of the working class.... They must act together; they must assert their combined power, and when they do this upon the basis of the class struggle, then and only then will they break the fetters of wage slavery."[72] *The Iron Heel* and "The Dream of Debs" effectively dramatize this idea, highlighting the potential for gains when individuals recognize their mutual interests and act accordingly to engender greater opportunity for the working class as a whole.

5

SOLIDARITY FOREVER

In Dubious Battle *and the Labor Movement in California*

John Steinbeck contributed to the development of American naturalism by incorporating a greater range of artistic and philosophical complexity into the social criticism that is central to naturalism. These ideas are especially prevalent throughout *In Dubious Battle*. The novel depicts an agricultural strike in Central California, illustrating the consequences that result from concentrated land ownership and examining how unbridled capitalism can adversely affect all levels of society. Jackson J. Benson and Anne Loftis have identified the work stoppages that Steinbeck used as the basis for the book, one at the Tagus Ranch in August 1933 and another that spread throughout the cotton industry in the San Joaquin Valley that October, yet few scholars have built on this research to connect these disputes with *In Dubious Battle*.[1] Instead, the criticism has focused largely on the portrayal of the organizers, Mac McLeod and Jim Nolan, questioning their motives or denouncing their methods during the strike. For instance, Warren French asserts that "Steinbeck refused to become a blind partisan and rather showed how struggles between laborers and employers—however provoked and justified—can inevitably prove only destructive and demoralizing to both parties and to society as a whole."[2] John H. Timmerman extends this argument by stating that "one wonders what difference there is between Mac and the growers themselves. Both have their own, separate ends, but the means differ hardly at all."[3] While Steinbeck does not necessarily present the workers and organizers favorably, *In Dubious Battle* does not suggest that the tactics of these individuals are equivalent to the measures undertaken by the landowners. Through the inclusion of episodes from California labor history, Steinbeck indicates that the responsibility for suffering rests on those who control the economic framework of the Torgas Valley, one that limits prosperity for the workers to the extent that they have no means to protect their interests save through practices that are ultimately destructive.[4]

Steinbeck's perspective is rooted in science and the close observation of the natural world, which shape his analysis of pressing societal ills. His outlook was indebted to Edward F. Ricketts, a marine biologist the author met in 1930 and whose philosophy was instrumental in forming Steinbeck's own.[5] Under Ricketts's guidance, Steinbeck shifted his attention to the experiences of common people, recognizing that their lives could supply the basis for literature. He first applied this lesson in *The Pastures of Heaven* (1932), a short story cycle that introduced both a California setting and the naturalistic method that would inform his greatest novels. This approach stems from the recognition that humans are the products of their environment and that their actions are governed by the same impulses as lower life forms. As Frederick Bracher notes, Steinbeck's writing reveals the belief that "man is formed of the same kinds of living cells, subject to the same primitive drives, and part of an ecological pattern as determinate as that of the tide pool, though infinitely more complicated."[6] This overview evokes the central tenets of naturalist fiction, emphasizing the representation of individuals shaped by both their biology and milieu. This position is further influenced by Steinbeck and Ricketts's conception of non-teleological thought, which "derives through 'is' thinking, associated with natural selection as Darwin seems to have understood it. They imply depth, fundamentalism, and clarity—seeing beyond traditional or personal projections. . . . Non-teleological thinking concerns itself primarily not with what should be, or could be, or might be, but rather with what actually 'is'—attempting at most to answer sufficiently difficult questions *what* or *how*, instead of *why*."[7] This theory relies on attempts to understand the totality of an event without blame or judgment and without recourse to broader principles of causation, and Steinbeck's emphasis on dispassionate investigation reflects the clinical detachment in Émile Zola's formulations of naturalism. Although non-teleological thinking situates Steinbeck's point of view within the parameters of this movement, he deviates considerably from these precepts in his literary output, most notably in *In Dubious Battle* and *The Grapes of Wrath,* which identify the dominant social institutions responsible for injustice and convey the need to address such outcomes.

Throughout his career, Steinbeck maintained a deep concern about the average citizens' struggles and protested against the power imbalance facing the working class.[8] In 1938, Steinbeck asserted, "I am actively opposed to any man or group who, through financial or political control of the means of production and distribution, is able to control and dominate the lives of workers."[9] After winning the Nobel Prize, he advanced a similar point, observing: "The thing that arouses me to fury more than anything else is the imposition of force by a stronger on a weaker for reasons of self-interest or greed. That arouses me to a fury. It's the one unforgiveable thing that I can think of."[10] These passages underscore Steinbeck's compassion for the oppressed and his antipathy toward the institutions and individuals who constrain the development of the masses. His fiction during the late 1930s suggests that working people should have the ability to manage their lives, and Steinbeck presented the conflict between labor and capital as an extension of the battle for security dating back to western expansion. He noted that since "the people will go on with their struggle, the writer still sets down that struggle and still sets down the opponents. The opponents or rather the obstacle to that desired end right now happens to be those individuals and groups of financiers who by the principle of ownership withhold security from the mass of the people."[11] In portraying the tension between the requirements of the population and the avarice of those who possessed the wealth, Steinbeck illustrates the causative agents that manipulate production in California to the detriment of the working class.

These concerns were especially urgent in the early decades of the twentieth century as conditions continued to deteriorate for working people, even during periods of general economic prosperity. In 1929, the thirty-six thousand richest families received as much income as the poorest twelve million, and two hundred companies controlled nearly half of all corporate wealth.[12] This affluence among the upper echelon of the economic system did not often lead to improvements for the masses. A majority of American families, 71 percent, earned less than twenty-five hundred dollars annually, and the top one-tenth had a combined income equal to that of the bottom 42 percent; overall, corporate profits rose by 62 percent, while wages experienced modest growth of 5 percent.[13] This figure, however, does not reflect the circumstances of a significant segment of laborers. Lizabeth Cohen observes that "wages advanced modestly if at all in big manufacturing sectors such as steel, meatpacking, agricultural implements, and the clothing industry, particularly for the unskilled and semi-skilled workers who predominated in this kind of work."[14] Further, gains for those employed in the automobile, electrical, and printing trades were offset by decreases for those in coal, shoes, and textiles.[15] This stratification existed even within industries, most notably for those employed by the railroads as the highly skilled brakemen experienced wage growth of 14 percent, yet their unskilled colleagues, who comprised one-third of the industry, found themselves earning 2.5 percent less.[16] The appearance of relative prosperity during the 1920s did not extend to the majority of the working class, whose members still found themselves laboring for meager compensation.

These hardships were intensified by the Great Depression, which provided another illustration of the instability of capitalism and its broader failure to meet human needs. The pervasive speculation of the previous decade, when share prices drastically outweighed the value of assets, led to the stock market crash in October 1929 and caused the general failure of the global economy.[17] John Kenneth Galbraith observes that the Depression resulted from the volatility of the economy as a result of unhealthy banking and corporate structures, an imbalance of trade, misinformation, and rampant inequality as the top 5 percent of the population received approximately one-third of all personal income.[18] In the immediate aftermath of the crash, five thousand banks failed, and a large number of businesses closed because of insufficient demand and the unavailability of credit.[19] Between 1929 and 1933, the gross national product fell by 29 percent with even more drastic declines in individual industries: construction dropped by 78 percent and investment by 98 percent.[20] These regressions led to disastrous consequences for laborers, and by the spring of 1933, nearly one in four wage earners was out of work.[21] Employment at the Ford Motor Company decreased from 128,000 people in the spring of 1929 to 37,000 by August 1931, and nearly 140,000 workers from textile mills in New England were unemployed by the end of 1930.[22] Those who managed to retain their jobs did not emerge from the Depression unscathed since companies, rather than fire all of their employees, reduced their days and hours with a commensurate decrease in their income. The Depression exemplified the inability of the free market to sustain the working class, further undermining the ability of citizens to subsist, let alone prosper.

In response, workers organized themselves into unions, utilizing the strike as a means to assert their collective strength and to promote their interests. Melvyn Dubofsky observes that by "the end of the nineteenth century ... the strike had become the wage worker's primary line of defense against employers' exactions. Together with the trade union, it served as the characteristic form of response by workers to an industrial society, their adoption of new rules for the game."[23] Labor strife intensified during the Depression. During 1933, there were 1,695 strikes nationwide, a twofold increase over the previous year, that involved 1.1 million workers; in 1934, there were another 1,856 work stoppages that featured 1.5 million individuals.[24] One of the most significant events happened in San Francisco during 1934, when a clash between police and longshoremen provoked a general strike involving 130,000 people that halted shipping on the West Coast.[25] This occurrence, in addition to disputes in Minneapolis and Toledo, led to the passage of the National Labor Relations Act of 1935. The legislation guaranteed that individuals could select their own representation, established the right to strike, and formed the National Labor Relations Board to arbitrate grievances. Despite this development, conflicts increased throughout the period as corporations routinely endeavored to cut wages. Employees responded by implementing a new tactic, the sit-down strike, that involved remaining in the factory instead of walking out. The longest dispute occurred at Fisher Body Plant #1 from December 1936 until February 1937, spreading to other General Motors plants in the area and forcing the company to recognize the United Automobile Workers.[26] The agitation of the period also led to important concessions, most notably the Social Security Act of 1935 and the Fair Labor Standards Act of 1938. The first supplied retirement benefits and unemployment insurance, while the second instituted the forty-hour week, a gain sought for five decades, and outlawed child labor. These measures contributed to the prosperity following World War II.

This period in California was also characterized by bitter conflicts that often turned violent when workers challenged the institutions and individuals that controlled the state. As Carey McWilliams observes: "The industrial character of California agriculture was firmly established. The industry was organized from top to bottom; methods of operation had been thoroughly rationalized; control tended more and more to be vested in the hands of the large growers; and the dominance of finance was greater than ever."[27] These men considered themselves to be businessmen rather than farmers as they presided over their vast estates, which relied on a migrant workforce to pick crops for low wages, often without union representation. Recognizing the limited opportunities for advancement, 48,000 people, the vast majority of whom were Mexican American, undertook 37 strikes in 1933, and there were

156 more between 1933 and 1939.[28] In response to these disputes, anti-union forces mobilized later that year, terrorizing agricultural districts in addition to beating organizers and their supporters. The most powerful anti-labor organization in the state was the Associated Farmers of California, a network of bankers, industrialists, chamber of commerce groups, shippers, utilities, and landowners with strong ties to local police.[29] During the Salinas lettuce strike of 1936, the Associated Farmers coordinated the resistance of the growers, assembling local police and sheriff's deputies, the California Highway Patrol, and local vigilantes to end the dispute through violent means.[30] The strike ended on November 3 with the complete victory of the growers and shippers, who replicated these tactics the following year in Stockton.

In Dubious Battle has its origins in specific labor struggles in the Central Valley during the 1930s, which resulted from the formation of the Cannery and Agricultural Workers Industrial Union (CAWIU). Since the demise of the IWW following the Palmer Raids of 1919, farmworkers were largely unrepresented until the Communist Party formed the CAWIU.[31] The impact of this union became evident during the strike at the Tagus Ranch in August 1933. In this dispute, 750 migrants walked off their jobs at one of the most industrialized agricultural operations in California, demanding a raise, a forty-hour week, and union recognition.[32] When the ranch manager rejected overtures to negotiate with the CAWIU and evicted employees from company-owned housing, organizer Pat Chambers threatened to call a general strike throughout the San Joaquin Valley; in response, two thousand laborers walked out at properties owned by the California Packing Corporation (Cal-Pak), which caused the firm to suspend its picking and canning operations.[33] Recognizing the threat posed by this disturbance, Cal-Pak executives increased compensation to twenty-five cents an hour, and the encouragement of state mediators led to officials from the Tagus Ranch accepting this pay scale on August 18.[34] These victories provided the impetus for many work stoppages throughout the San Joaquin Valley. As a result of these conflicts, growers throughout the region also raised rates to twenty-five cents an hour, a figure that soon became the prevailing wage for fruit pickers.[35]

Labor strife intensified two months later when a cotton strike informed by similar economic tensions spread throughout California, featuring an intensification of violence from the growers. This struggle originated from the fluctuating prices of cotton: while rates declined from 1929 to 1932 and compensation decreased accordingly, by 75 percent, over this period, the total value of this commodity increased by 150 percent in 1933.[36] In response to wages that would barely meet the pickers' physical requirements, CAWIU members voted to strike on October 4, and twelve thousand employees had walked off their jobs in Tulare, Kings, and Kern Counties by October 9.[37] Undeterred, armed men aligned with landowners organized patrols to intimidate individuals who refused either to work under existing conditions or to leave the area. On October 10, growers opened fire on a peaceful demonstration, killing two people in addition to wounding seven more.[38] As a result of this event and the inability of local law enforcement to control the situation, George Creel, chair of the Regional Labor Board, appointed a fact-finding commission to determine a basis for settlement. This panel ultimately decided that seventy-five cents per hundred would be a fair compromise.[39] Pickers initially held out for eighty cents and formal recognition of the CAWIU by employers; however, union leaders eventually persuaded membership to call off the dispute, recognizing that "the government will not recognize any union that has a militant policy of struggle in the interests of the working class" and that no additional benefit would come from prolonging the conflict.[40]

Steinbeck was familiar with these disputes and some of their organizers. Writing to Harry Thornton Moore about the historical sources for the book, Steinbeck noted that as "for the Valley in *In Dubious Battle*—it is a composite valley as it is a composite strike. If it has the characteristics of Pajaro nevertheless there was no strike there. If it's like the cotton strike, that wasn't apples."[41] As Benson and Loftis have argued, Steinbeck combined the setting and underlying causes of the walkout at the Tagus Ranch with occurrences from the struggle in the cotton industry, deviating from their particulars to present his work stoppage in more universal terms.[42] Discussing the basis for his representation of events, Steinbeck wrote his agents that "my information for this book came mostly from Irish and Italian communists whose training was in the field."[43] Through Sis Reamer, the author became acquainted with Cicil McKiddy and Carl Williams when they were hiding in Monterey to evade arrest for their activities during the cotton strike.[44] Reamer introduced Steinbeck to the men at their boardinghouse, and the writer offered them a small sum of money for their stories, which he planned to use for a nonfiction account from the perspective of a Communist organizer. Steinbeck, however, decided that a first-person narrative from a union leader's point of view would not be the most effective use of this material, a decision that marked the start of the initial conception of *In Dubious Battle*.

Steinbeck began writing the novel in September 1934, shortly after completing *Tortilla Flat,* and after an earlier rejection, Covici-Friede released *In Dubious Battle* on January 15, 1936, to largely favorable reviews.[45] Describing his narrative method in this work, Steinbeck wrote to George Albee, "I merely wanted to be a recording consciousness, judging nothing, simply putting down the thing."[46] This desire for impartiality manifests through the absence of an intrusive narrator who explains occurrences in terms of a deterministic thesis; instead, Steinbeck develops his treatment of the work stoppage through action and dialogue. In the same letter, Steinbeck discussed his aims with *In Dubious Battle:* "I have used a small strike in an orchard valley as the symbol of man's eternal, bitter warfare with himself" and elaborated that "I'm not interested in strike as a means of raising men's wages, and I'm not interested in ranting about justice and oppression, mere outcroppings which indicate the condition. But man hates something in himself. He has been able to defeat every natural obstacle but himself he cannot win over unless he kills every individual. And this self-hate which goes so closely in hand with self-love is what I wrote about."[47] While Steinbeck deemphasizes the concrete aims of labor struggles, they do provide the context for the representation of issues fundamental to the human enterprise, an approach that expands the project from a mere muckraking book to an exploration of the forces that animate behavior. The use of elements from specific strikes, however, contextualizes the events of *In Dubious Battle,* and the power of the narrative emerges through its representation of the struggle between labor and the forces responsible for economic injustice.

In developing these themes, Steinbeck highlights the need for a unified working class to effectively challenge the landowners, who dictate the conditions facing the laborers, limit their possibilities for survival, and necessitate the strike. Describing the men who wield power in the region, Mac states that they "got this valley organized. God, how they got it organized. It's not so hard to do when three men control everything, land, courts, banks. They can cut off loans, and they can railroad a man to jail, and they can always bribe plenty."[48] The workers' plight stems from the practices of these individuals, who manipulate economic activity within the Torgas Valley. Since the pickers have few alternatives for employment, they have limited means to alter the nature of their labor or to increase their compensation. These consequences are exacerbated by the landowners' dominance over the fiscal structure of the area, and Steinbeck illustrates this point through the example of Mr. Anderson, a small farmer whose interests are threatened by the growers. He pays wages at the rates stipulated by the Growers' Association, owned by the Torgas Finance Company, which also holds his mortgage (81–82). When Mac proposes that he allow the strikers to camp on his property, Mr. Anderson responds: "I own this place. I got to get along with my neighbors. They'd raise hell with me if I did a thing like that" (81). Through this control over the financial system, the planters can subordinate small farmers by foreclosing on their land. Mr. Anderson agrees to Mac's proposal because having his apples picked for free would enable him, theoretically, to pay off his debts and to escape from the decrees of the Growers' Association.

The depiction of these concerns incorporates aspects of the labor disputes at the Tagus Ranch and in the cotton industry, which Steinbeck uses to explicate the circumstances that lead to the inevitable conflict throughout *In Dubious Battle*. Mac explains his decision to travel to the Torgas Valley, stating that "the Growers' Association just announced a pay cut to the pickers. They'll be sore as hell. If we can get a good ruckus going down there, we might be able to spread it over to the cotton fields in Tandale" (20). This passage alludes to the immediate cause of the cotton strike. On September 19, the Agricultural Labor Bureau of the San Joaquin Valley, comprised of growers and representatives from local finance companies, set wages at sixty cents per hundred pounds, well under the figure the pickers desired.[49] The incorporation of this reference heightens the realism of the narrative, reinforcing the landowners' ability to shape economic conditions. This causative function manifests further through the pay scale of fifteen cents, which parallels the compensation offered to the employees at the Tagus Ranch (36). The combination of these sources denotes the universal dimensions of the struggle since the disturbance in the book does not signal an isolated instance in the skirmish between labor and capital. Instead, the novel reproduces elements common to the intense clashes throughout California during the 1930s. In addition, Mac's statement about the spread of the strike reflects the relationship between the two work stoppages that formed the basis for *In Dubious Battle* as the militancy at the Tagus Ranch inspired the pickers in the cotton fields to walk off their jobs.

Steinbeck incorporated other elements from these strikes that reinforce the socioeconomic themes of the novel. In a broader critique of the circumstances confronting the workers, an unnamed man states that the pickers have decided to walk off their jobs because "we're gettin' screwed, that's why.

The bunk houses is full of pants rabbits, and the company's store is takin' five per cent house-cut, and they drop the pay after we get here, that's why! And if we let 'em get by with it, we'll be worse in the cotton. We'll get screwed there, too; and you know it damn well" (63–64). The reference to the company store is significant in that it alludes to one of the principal grievances of the laborers at the Tagus Ranch, who were paid not in cash but in scrip at an establishment owned by the firm that charged 25 to 30 percent higher than those in the surrounding areas.[50] The actual work stoppage does not provide a direct antecedent for the event that triggers the fictional dispute: an injury to a worker named Dan, who breaks his hip when an antiquated ladder breaks under his weight. However, this episode effectively dramatizes the substandard conditions in California agriculture. Dan's injury reveals the potential consequences that could result from allowing employees to engage in dangerous tasks with unsafe equipment, and these conditions indicate the growers' view of their workforce as replaceable commodities that do not merit decent treatment.

The portrayal of the causes underlying the strike highlights the inevitable nature of the conflict, which reinforces the representation of the causative agents in the narrative. Mac notes that the Party did not provoke the work stoppage; its members merely responded to conditions created by the landowners. He states that they "cut the wages before we showed up, don't forget that. Hell, you'd think that we started this strike, and you know damn well we didn't. We're just helpin' it to go straight instead of shootin' its wad" (109–10). In a related vein, London, a migrant worker who initially takes on a leadership role in the strike, observes that the walkout stems from a desire to protect the pickers' children from starvation by "usin' the only way a workin' stiff's got" (180). Mac and London view the dispute as a necessary response to the economic subordination that threatens the pickers' survival, and Mac's final sentence indicates the role of the organizers, who merely respond to existing circumstances in order to give the industrial action some potential for success. Mac clarifies this point when he asserts that the owners "say I started this strike. Now get me straight. I would have started it if I could, but I didn't have to. It started itself" (188). The last sentence underscores the workers' lack of agency since they are reacting to the economic context that shapes their labor and opportunities, which limits their culpability for the disturbance.

The early stages of Steinbeck's labor dispute feature additional elements of the work stoppages at the Tagus Ranch and in the cotton fields, and these events further illustrate the landowners' power while also conveying the potential for progress through concerted action. The cotton growers, learning from the example of the Tagus Ranch, evicted striking workers from company housing. In response, twenty-five hundred people settled on a farm outside Corcoran, which parallels the encampment at Mr. Anderson's orchard in the narrative.[51] Benson and Loftis have noted that this property was donated by a sympathizer named Morgan, a small farmer who owned a tract of land on the outskirts of town and whose actions, like his counterpart in the book, caused him to live in fear of reprisals.[52] Further, the *Visalia Times-Delta* observed that five hundred men remained after the disturbance to pick Morgan's "cotton free of charge since he furnished the land on which their camp is located," which approximates the men harvesting Anderson's apples in exchange for the right to stay on his holdings.[53] In addition, the local authorities' reactions were similar in both instances as press accounts presented Morgan's camp as a health threat. A reporter for the *San Francisco Chronicle* asserted that the tent colony constituted a "menace to the health of the community because of the lack of sanitation. With food and water running short and some growers urging that the strikers be 'starved out,' the situation is watched with growing alarm by State officials."[54] Further developing these problems, another correspondent reported that the "deplorable conditions among the more than 2,000 striking cotton pickers . . . were emphasized here today with the death of a 3-months-old child from malnutrition . . . and a dozen other persons are known to be suffering similarly."[55] These illustrations stress the hypocrisy of the economic elite, who profess concern for the poor only when expedient. Mac comments that "they let us live like pigs in the jungle, but just the minute we start a strike, they get awful concerned about the public health" (89–90). Further, the attempts of the strikers to prevent the closure of the settlement parallel their counterparts' efforts in the novel. In both the fictional strike and its factual antecedent, a doctor named Burton set up sanitary facilities with running water, toilets, and a piping system that enabled the temporary lodgings to remain available throughout the disputes.[56]

Episodes from the work stoppage at the Tagus Ranch further develop the power of those aligned against the pickers, accentuating their inability to improve conditions within the legal framework of the Torgas Valley. In the novel, the owners secure an injunction against picketing, a tactic that undermines the effectiveness of the walkout since the laborers cannot access company property in order to demonstrate against the employers. H. G. Merritt Jr., the manager of the Tagus Ranch, employed comparable practices, obtaining a similar edict and ordering the eviction of anyone who refused to work from company-owned housing.[57] The Tulare County district attorney doubted the legality of this ruling, so authorities made no attempts to halt protests outside the gates. However, guards at the Tagus Ranch, using automatic rifles on loan from the Tulare Police Department, evicted several families on August 15, dumping their belongings along the highway north of the county.[58] The fictionalization of this incident stresses the seemingly insurmountable barriers to the workers' objectives as a result of local law enforcement protecting the interests of capital, which limits the pickers' ability to effectively challenge the employers. The actions of the vigilantes operate in this context, and their display of force to frighten the protesters also has its origins in the Tagus Ranch dispute. A reporter for the *San Francisco Chronicle* referred to high-powered weapons being used "in intimidating strikers" and further noted that a machine gun "had been purchased by the Tulare Chamber of Commerce and manned by Ray Edwards, former Tulare police officer."[59] Steinbeck alludes to this incident through the vigilantes' use of artillery to threaten the strikers in chapter 15, which provides another illustration of the landowners' practices that minimize the potential for a peaceful resolution of the conflict.

The conduct of Steinbeck's landowners has its precursor in the climate of hostility engendered by their predecessors during the cotton strike, who suppressed labor to reassert control of the region's economic activity. Early in this conflict, the ranchers agreed to employ whatever force was necessary, forming protective associations and attempting to drive the so-called radicals out of the San Joaquin Valley.[60] During a mass meeting on October 9, L. D. Ellett, chairman of the Kings County Growers' Committee, stated that the "time has come when we have to take the law into our own hands. We will have to use force to get rid of these workers and get new ones."[61] Toward these ends, the men who owned large farms took up arms to patrol the district, which caused a reporter for the *San Francisco Chronicle* to observe that the San Joaquin Valley had become "a veritable powder keg likely to explode at any instant."[62] This eruption of violence occurred in Pixley on October 10, when forty armed growers arrived at the CAWIU hall where workers had congregated to protest the arrests of several pickets from a nearby ranch. As

Chambers called the meeting to an end, one landowner fired into the crowd, and when a striker, Dolores Hernandez, attempted to take the gun, he was clubbed to the ground and riddled with bullets.[63] The rest of the farmers immediately discharged their weapons at the fleeing men, women, and children. The growers continued to shoot into the building until their ammunition ran out, killing Delfino D'Avila and wounding seven more people.[64] These homicides aroused widespread condemnation of the landowners and, in addition to further acts of aggression from vigilante groups, provided the pretext for the government mediation that ended the dispute.

Although *In Dubious Battle* adheres to the general contours of its historical models, Steinbeck deviated from these events in his representations of the striking employees and organizers. The book devotes considerable attention to the violent practices of the strikers, describing these acts, most notably the beating of the young man and the attack on the strikebreakers, in graphic terminology.[65] However, the landowners and vigilantes were largely responsible for bloodshed in the actual strikes, and the workers defended themselves without evidence of the tactics that Steinbeck associates with his fruit pickers. In fact, the absence of such responses contributed to the success of the historical models for *In Dubious Battle*. During the dispute at Tagus Ranch, the sheriff of Fresno County, George Overholt, said that his police "are well equipped to handle riots. We are not afraid of any overt act [strikers] might commit. In fact, that is the thing that troubles us; they don't commit any overt act, don't give us a chance to help ourselves by legally getting out and getting them by the neck. They just agitate and agitate and keep the farmers unsettled."[66] Further, the CAWIU leadership, unlike their counterparts in the text, did not incite laborers to violence or threaten growers after the murders of D'Avila and Hernandez; by contrast, the union largely prevented reprisals against landowners. By including episodes of brutality that were not present in the actual conflicts and de-emphasizing successful efforts to avert such aggression, *In Dubious Battle* avoids the tendency of other proletarian novels to idealize the working class or to portray labor disputes in broad strokes, with predatory owners oppressing the aggrieved masses. Instead, Steinbeck highlights the consequences that could emerge in response to the apparent hopelessness of the pickers' situation, which expresses the need to alter these conditions before they facilitate the course of action in the narrative.

This emphasis also reinforces the principles of causation underlying the novel, with the strikers' violence as the predictable result of the landowners' attempts to reassert control over the region. Doc Burton posits that "the end is never very different in its nature from the means" and that "you can only build a violent thing with violence" (184). Though Doc focuses his attention on the workers' methods, his analysis seems more accurately to suggest the landowners' tactics. Mac clarifies this point when he warns a representative of the ranchers that "if any of your boys touch that property or hurt Anderson, if you hurt one single fruit tree, a thousand guys'll start out an' every one of 'em'll have a box of matches. *Get it, Mister?* Take it as a threat if you want to: you touch Anderson's ranch and by Christ we'll burn every fucking house and barn on every ranch in the Valley" (94). Mac traces a strictly causal relationship between the practices of the growers and those of the pickers with violence as the logical result of the measures undertaken by the affluent. Mac highlights the character of these procedures when he notes that the vigilantes "like to hurt people, and they always give it a nice name, patriotism or protecting the constitution. But they're just the old nigger torturers working. The owners use 'em, tell 'em we have to protect the people against reds. Y'see that lets 'em burn houses and torture and beat people with no danger" (120). The conventional platitudes associated with these individuals supply the rhetorical justification to employ brutal means in order to quell any popular disturbances under the guise of promoting freedom, liberty, and other cherished American values. However, the allusion to these men as plantation overseers expresses the nature of the vigilantes' activities, underscoring the imbalance of power between the parties in the strike.

The exchange among the organizers and Bolter, the president of the Growers' Association, emphasizes this dynamic by drawing on the landowners' methods during the cotton strike. After the laborers reject an offer for a pay increase, Bolter declares that he and the other growers "have a right to protect our property, and we'll do it. . . . From now on the roads are closed. An ordinance will go through tonight forbidding any parading on the country roads, or any gathering. The sheriff will deputize a thousand men, if he needs them" (182). His threats correlate to events in October 1933. A reporter for the *Visalia Times-Delta* observed that pickers, "hitherto allowed to hold meetings on public roads in front of ranches where picking is in progress, are now being denied that privilege. They are allowed to parade through the cotton districts in automobile caravans, but are not allowed to stop and hold meetings."[67] While the book differs from the actual events since the strikers were able to parade on local roads, *In Dubious Battle* accurately reflects the limited nature of these demonstrations. Sheriff Robert Hill of Visalia passed an ordinance stipulating that workers "will not be allowed to stop on roads, they will not be allowed to double back on roads," and "none of the strikers will be allowed to get out of their automobiles."[68] These measures effectively prevented men and women from protesting against their former employers or destabilizing the importation of strikebreakers. The narrator underscores this point through the reference to the sheriff deputizing a thousand men. This figure represents an exaggeration in that the *Visalia Times-Delta* reported that Hill could appoint approximately 250 people, yet this number was augmented by citizens who were granted permission to carry concealed weapons in the strike districts, including 600 individuals in nearby Kern County.[69] These references express the authorities' role in perpetuating inequitable conditions and contextualize the practices employed by the workers in the novel.

In Dubious Battle continues to illustrate the causal relationship between the aggression of capital and that of labor, which buttresses the consequences fostered by the economic relations in the valley. Expanding on this idea, Mac observes that the strikers have "no money and no weapons, so we've got to use our heads, London. See that? It's like a man with a club fighting a squad with machine-guns. The only way he can do it is to sneak up and smack the gunners from behind. Maybe that isn't fair, but hell, London, this isn't any athletic contest. There aren't any rules a hungry man has to follow" (206–7). This disparity, evident through the juxtaposition between a club and machine guns, necessitates methods that deviate from ideal conduct, and the final sentence further connects the actions of the pickers to the practices of their employers. This pattern manifests throughout *In Dubious Battle*. For instance, Sam, a young striker, burns down a grower's house after vigilantes destroy Anderson's barn, and the pickers attack the strikebreakers since their presence threatens the success of the labor dispute. Even the most disturbing episode of brutality, Mac's thrashing of a high school student, originates within the climate produced by the individuals who control the Torgas Valley. Jim states that the boy, a sniper with a deadly weapon, "wasn't a scared kid, it was a danger to the cause. It had to be done, and you did it right. No hate, no feeling, just a job" (199). The conditions in the Torgas Valley create an environment in which violence offers the only means to protect the laborers' interests. Further, the casualties produced by the working-class characters pale in comparison to those of the owners and allies, who kill Jim and Joy, another organizer for the Party; severely beat Al, who is sympathetic to the workers' cause; and burn down his restaurant, in addition to harassing countless people.

The portrayal of violence parallels the formation of a collective consciousness that offers labor a means to combat the landowners, which reflects Steinbeck's phalanx theory. Jeffrey Wayne Yeager asserts that this concept was a product of the novelist's "engagement with the social tensions of the late 1930s and early 1940s" that helped him "to capture the labor issues occurring around him" during this period.[70] Discussing the phalanx in a letter to Carlton A. Sheffield, Steinbeck wrote that the "fascinating thing to me is the way the group has a soul, a drive, an intent, an end, a method, a reaction and a set of tropisms which in no way resembles the same things possessed by the men who make up the group. These groups have always been considered as individuals multiplied. And they are not so. They are beings in themselves, entities."[71] In this formulation, the dynamic of the unit establishes an identity that differs from those of the people who comprise the collective organism through tapping into its knowledge and strength. Steinbeck further explained this concept in "Argument of Phalanx." He observed that once a man becomes a part of such an entity, "his nature changes, his habits and desires. . . . Phalanx resistance to circumstance is far greater than individual man's resistance. Once a man has become a unit in a phalanx in motion, he is capable of prodigies of endurance of thought or of emotion such as would be unthinkable were he acting as individual man. . . . All life forms from protozoa to antelopes and lions, from crabs to lemmings form and are part of phalanxes, but the phalanx of which the units are men, are more complex, more variable and powerful than any other."[72] This description provides the basis for Steinbeck's representation of characters who, although they are largely helpless by themselves, can potentially improve conditions by acting in unison with one another. Through merging the individual with something larger than himself, the common people possess a range of defense that would not be possible for isolated men and women. The portrayal of the phalanx in Steinbeck's major fiction reinforces the power of milieu since it both necessitates the formation of the group as a means of protection and shapes the nature of the structure that emerges, which can have either positive or negative implications that are largely dependent on environmental pressures.

In this context, *In Dubious Battle* posits a framework to confront these deterministic agents through concerted action, which introduces greater agency and complexity into the novel. When operating as a unit, the pickers possess a combined strength that enables them to restrain their adversaries' repressive inclinations and temporarily destabilize the conventional power relations in the Torgas Valley. This tendency manifests in chapter 9 when the slaying of Joy provides the impetus for the group's unification. In a passage that echoes Sheriff Overholt's statement about the people who walked off their jobs during the Tagus Ranch dispute, the narrator states that the "guards were frightened: riots they could stop, fighting they could stop; but this slow, silent movement of men with the wide eyes of sleep-walkers terrified them. They held to their places" (118). This episode also originates from the cotton strike. Following the murders of D'Avila and Hernandez, fifteen hundred people gathered in Tulare for the funeral services at St. Aloysius Catholic Church, and this number increased to five thousand as they marched to the cemetery. A correspondent for the *San Francisco Chronicle* noted that the protesters maintained a "military marching order" with "armed police in close attendance," which parallels the public funeral and demonstration for Joy.[73] The fact that this silent procession of men prevents the guards from their usual violent tactics demonstrates the power of both Steinbeck's workers and their historical antecedents, who were able to avert the outcomes usually associated with disobedience. The benefits of the strategy are fortified through the efficacy of the funeral procession for Hernandez, a demonstration that galvanized popular support for the strikers and contributed to the success of the cotton strike.

While concerted action allows the laborers to promote their interests and to defy the agents of capital, *In Dubious Battle* also indicates the destructive potential of the phalanx since the conduct of the group reflects pressures within the immediate environment of its members. Through the desperation engendered by the strike, coupled with the continued aggression on behalf of the landowners, the phalanx shifts from its earlier form when the workers attack the strikebreakers in chapter 10. The narrator states that "Jim looked without emotion at the ten moaning men on the ground, their faces kicked shapeless. Here a lip was torn away, exposing bloody teeth and gums; one man cried like a child because his arm was bent sharply backward, broken at the elbow. Now that the fury was past, the strikers were sick, poisoned by the flow from their own anger glands" (131). This graphic description highlights the destructive capability of the masses and evidences Steinbeck's refusal to portray the proletarians as innocent victims. However, the broader representation of this scene emphasizes the operations of the growers: if the replacement workers harvest the apples, then the pickers will lose their only potential advantage against the owners, who will assuredly emerge victorious. Further, the strikers' remorse suggests that their actions have been determined by insuperable forces, which is heightened by the reference to biological processes in the final sentence, yet the potential for such drastic consequences indicates the need to guide the collective toward constructive ends.

Steinbeck's animal imagery reiterates the causative function of the landowners, signifying that the laborers have been reduced to their present condition by the practices of the powerful. Many instances, such as the reference to Al as a "ruminating cow" or the statement that London has the eyes of a gorilla, emphasize the insignificance of human beings and the peripheral roles of these people to the strike, which denotes the limited potential of individual action (32, 38). The further instances of such images display the consequences engendered by the wealthy, most notably when Dan observes that the "stiffs don't know what's happenin', but when the big guy gets mad, they'll all be there; and by Christ, I hate to think of it. They'll be bitin' out throats with their teeth, and clawin' off lips. . . . That big guy'll run like a mad dog, and bite everything that moves. He's been hungry too long, and he's been hurt too much" (48). The reference to the men as mad dogs evokes the responsibility of the growers for this development since they have created the circumstances that have brought these elements to the forefront. Dan recognizes the problematic nature of this development: when united through their anger toward capital, the workers might employ violence indiscriminately. This depiction reinforces Mac's assertions about the need to direct labor in order for the walkout to have any chance of success.

The deterministic nature of the references to the characters as animals manifests in the breakdown of Dakin, a striker known for being particularly levelheaded. After the vigilantes destroy his truck, he "crawls for 'em, slavering around the mouth like a mad dog—just nuts, he just went *nuts!* I guess he loved that truck better'n anything in the world. The guy that came back said it was just awful, the way he crawled for 'em. Tried to bite 'em. He was snarling—like a mad dog" (134). The use of Dakin is important in that he had a calm demeanor that distinguished him from the other strikers, and his descent provides a clearer illustration of the problems that could occur because of the tensions in the valley. Further, Dakin is separated from his fellows since he has a stake in society resulting from his ownership of a new truck and well-appointed tent. These possessions indicate that he has more to lose during the struggle, while his fate reveals that even those who profit from an inequitable economic system will suffer its consequences. Mac clarifies this point when he reflects on the potential ramifications of the labor dispute by noting that the workers "are straight now. They know how much capital thinks of 'em and how quick capital would poison 'em like a bunch of ants" (234). The reference to the poor as creatures that must be exterminated signals the owners' view of the pickers, one that shapes the treatment that they must endure and ultimately seek to eradicate in order to survive.

The continuing portrayal of violence contextualizes the perspective and corresponding tactics embraced by Mac, who emphasizes the perils of the existing economic framework in addition to the need for an alternate social structure to ameliorate these circumstances. Critics have often condemned Mac for viewing the workers as mere abstractions in his pursuit of broader revolutionary ends, yet Steinbeck's representation of this character focuses on his basic humanity amid what seem to be examples of his calculating nature.[74] After the destruction of Al's diner, the labor organizer asks: "How's it feel to be a Party man now, Jim? . . . That poor guy. . . . I feel responsible for that." Though Al declares allegiance to the Party, Mac's response demonstrates his sensitivity and an awareness of his role in this outcome. As a result of Al's fate, Mac states that it is "awful hard to keep your eyes on the big issue," which reveals an individual who is deeply concerned with the ramifications of his undertakings (124). *In Dubious Battle* features a parallel illustration of this conception through Mac's interactions with Mr. Anderson. After the vigilantes burn down the farmer's barn, Mac looks "weak and sad," tries to console Anderson, and tells London: "I wish it hadn't happened. Poor old man, it's all his crop" (190). This response is inconsistent with an interpretation of Mac as one who views people as mere pawns in the revolution; instead, he exhibits compassion for a man who has lost everything during the work stoppage and shows remorse for bringing about this occurrence. Mac's use of Joy's murder to inflame the strikers further dramatizes this idea. Far from exploiting the death of his friend, Mac takes an approach that is consistent with his colleague's desire to help the cause. As such, the organizer's use of Joy's corpse to illustrate the growers' practices provides a means to honor his friend by further serving the struggle to which both men had dedicated their lives.

This devotion does not supersede the immediate aims of the work stoppage as these are inextricably linked with Mac's grander aspirations and further demonstrate his compassion for the laborers. The illustrations of Mac's apparent tendency to prioritize Party objectives over the strikers' needs give credence to this point. Before traveling to the Torgas Valley, he informs Jim that a "strike that's settled too quickly won't teach the men how to organize, how to work together. A tough strike is good. We want the men to find out how strong they are when they work together" (22). While the first sentence expresses a limited concern with the outcome of the walkout, Mac's formulation links the fate of the individual to that of the group, coupled with the realization that collective endeavors offer the men a means of confronting a more powerful force. Connecting these larger ambitions to the existing conflict, Mac observes that "we made the men work for themselves, in their own defense, as a group. That's what we're out here for anyway, to teach them to fight in a bunch. Raising wages isn't all we're after" (42). The final statement illustrates that Mac does not lose sight of the particular target of the strike, and his desire to facilitate radical change does not preclude improving compensation. The current struggle is intimately related to the future vision as the former would increase wages for the apple pickers and prevent a cut in the cotton industry while also teaching the workers how to organize themselves. This development can supply a framework for broader action within the pursuit of more concrete goals since these are not divorced from the ends embraced by the Party. Mac clarifies this point when he tells Doc that there is "an end to be gained; it's a real end, hasn't got anything to do with people losing respect. It's people getting bread into their guts. It's *real,* not any of your high-falutin ideas" (146). This focus on basic requirements conveys the nature of Mac's interest in the labor dispute and the perspective that governs his undertakings, which center on providing an organizational structure that will enable the working class to prosper.

As a result of this outlook, Mac contrasts with Doc Burton, who views the workers in terms of abstract categories that ignore the particulars of the strike. Although many critics interpret Doc as a preferential alternative to the veteran organizer, and Steinbeck does associate some of his ideas with the former, he is not the writer's spokesman.[75] Instead, Doc illustrates the problematic nature of imposing theoretical formulas on existence. He exhibits a concern for individual suffering, apparent through his efforts to aid the strikers despite not believing in their cause, yet his interest in the strikers does not correlate to their concrete objectives. Doc asserts: "I want to *see*, Mac. I want to watch these group-men for they seem to me to be a new individual, not at all like single men. A man in a group isn't himself at all, he's a cell in an organism that isn't like him any more than the cells in your body are like you. I want to watch the group, and see what it's like" (104). This passage reflects Steinbeck's theory of the phalanx; however, Doc's perspective differs considerably from that of Steinbeck, whose Depression-era fiction presents the power of concerted effort to protect labor. Doc, by contrast, advances this proposal as a mere scientific postulate, one detached from the practical world since he perceives the exploitation of human beings in a manner similar to the operations of bacteria under a microscope. This viewpoint gives him a position divorced from the conflict as evident through his emphasis on ocular tropes. Doc's desire to watch and to investigate an event from all possible angles, which evokes non-teleological thinking, creates a paralyzing sense of objectivity that prevents him from operating with any broader purpose.[76] In his last conversation with Jim, Doc states that everything "seems meaningless to me, brutal and meaningless" and later admits: "I'm lonely, I guess. I'm awfully lonely. I'm working all alone, towards nothing" (183, 186). Doc's assertions and his subsequent disappearance highlight the limitations of his position, conveying that intellectual neutrality only leads to isolation and prevents meaningful action.

Steinbeck also underscores the constraints governing the perspective of Jim Nolan, who is preoccupied by individualistic concerns despite his apparent absorption in the pickers' cause. While critics have viewed Jim as an illustration of the loss of individuality that results from the phalanx, he fixates on himself throughout the novel, which the narrator accentuates through an emphasis on Jim's eyes and his act of looking into the mirror during the opening paragraphs.[77] This description provides the initial manifestation of Jim's inability to transcend the confines of the self, and his decision to join the Party largely stems from his personal aspirations. After initially asserting that he wishes to become an organizer because his "whole family has been ruined by this system" (4), he finally admits: "I want to work toward something. I feel dead. I thought I might get alive again" (6). Instead of addressing the systemic forces that condition the laborers' plight, Jim views the class struggle in terms of his fulfillment. This idea also manifests when he gains a measure of power over others and says: "I'm happy. . . . And happy for the first time" (145). Jim again focuses on his impressions and needs after the brutal beating of several workers; unlike Mac, the youth does not identify with the men or regard them with compassion, instead prioritizing what such occurrences mean in relation to him. After Mac thrashes the would-be sniper, Jim states: "I'm stronger than you, Mac. I'm stronger than anything in the world, because I'm going in a straight line. You and the rest have to think of women and tobacco and liquor and keeping warm and fed" (199). This stress on separating himself from Mac and the strikers expresses that he still acts within the confines of his ego rather than through a communal entity. This reading gains additional credence because he is not motivated by the drives that animate everyone else. His limited interest in human companionship or basic requirements highlights his alienation from the aims of the dispute, which serves as a vehicle for his self-discovery rather than a means to improve the conditions facing the working class.

The conclusion reinforces these themes by deviating from the factual antecedents for the novel and underscoring the requirements of the group. The peach and cotton strikes both resulted in victories for the CAWIU plus higher wages for the affected laborers, yet the novel ends with Jim's murder amid the almost certain defeat of the work stoppage. Describing Mac's efforts to prevent this outcome, the narrator states that the veteran organizer's "hands gripped the rail. His eyes were wide and white. In front he could see the massed men, eyes shining in the lamplight. Behind the front row, the men were lumped and dark. Mac shivered. He moved his jaws to speak, and seemed to break the frozen jaws loose. His voice was high and monotonous. 'This guy didn't want nothing for himself—' he began. His knuckles were white, where he grasped the rail. 'Comrades! He didn't want nothing for himself—'" (250). The repetition of Jim's supposedly selfless motives presents an ironic commentary on his egotistical impulses, and the double negative, with the implication that he did want something for himself, stresses the selfish ends that he had hoped to realize through the struggle. The narrator provides a counterpoint to Jim through the portrayal of the strikers as indistinguishable from one another. Further, the reference to their "eyes shining in the lamplight" suggests that the identification of a common fate and undertakings based on this realization offer the potential for a future victory that will alter the conditions that have determined the pickers' outcomes. The narrator highlights this point through Mac, who is able to reconcile his interest in the individual with his obligation to the collective. His concern for the individual manifests through his grief, apparent through the emphasis on his eyes, the movement of his "frozen jaws," and his efforts to steady himself on the rail. On the other hand, his recognition of the need to use Jim's corpse in an attempt to prolong the strike indicates a willingness to subordinate his personal impulses to the requirements of the conflict, which illustrates the perspective necessary to transform society.

While this ending deviates from the particulars of the labor disputes that served as the historical foundation for the novel, the conclusion reflects the social context of the following period, which was characterized by the concerted efforts of capital to undermine the progress that had emerged from these victories. The success of the cotton strike provided the impetus for the destruction of the CAWIU as its continued emphasis on agricultural conditions aroused the wrath of the Associated Farmers, and this group began a program of violence and intimidation against workers.[78] These tendencies manifested during a lettuce strike in the Imperial Valley in January 1934, when landowners intensified their vigilante tactics from 1933 to end the walkout, and again during another clash in Brentwood in the spring of 1934.[79] Following the San Francisco general strike, the Associated Farmers embarked on a renewed crusade to weaken labor. The organization was able to effectively eradicate the CAWIU through the convictions of its leaders, including Chambers, under the California Criminal Syndicalism Act, which offered a pretext for imprisoning radicals.[80] After the demise of the CAWIU, the Associated Farmers continued to wage bitter and violent campaigns against unions, most notably in Sonoma County during June 1935, Los Angeles in April and May 1936, Orange County during June and July 1936, Salinas in September 1936, and Stockton in April 1937.[81] These conflicts all ended in defeat for the strikers, erasing the gains from the struggles that formed the basis for *In Dubious Battle,* and the tactics adopted by the Associated Farmers illustrated the growers' control over the machinery of the state, actions that highlighted the need for a collective response to combat such forces.

The strikes at the Tagus Ranch and in the cotton industry provide an effective foundation for portraying the possible consequences if the grievances of the working class are not ameliorated. Steinbeck also addressed these topics in "Dubious Battle in California," asserting that it "is fervently to be hoped that the great group of migrant workers so necessary to the harvesting of California's crops may be given the right to live decently, that they may not be so badgered, tormented, and hurt that in the end they become avengers of the hundreds of thousands who have been tortured and starved before them."[82]

Steinbeck's statement correlates with the dominant concerns of *In Dubious Battle,* which depicts the destructive outcomes of owners' unfair treatment of labor. The connection between the article and the novel also clarifies the significance of Steinbeck's title, a line taken from John Milton's *Paradise Lost* (1667), when Satan addresses his followers about their warfare against God. By using this phrase, Steinbeck does not express a broader critique of these workers and advances instead an indictment of the growers. The conflict in the novel is not dubious in the sense that the strike is questionable or specious but that the employees are unlikely to prevail in this particular instance, which does not undermine the validity of the work stoppage or its underlying concerns. Even though the outcome of the particular strike is an almost certain defeat, *In Dubious Battle* suggests the clash must inevitably take place despite the vast obstacles against the victory of labor in order to alter socioeconomic conditions that adversely impact the working population.

6

A REVOLUTION OF VALUES

Economic Themes in The Grapes of Wrath

The Grapes of Wrath advances a similar view of people victimized by a restrictive social structure and reflects the underside of the American dream. Louis Owens observes that "Steinbeck's California fiction—all of his finest work—represents a lifelong attempt to open this 'new eye,' to awaken America to the failure at the heart of the American Dream and provide an alternative to that dream. . . . In nearly every story or novel he wrote, Steinbeck strove to hold the failed myth up to the light of everyday reality."[1] These concerns are closely related to the ideas of naturalism that emerge in *The Grapes of Wrath,* which focuses on the plight of the Joad family as they lose their farm in Oklahoma and must travel to California in search of a better life. Few recent critics have devoted serious attention to the placement of this novel within the trajectory of American naturalism, and the existing scholarship has often confused the relationship between the text and this literary movement.[2] For instance, Charles L. Etheridge Sr. asserts that "Steinbeck's narrative technique grows directly out of his Naturalism when the term is understood as a biological term rather than a literary one."[3] Alan Gibbs posits that Steinbeck incorporates the diverse strands of Transcendentalism and Marxism that are responsible for "affecting or diluting his Naturalistic tendencies," elements that Gibbs also defines in a chiefly biological sense.[4] While *The Grapes of Wrath* contains a range of discursive patterns and forms, they are all closely related to the socioeconomic themes of the text, which traces the causative agents that drive the Joads from their ancestral home and necessitate their migration to California. This emphasis on identifying the causative forces that limit the range of action available to the migrants situates *The Grapes of Wrath* within the naturalist tradition.

In its portrayal of the institutional forces that imperil the protagonists, *The Grapes of Wrath* provides a framework to engage with the consequences of economic exploitation and the concentration of essential resources while also suggesting the capacity for the common people to collectively challenge powerful economic institutions.

The Grapes of Wrath has its origins in the conditions facing agricultural workers during the early twentieth century. According to Carey McWilliams, the distress of the rural populace and their movement to the West resulted from "a process of social disintegration set in motion as early as 1900. Their problem is a distinctly man-made problem. Their tragedy is part of a greater tragedy,—the wasteful and senseless exploitation of a rich domain,—the insane scrambling of conflicting group interests which frustrated the promise of the frontier and (within a decade) converted a pioneer territory into a sink of poverty."[5] The immediate plight of people like the Joads emerged from rising wheat prices during World War I, which caused small farmers to expand their operations, and these individuals took out mortgages on their land to purchase new machinery in order to maximize profits.[6] After the war, landowners increased the scope of their undertakings and further eroded the soil by placing an additional million acres in the southern plains under cultivation between 1925 and 1930.[7] Because of an abundance of produce glutting the market by the end of the decade, net agricultural income plummeted between 1929 and 1932, with the value of cotton falling by more than two-thirds and wheat declining by half.[8] As a result, many growers could not meet their payments and lost their holdings. These individuals either remained behind as tenants, who operated 61.2 percent of the small farms in Oklahoma by 1935, or went elsewhere as 28 percent of the rural population worked different land each year.[9] These developments situate westward migration within a larger system of exploitation and underscore the predicament of the Joads, who have followed a similar trajectory from independent farmers to migrants due to economic injustice and ecological catastrophe.

These consequences were exacerbated by the destructive farming techniques employed throughout the Great Plains. Farmers in this area extended production to unsustainable levels through mechanized plowing, a procedure that was responsible for eliminating the grasses that kept the topsoil in place; in addition, homesteaders left their fields bare during the winter, with little protection from the elements.[10] As a result of expanding these practices during the 1920s and a prolonged drought throughout the 1930s, severe dust storms emerged, lasting from an hour to several days, with clouds of dirt as high as eight thousand feet often accompanied by thunder, lightning, and powerful winds. One particular episode in March 1935 carried off twice as much earth as had been dug up during the construction of the Panama Canal, and these storms destroyed half of the wheat harvest in Kansas and the entire wheat crop in Nebraska.[11] Since the residents could no longer survive in this part of the country, between 315,000 and 400,000 people moved to California during the 1930s and sought employment in its agricultural industry.[12] However, the movement of individuals from the Dust Bowl region, which accounted for 16,000 migrants, or 6 percent of the total, was only part of a broader exodus to the West.[13] James Gregory observes that most people came to California due to droughts throughout the Southwest that had rendered the land unable to sustain its inhabitants, in addition to an increase in foreclosures and a decrease in the prices for crops.[14] These developments contextualize the plight of the Joads, whom Steinbeck locates in Sallisaw, a town near the Arkansas border that was thereby not affected by dust storms.[15]

Steinbeck became acquainted with the struggles of these migrants, all of whom were viewed as Okies regardless of their state of origin, through a series of articles that he wrote for the *San Francisco News,* which ran from October 5 through 12, 1936. Explaining the purpose of these pieces, Steinbeck observed that "we shall try to see how [the migrants] live and what kind of people they are, what their living standard is, what is done for them and to them, and what their problems and needs are," and he asserted that "while California has been successful in its use of migrant labor, it is gradually building a human structure which will certainly change the State, and may, if handled with the inhumanity and stupidity that have characterized the past, destroy the present system of agricultural economics."[16] To conduct the research for this assignment, Steinbeck began touring the Central Valley, interviewing migrant workers, and coming into contact with their widespread poverty and desperation. In his travels, Steinbeck visited the Arvin Sanitary Camp, established by the Resettlement Administration to offer a model that landowners could emulate. He continued to explore the area with camp manager Tom Collins, drawing on his reports for the series in the *San Francisco News* and eventually for *The Grapes of Wrath,* to further understand the experiences of the migrants amid their battle to survive in California.[17] After the publication of his articles, Steinbeck embarked on another research trip with Collins in late 1937 and started a narrative that he titled *The Oklaho-*

mans. However, Steinbeck stopped working on this project during January 1938, and Robert DeMott doubts that the author made much progress on the manuscript, which has never been discovered.[18]

In February 1938, Steinbeck began drafting *L'Affaire Lettuceberg,* a satire aimed at the affluent citizens of Salinas who had taken a leading role in the lettuce strike of 1936. However, he abandoned the project by May, informing his agent and editor that he would not be delivering the manuscript. Explaining his rationale, Steinbeck wrote that "this book is finished and it is a bad book and I must get rid of it. It can't be printed. It is bad because it isn't honest. Oh! these incidents all happened but—I'm not telling as much of the truth about them as I know. . . . My whole work drive has been aimed at making people understand each other and then I deliberately write this book the aim of which is to cause hatred through partial understanding."[19] Steinbeck's decision to destroy the draft communicates the vision animating his fiction, one that centers on telling the truth about issues of human importance rather than simply condemning those viewed as the oppressors. Accordingly, Steinbeck developed an alternate conception for the project that portrayed the struggles of the migrants and their underlying dignity against overwhelming obstacles. Writing approximately six pages a day on oversize ledger paper that held nearly twelve hundred words, Steinbeck began *The Grapes of Wrath* on May 31, 1938, and completed his manuscript of 200,000 words by October 26. After Steinbeck made minor revisions, Viking published the novel in April 1939, selling 83,000 copies by the middle of May and shipping 430,000 by the end of the year; since then, the work has never been out of print or had an annual sale of less than 50,000.[20]

In its portrayal of the migrants, *The Grapes of Wrath* presents characters whose experiences are shaped by pressures within both the natural world and the economic system. Steinbeck introduces the former through the impressionistic opening paragraphs, which trace the ruination of the soil and its impact on those who inhabit the land. The narrator states that to "the red country and part of the gray country of Oklahoma, the last rains came gently, and they did not cut the scarred earth. The plows crossed and recrossed the rivulet marks. The last rains had lifted the corn quickly and scattered weed colonies and grass along the sides of the roads so that the gray country and the dark red country began to disappear under a green cover. . . . The sun flared down on the growing corn day after day until a line of brown spread along the edge of each green bayonet. . . . The surface of the earth crusted, a thin hard crust, and as the sky became pale, so the earth became pale, pink in the red country and white in the gray country."[21] As Owens observes, this movement from the panoramic first line to a specific focus on the landscape and back reflects the structural principle of the novel as it alternates between a generalized treatment of the conditions facing the migrants and the plight of the Joads, whose experiences mirror those of the group.[22] Further, this passage illustrates the hostility of nature, which no longer promotes human welfare because of destructive farming practices and changing weather patterns. Steinbeck develops this point through the references to the corn as "bayonets" and the sun that is "red as ripe new blood" (3). The corn, which once supplied the farmers with the means to sustain their physical existence, now emerges as something antagonistic, with the bayonets implying that the crops no longer serve a beneficial function. The narrator bolsters this point through the reference to the bloody sun that brings death rather than life. This state of affairs highlights the elements that necessitate the movement of families like the Joads, who cannot alter their fates in Oklahoma and have no options other than to leave their homes.

Steinbeck heightens the necessity of this movement through the turtle in chapter 3, which establishes a parallel to the Joads and foreshadows their migration to California. The narrator connects Tom Joad to the creature through a reference to its "yellow-nailed feet," a description that evokes the protagonist's "dusty yellow shoes" (14, 8). The narrator reinforces this link by referring to Tom's "new yellow shoes" from which "the yellowness was disappearing under gray dust" (17). Like the family, the tortoise is beset by both environmental forces, as symbolized through the red ant, and mechanical ones, as manifest through the truck that tries to push the reptile off the road when he transports the wild oat across the highway. From this correspondence, Steinbeck develops a series of connections with the characters: the turtle has been moving southwestward, which anticipates the Joads' journey to California; Tom picks it up as a present to the family; and the creature continues in the same direction when released on land once owned by the Joads. This progression exhibits an instinct for survival and a sense of determination that parallel the migrants' undertakings, situating the Joads' actions within the patterns of the natural world. Further, the representation of the tortoise transporting the seed, with its associations of fertility and growth, expresses the potential for a new life at the end of the Joads' journey, one that offers an alternative to the hostility of their current environment. However, Steinbeck contrasts the movement of the turtle, which is fulfilling its biological role within the cycle of nature, with the forced migration of the Joads, whose departure results from the operations of financial institutions.

Accordingly, the representatives of capital comprise the primary deterministic agents in *The Grapes of Wrath,* dictating the course of action available to the central characters in accordance with the imperatives of the marketplace. Steinbeck develops this point in chapter 5 through the use of indirect discourse, which supplies a commentary on the new landowners' justifications for their practices. The representative of the banks asserts that they "breathe profits; they eat the interest on money. If they don't get it, they die the way you die without air, without side-meat. It's a sad thing, but it is so" (32). The use of personification suggests that the banks have an organic existence, yet the underlying logic indicates that these firms sustain themselves by exploiting the efforts of others and consuming the resources of the region. Through the substitution of profits and interest for air and meat, the banker expresses the relationship between the farmers and the current owners of the land with the practices of the new owners undermining the ability of the workers to survive. The people will die without nourishment; however, the consumption favored by the financiers prioritizes acquisition rather than the satisfaction of basic needs. Echoing Shelgrim's arguments in *The Octopus,* an anonymous speaker asserts that the "bank is something else than men. It happens that every man in a bank hates what the bank does, and yet the bank does it. The bank is something more than men, I tell you. It's the monster. Men made it, but they can't control it" (33). While this person suggests that these destructive actions result from abstract laws of exchange without any individual agency, this assertion does not match the reality of the situation. As one tenant observes, there must be "some way to stop this. It's not like lightning or earthquakes. We've got a bad thing made by men, and by God that's something we can change" (38). The contrast with natural disasters highlights that people motivated by economic self-interest are responsible for injustice. As a result, the fiscal concerns that often govern the human enterprise can be challenged by popular pressure, an idea that the narrator reinforces through making this the final line of dialogue in the chapter.[23]

The narrative further highlights the negative effects facilitated by the deterministic agents' myopic view of the natural world. Barbara A. Heavilin notes: "There is no love for the land here—no sense of obligation to give something back, of reciprocity. Just as the migrants are dispossessed of their homes, so the land is depleted of the minerals of its life-giving essence—both victims of greed and ignorance."[24] In developing this idea, the narrator reflects the positions of the owners by noting that they have "got to take cotton quick before the land dies. Then we'll sell the land. Lots of families in the East would like to own a piece of land" (33). This perfunctory presentation of the destruction of the earth implies that it is a disposable resource to be exploited in order to maximize earnings, which does not encourage the use of practices that would enable the survival of the soil for future generations. *The Grapes of Wrath* provides another illustration of this point in chapter 11 through a man hired to work on acreage now owned by the bank. The narrator states that so "easy that the wonder goes out of the work, so efficient that the wonder goes out of the land and the working of it, and with the wonder the deep understanding and the relation" and that "nitrates are not the land, nor phosphates and the length of fiber in the cotton is not the land. Carbon is not a man, nor salt nor water nor calcium. He is all these, but he is much more, much more; and the land is so much more than its analysis" (115). The reduction of the earth to a source of wealth undermines an understanding of the complexity of the land and its significance to focus on elements conducive to capital accumulation. The narrator intensifies this perspective when he notes that "the machine man, driving a dead tractor on land he does not know and love, understands only chemistry; and he is contemptuous of the land and of himself. When the corrugated iron doors are shut, he goes home, and his home is not the land" (116). The emphasis on the tractor operator's dehumanization reveals the consequences for those aligned with dominant financial institutions, which results in alienation from others and the natural world, a theme that the narrator strengthens through the final clause.

Steinbeck, however, heightens the moral complexity of the novel by connecting the deeds of the migrants to the corporate outlook on the soil. In expressing the nature of this relationship, the narrator states that the current inhabitants' fathers "had to kill the Indians and drive them away" and that "Grampa killed Indians, Pa killed snakes for the land" (33, 34). These references indicate that the conditions facing families like the Joads are deeply rooted within the national archetype through the removal of the indigenous population and the seizure of their resources. These acts make the migratory workers complicit in the process of expropriation that characterized the founding of the nation.[25] Through such undertakings, these individuals practice on a small scale what the banks and large growers employ on a larger one.

Further, this view of the natural world as a commodity animates the share-croppers' engagement with their property: economic motives have dictated the use of agricultural techniques that created the circumstances in the first chapter. Steinbeck clarifies this point when the tenants plead for a chance to remain on their land by exclaiming that maybe "the next year will be a good year. God knows how much cotton next year. And with all the wars—God knows what price cotton will bring.... Get enough wars and cotton'll hit the ceiling" (32). This emphasis on financial gain, especially on profits from war, highlights how capital has formed the perspectives of the farmers, although they have no means of bringing about their desired outcome.

While these agents shape the perspectives of the migrants, their en-gagement with the land runs deeper than the purely monetary significance imposed by capital. Steinbeck develops this idea when Tom returns to his family's former farm. The narrator observes that "the dooryard had been pounded hard by the bare feet of children and by stamping horses' hooves and by the broad wagon wheels" (40). Despite the economic impetus of their pro-duction, the Joads and other small farmers in Oklahoma perceive their for-mer holdings as records of their pasts that confer a more authentic basis for ownership than the titles at financial institutions since these documents only have an arbitrary relation to the soil. Through their experiences and labor, the migrants find that their lives are intertwined with the earth, which Stein-beck reinforces through Tom's recollection of why his mother always shut the gate and the discussion of the spot where the protagonist was baptized.

Steinbeck provides another illustration of this point through Muley Graves, a neighbor of the Joads who refuses to leave his family's land after the bankers have foreclosed. Reflecting on such practices, he states: "What'd they get so their 'margin a profit' was safe? They got Pa dyin' on the groun', an' Joe yelling his first breath, an' me jerkin' like a billy goat under a bush in the night.... But them sons-a-bitches at their desks they jus' chopped folks in two for their margin a profit. They just cut 'em in two. Place where folks live is them folks." Muley's examples of coupling, birth, and death highlight the fundamental connection between the characters and their property, which he reiterates through the final line. The parallel between Muley's and Tom's perceptions of the land, along with the allusion to chapter 5 through the reference to the bank having "tractored the folks off the lan'," heightens the tragedy of the work by conveying the universal dimensions of the migrants' struggle (52).

The narrator reinforces this idea in the chapters surrounding the Joads' migration and the attempts of others to sell their belongings before undertaking similar journeys. In chapter 9, one man asserts: "You're not buying only junk, you're buying junked lives. And more—you'll see—you're buying bitterness. Buying a plow to plow your own children under, buying the arms and spirits that might have saved you" (86–87). These possessions have a value that cannot be measured in money since they reflect the lives of their former owners and cannot be disassociated from their experiences. The speaker develops this point when he asserts that the "anger of the moment, the thousand pictures, that's us. This land, this red land, is us; the flood years and the dust years and the drought years are us" (87). This further correlation between the land and the migrants' conception of selfhood dramatizes the profound sense of loss tied to the sale of their former homes, which estranges them from the experiences of generations who have worked the same fields amid similar catastrophes. These experiences anticipate the Joads' disposal of their household goods in the following chapter. The narrator states that after the Joads sell everything from the farm for a mere eighteen dollars, "they were weary and frightened because they had gone against a system that they did not understand and it had beaten them. They knew the team and wagon were worth much more. They knew the buyer man would get much more, but they didn't know how to do it" (97). The family's dispossession reiterates the fundamental conflict with the forces of the deterministic world as the broader spiritual connection to the environment has been severed by an individualistic and predatory social order.

Steinbeck provides an alternative to this perspective through the formation of a consciousness that connects the individual to the collective and offers the potential to overcome entrenched power. Jim Casy, a former preacher who no longer believes in organized religion, articulates this theme when he posits that maybe "all men got one big soul ever'body's a part of" (24).[26] As Frederic I. Carpenter has noted, this opinion situates Casy's outlook within the context of American Transcendentalism and Ralph Waldo Emerson's conception of the Over-Soul, the belief that all humans are joined in one indivisible soul.[27] The former preacher, however, shifts this formulation from the metaphysical realm to the material one, linking the eradication of the unity of life to economic self-interest. Casy observes that "we was holy when we was one thing, an' mankin' was holy when it was one thing. An' it on'y got unholy when one mis'able little fella got the bit in his teeth an' run off his own way," and the former preacher goes on to assert that when people are "all workin' together, not one fella for another fella, but one fella kind of harnessed to the whole shebang—that's right, that's holy" (81). The narrative illustrates this process of removal from the group through the poverty and the lust for possessions that shape the lives of the working class. The tractor driver in chapter 5 illustrates this idea, placing his family's needs over the good of the collective. In this context, the man's actions serve a destructive function since his attempts to support his family prevent others from doing the same by forcing them from the land that once provided a means of subsistence. The narrator reinforces this point when the children of the dispossessed eat fried dough while watching the tractor operator consume a Spam sandwich and a "piece of pie branded like an engine part" (36). The contrast between the meals of the youths and that of the worker emphasizes his separation from the group as his actions have supplied a higher standard of living, evident through his store-bought food, yet these references signify the artifice of the man's perspective through his association with machine-made products.

While self-interest has fractured the unity of life, the novel indicates that concerted action offers the potential to recover this harmony through fostering a shared sense of purpose. Steinbeck develops this movement through Ma Joad, who advances an outlook that encompasses the requirements of the broader human community.[28] This idea manifests when she offers to feed Tom and Casy, whom Pa tells her are strangers in need of a meal, and Steinbeck extends this theme when the matriarch argues in favor of the former preacher accompanying them to California. She asserts that "I never heerd tell of no Joads or no Hazletts, neither, ever refusin' food an' shelter or a lift on the road to anybody that asked. They's been mean Joads, but never that mean" (102). Ma's willingness to assist others contrasts with the endeavors of the used-car salesmen who fleece the migrants in chapter 7 and the men who purchase the tenants' belongings for less than their real value in chapter 9. Her kindness attains a deeper significance given the poverty of the Joads as they barely have the means to sustain themselves on their journey. Steinbeck also illustrates this progression through the Joads' interactions with the Wilsons, who accompany the Joads to the West Coast and offer their mattress to Grandpa Joad as he is dying. Reflecting on the importance of this occurrence, Sarah Wilson states: "We're proud to help. I ain't felt so—safe in a long time. People needs—to help" (141). This response expresses a sense of compassion that the Joads have not received from others up to this point, while the connection between security and assisting others highlights the importance of the families working together, sharing resources to enable the voyage to proceed. The incorporation of the Wilsons into the traveling party, much like the earlier addition of Casy, denotes the expansion of the family to a unit that incorporates the interests of a larger community based on the recognition that the fate of one is linked to the circumstances facing others.

The narrator clarifies the significance of this progression in chapter 14 when he offers a broader commentary on the threat that the union of families like the Joads and Wilsons poses to the economic elite. He notes that in the connection between individuals, "'I lost my land' is changed; a cell is split and from its splitting grows the thing you hate—'We lost *our* land.' The danger is here, for two men are not as lonely and perplexed as one. And from this first 'we' there grows a still more dangerous thing: 'I have a little food' plus 'I have none.' If from this problem the sum is 'We have a little food,' the thing is on its way, the movement has direction.... This is the beginning—from 'I' to 'we.'" (151–52). The reference to the splitting of cells indicates that the shift from "I" to "we" is the organic result of present conditions and that aligning the interests of the individual with those of the group is necessary for survival. When the downtrodden act on the basis of their shared circumstances and pursue common objectives, these people can challenge the dictates of powerful social institutions and promote human needs, evident through the narrator's specific examples of the food necessary to sustain life and the land that would provide financial security. Steinbeck reinforces this theme when Ma observes that all "we got is the family unbroken. Like a bunch of cows, when the lobos are ranging, stick all together. I ain't scared while we're all here, all that's alive, but I ain't gonna see us bust up" (169–70). The use of animal imagery provides a further example of the strength that occurs through the operations of the group rather than as isolated men and women, who would become prey for forces that the collective could withstand.

The surrounding interchapters extend this theme through juxtaposing an individualistic outlook against the benefits of mutual aid. Steinbeck presents the selfish view through the mechanic in chapter 12, who states: "I ain't in business for my health. I'm here a-sellin' tires. I ain't givin' 'em away. I can't help what happens to you. I got to think what happens to me" (120). This selfish position emphasizes the perspective responsible for exacerbating the plight of the poor; however, the narrator provides a counterpoint through the man who picks up a family on the side of the road, towing them to California and feeding them throughout their travels. These deeds parallel Ma's insistence on taking Casy to the West Coast and the Wilsons sharing their resources with the Joads on their journey. Chapter 15 reiterates this point while also alluding to previous occurrences. For instance, Mae's conversation with the truckers reflects Tom's interactions with the truck driver from chapter 2. Both episodes emanate from a need for human contact, yet Tom demonstrates a hostility toward the driver that is not apparent in Mae's interplay with her customers. Further, the sympathy of Mae and Al, who sell food to the migrants at a reduced price, contrasts with the actions of the car salesman in chapter 7 and gas station attendant in chapter 13, both of whom prey on the downtrodden. Accordingly, the kindness of Mae and Al anticipates Ma sharing her meager rations with the hungry children in addition to the shopkeeper at the Hooper Ranch taking money out of his pocket so that the matriarch could obtain more sugar. Through its presentation of the correspondences among events, chapter 15 reinforces the structures that determine the Joads' circumstances and the parallel movement toward a collective consciousness that could transcend these constraints.

The Joads' arrival in the Central Valley connects the narrative to the American Dream as the natural abundance of this locale evokes the potential for fiscal progress. As Owens observes, Steinbeck develops the portrayal of the West through a prominent Eden motif.[29] Contrary to the religious readings of *The Grapes of Wrath,* Steinbeck situates the family's movement within a clearly demarcated economic context, and their desire for renewal focuses less on spiritual aims than broader monetary concerns.[30] For instance, Ma exclaims: "I like to think how nice it's gonna be, maybe, in California. Never cold. An' fruit ever'place, an' people just bein' in the nicest places, little white houses in among the orange trees" (91). The emphasis on the plentiful crops contrasts with conditions in Oklahoma, suggesting that California could be a land of rebirth where the family could obtain financial security. This idyllic vision correlates to conventional ideas of the West as a place that affords opportunities to all comers, a point that the narrator reinforces when the Joads enter the Central Valley: "They drove through Tehachapi in the morning glow, and the sun came up behind them, and then—suddenly they saw the great valley below them. . . . The vineyards, the orchards, the great flat valley, green and beautiful, the trees set into rows, and the farm houses. . . . The grain fields golden in the morning, and the willow lines, the eucalyptus trees in rows.... The peach trees and walnut groves, and the dark green patches of oranges" (227). The narrator's emphasis on such vast natural resources reflects the material possibilities of the region, which should offer better prospects to the migrant family than the barren ground of Oklahoma. This passage, however, reveals the illusions that govern the Joads' perceptions of their new home to suggest that their new surroundings will offer a limited chance for mobility.

The reality underlying this idyllic portrayal of California materializes through the growers' attempts to attract a large supply of laborers in order to decrease wages, a process that pits individuals against one another for limited resources. Regarding these actions, one man describes an employment contractor's use of handbills, noting that he "wants eight hundred men. So he prints up five thousand of them things an' maybe twenty thousan' people sees 'em. An' maybe two-three thousan' folks gets movin' account a this here han'bill"; he observes that the "more fellas he can get, an' the hungrier, less he's gonna pay" (189, 190). These advertisements provide a means to exert downward pressure on compensation by inflating the workforce, and the promise of employment would be likely to engender migration given the extreme poverty in the Dust Bowl region.

While Kevin Starr has challenged the accuracy of this representation, the empirical foundation for these references seems to have their basis in the reports that Tom Collins assembled for the Farm Security Administration (FSA).[31] He referred to the attempts of the management at DiGiorgio Farms to quell a strike by telling employees "that an advertising campaign in the Oklahoma and Arkansas press would bring out, on short notice, hundreds, and probably thousands of wor[k]ers from those states and that those workers would be quite happy to work for the 25¢ per hour scale," and Collins later asserted that the "threat of Di Georgio [sic] to bring to California, drought stricken farmers and sharecroppers from Oklahoma, Arkansas, and Texas can be taken quite seriously."[32] Further, the use of circulars to draw transient workers to various parts of the state during harvest season was common practice in the agricultural industry at the time. For instance, the owners of the Durst Ranch advertised jobs throughout California and Nevada, luring twenty-seven hundred people to the fields in Wheatland when only about fifteen hundred positions were available, a course of action that approximates the logic of the handbills in *The Grapes of Wrath*.[33] As such, the leaflets reinforce the operations of the deterministic agents in the narrative, and these references serve a structural function through demonstrating that life in California does not accurately reflect the myths associated with this locale.

This tension between the potential for prosperity and the harsh reality of the state continues for the remainder of *The Grapes of Wrath*. For instance, when the male Joads bathe in the Colorado River in chapter 18, they encounter a father and son returning to Oklahoma, and the father exclaims that California is "a nice country. But she was stole a long time ago.... An' you'll pass lan' flat an' fine with water thirty feet down, and that lan's laying fallow. But you can't have none of that lan'" (205). Steinbeck connects the failed promise of the region to a concentration of land ownership that limits the ability of the earth to sustain the population, which manifests through the reference to the fertile ground left fallow and anticipates the destruction of oranges to support prices. This inequity has its foundation in the history of California. Regarding the Americans who settled this area, the narrator states that "such was their hunger for land that they took the land—stole Sutter's land, Guerrero's land, took the grants and broke them up and growled and quarreled over them" (231). The reference to the cancellation of the Mexican-era grants evokes the period immediately following the gold rush, which Steinbeck conveys through the reference to John Sutter, who owned the property where James W. Marshall found this precious metal in 1848. The narrator also presents the alternate conception of the environment that emerged during this period, noting that those who commandeered resources lost an appreciation for the natural world: as the farms became bigger, "the owners no longer worked on their farms. They farmed on paper; and they forgot the land, the smell, the feel of it, and remembered only that they owned it, remembered only what they gained and lost by it" (232). Further, this context establishes the growers in California as the counterparts to the banks in Oklahoma since both view the earth through the calculus of the marketplace, negating any connection between the soil and its inhabitants.

The representation of the migrants connects their exploitation to the concentration of resources. The narrator observes that the Dust Bowl refugees "streamed over the mountains, hungry and restless—restless as ants, scurrying to find work to do—to lift, to push, to pull, to pick, to cut—anything, any burden to bear, for food. The kids are hungry. We got no place to live. Like ants scurrying for work, for food, and most of all for land" (233). The references to these individuals as ants evoke their dehumanization, and the narrator situates this process within a socioeconomic arrangement that ties the wealth of the growers to the poverty of the workers. The narrator states that "when property accumulates in too few hands it is taken away. And that companion fact: when a majority of the people are hungry and cold they will take by force what they need. And the little screaming fact that sounds all through history: repression works only to strengthen and knit the repressed" (238). This passage serves as a warning to the large landowners responsible for the plight of the poor, yet the narrator's clinical, dispassionate tone establishes this development as the logical outgrowth of poverty and desperation. By hoarding the abundant crops of California and repressing labor, the owners facilitate conditions that destabilize the economic system. Accordingly, Steinbeck suggests that this emphasis on profit will ultimately arouse widespread animosity, which will produce the circumstances necessary for the transformation of society, potentially through a violent upheaval if the conditions facing labor are not improved.

These ideas also emerge through the novel's title, one that places *The Grapes of Wrath* within a tradition of militant protest while also linking the work to central American values. Carol Steinbeck thought of the title for the book, which comes from "The Battle Hymn of the Republic." Regarding the significance of this reference, Steinbeck wrote to Elizabeth Otis: "I think it is Carol's best title so far. I like it because it is a march and this book is a kind of a march—because it is in our own revolutionary tradition and because in reference to this book it has a large meaning. And I like it because people know the Battle Hymn who don't know the Star Spangled Banner."[34] This title provided a means of situating the narrative within the broader currents of U.S. history, linking the migrants' plight to other struggles for justice throughout the country's past and suggesting that *The Grapes of Wrath* involves a conflict central to the American experience, one that pits the powerful against the powerless in order to determine whether the ideals of the nation would truly apply to all. The use of "The Battle Hymn of the Republic" had a further advantage as Steinbeck observed in a letter to Pascal Covici that the "fascist crowd will try to sabotage this book because it is revolutionary. They try to give it the communist angle. However, the Battle Hymn is American and intensely so. Further, every American child learns it and then forgets the words."[35] By invoking a song so commonly associated with patriotic sentiment, Steinbeck could preempt claims that *The Grapes of Wrath* was Communist propaganda. Instead, he could present the work as one that dealt with uniquely American characters, conditions, and experiences to reveal how the practices of the growers are antithetical to the values that supposedly animate the American experience.

Chapter 20 supplies a further illustration of this theme through the introduction of Floyd Knowles, who stands up for the migrants and provides the impetus for Casy's interest in unionization. When Floyd insists that the labor contractor stipulate in writing the compensation for prospective employees, the deputies try to detain this worker, which leads to a woman being badly injured. This exchange reflects an important strain in California history as labor contractors featured prominently within the state's agricultural industry. In her notes on the FSA camps, Sanora Babb discussed the actions of those employed by large landowners to recruit workers: "He drives along the camps, talks to the 'Okies' and tells them all to go to a certain farm where several hundred men are needed, at good wages (perhaps at 80 cents), etc. Then he drives to another camp and repeats the offer, and more men go to these farms. Finally where 300 men are actually needed 1,000, or 2,500 men will appear. The offered price at once comes down, and most of them leave without work. They have arrived with their last bit of gas and no food at 'home' so that they are forced to take anything."[36] This explanation parallels Floyd's account in *The Grapes of Wrath*, which also suggests the logic underlying the handbills that attract the migrants to California, and these elements convey the serious obstacles to the Joads' attainment of material progress in their new environment. This episode also demonstrates the need for people to work together in order to eliminate the conditions that cause such outcomes. Casy develops this contention when he takes the blame for Tom attacking the police officer. He states: "I got no kids. They'll jus' put me in jail, an' I ain't doing nothin' but set aroun'. . . . If you mess in this your whole fambly, all your folks, gonna get in trouble" (265–66). Through this self-sacrifice, Casy places the concerns of others over his own, echoing the movement toward a collective consciousness that contravenes the economic self-interest of the growers while also allowing the Joads to remain united.

The following interchapter underscores the need for such structures by emphasizing the practices of those who oppose the migrants despite having similar interests, which presents the negative implications of the phalanx. The narrator observes that "the hostility changed them, welded them, united them—hostility that made the little towns group and arm as though to repel an invader, squads with pick handles, clerks and storekeepers with shotguns, guarding the world against their own people" (282). While similar circumstances adversely impact both Dust Bowl refugees and working-class Californians, the arbitrary divisions among laborers undermine the possibility that they will recognize their shared predicament, an outcome that illustrates how the imperatives of capital pervade all levels of the social order. Within this context, many Californians, who were only slightly removed from the fates of the impoverished, internalized the perspectives of the landowners and demonized the migratory workers.[37] The narrator conveys this point when he adopts the perspectives of those aligned with the growers: "Okies are dirty and ignorant. They're degenerate, sexual maniacs. These goddamned Okies are thieves. They'll steal anything. They've got no sense of property rights." These arbitrary differences allow the owners to divide potential allies by causing one group to perceive the others as invaders coming to jeopardize what the townspeople have attained or hope to achieve. This perspective enables their mutual adversary to plunder with impunity. The narrator reinforces this idea when he asserts that the vigilantes think they "own the country. We can't let these Okies get out of hand. And the men who were armed did not own the land, but they thought they did. And the clerks who drilled at night owned nothing, and the little storekeepers possessed only a drawerful of debts" (283). The contrast between the exalted estimation of their positions and the reality of their situations illustrates that the inequitable division of resources adversely affects those who believe that they benefit from the present system. Since they seem to gain from the smooth operation of society, they are less likely to unite against the large landowners, which perpetuates the structural inequity that impacts all workers.

The chapters set in Weedpatch convey an alternative to this scenario. Steinbeck discussed the inspiration for this locale, the Arvin Sanitary Camp, in his fourth article for the *San Francisco News*, asserting that "the intent of management has been to restore the dignity and decency that had been kicked out of the migrants by their intolerable mode of life," a pattern of existence that "does reduce his responsibility and does make him a sullen outcast who will strike at our Government in any way that occurs to him."[38] This description posits a model of organization that challenges the broader inequities that have shaped the migrants' predicament, providing access to basic services from sanitary facilities to health care while also engendering a sense of solidarity. This development occurs through the shared use of resources when the family next to the Joads splits their meager breakfast with Tom, which offers a parallel to Ma sharing food with the children at the squatter's camp. These episodes reflect the structural function of Weedpatch in *The Grapes of Wrath* as a further movement away from the individual consciousness of the landowners. The family also helps Tom find a job, yet this episode highlights the distinction between Weedpatch and dominant society through the material tensions that govern the men's employer, who reduces wages after an officer at the Bank of the West intimates that a refusal to do so will cause the bank to withhold a loan (294–95). The bank pressure on small farmers to depress wages supplies a further illustration of the economic control over the region and the resulting need to address these constraints.

In this context, Weedpatch offers an opportunity for the rediscovery of the migrants' common humanity and a means for self-preservation. One tenant asserts that the "folks in the camp are getting used to being treated like humans. When they go back to the squatters' camps they'll be hard to handle" (296). The democratic structure of this setting and management's emphasis on providing basic services transform its inhabitants, and the camp establishes a model for organization that could potentially lead to meaningful social change if these practices were enacted on a broader scale. Developing the importance of Weedpatch, Ma states that the growers and their functionaries "done somepin to us. Ever' time they come seemed like they was a-whippin' me—all of us. An' in Needles, that police. He done somepin to me, made me feel mean. Made me feel ashamed. An' now I ain't ashamed. These folks is our folks—is our folks. An' that manager, he come an' set an' drank coffee, an' he says, 'Mrs. Joad' this, an' 'Mrs. Joad' that—an' 'How you gettin' on, Mrs. Joad?' . . . Why, I feel like people again" (307). Ma's statements illustrate the role of this locale in the restoration of her humanity, which threatens the owners' interests as the workers' belief that they should be treated like human beings rather than beasts would make them less likely to tolerate their subordination. The narrator develops this idea when the police attempt to provoke a riot during the dance, yet the residents prevent this outcome through a unified response that maintains order. By forming committees to stop the interlopers and refraining from the acts of violence that would enable law enforcement to enter Weedpatch, the migrants demonstrate their capacity to manage their own affairs. One man underscores this point when he tells a gate-crasher: "Don't knife your own folks. We're tryin' to get along, havin' fun an' keepin' order. Don't tear all that down. Jes' think about it. You're jes' harmin' yourself" (344). This focus on the concerns of the individual separate from those of the group reinforces the ability of capital to pit natural allies against one another, yet the actions of the migrants express the power of labor to challenge these constructs.

Chapter 25 provides a further illustration of the need to challenge entrenched power through juxtaposing the consequences wrought by the pursuit of capital accumulation against the material possibilities of California. The references to spring throughout this interchapter signify the potential for rebirth, a progression tied to the cycle of the natural world, with grapes "swelling from the old gnarled vines" and produce so heavy that "the limbs bend gradually under the fruit." These crops promise the ability to sustain the residents, and the description of the hills as "round and soft as breasts" evokes the potential for the countryside to nurse the migrants back to health, which thereby anticipates Rose of Sharon's actions at the end of the novel (346). This abundance is further intensified by scientific advances that enable people to transform "the world with their knowledge," causing "short, lean wheat" to become "big and productive" and making "little sour apples ... large and sweet" (347). However, men undermine the capacity of the earth to support the population by allowing these commodities to decay in order to keep prices high. The inability of industry to direct these innovations to satisfying hunger reiterates that the plight of the impoverished stems from the practices of the elite. The narrator reinforces this theme through the burning of oranges, asserting that there "is a crime here that goes beyond denunciation. There is a sorrow here the weeping cannot symbolize. There is a failure here that topples all our success. The fertile earth, the straight tree rows, the sturdy trunks, and the ripe fruit.... And coroners must fill in the certificates—died of malnutrition—because the food must rot, must be forced to rot" (349). This misuse of resources highlights the inadequacy of the present system to meet human needs and indicates the necessity of an economic model that would minimize such unnecessary tragedies.[39] As Susan Shillinglaw observes, "Capitalism has failed because self-interest and greed have trumped compassion, certainly when mounds of oranges are burned to keep prices high. And while the grapes of wrath are not yet harvested, the vintage not yet bottled, collective rage might make it so—revolution simmers. Change hovers."[40] By connecting the plight of the poor to prevailing economic conditions, Steinbeck places the onus on those who preside over the social system to ameliorate the forces they have set in motion.

The Joads' departure from Weedpatch highlights the further obstacles to meaningful social change. When Ma observes the fertile landscape on the way to the Hooper Ranch, she states: "I ain't really felt so good for a long time. ... 'F we pick plenty peaches, we might get a house, pay rent even, for a couple months. We got to have a house" (366). This perspective reflects a return to her past illusions by alluding to the rationale underlying the journey to California. The narrator accentuates the forces that will prevent the Joads' progress when they become strikebreakers, aligning themselves with capital to survive. The narrator buttresses this point through the reintroduction of Casy, whose new vocation as a labor leader contrasts with undertakings of the Joads, who have deviated from a collective consciousness out of economic necessity. Explaining why they are willing to cross a picket line, Tom notes: "Tonight we had meat. Not much, but we had it. Think Pa's gonna give up his meat on account a other fellas? An' Rosasharn oughta get milk. Think Ma's gonna wanta starve that baby jus' 'cause a bunch of fellas is yellin' outside a gate?" (384). Tom's focus on the Joads' requirements illustrates the deprivation that perpetuates inequality, reinforces arbitrary distinctions among individuals, and minimizes the likelihood that they will operate in concert with their fellows.

This tension between the individual and the group frames both the murder of Casy and Tom's killing of the deputy, events that further develop the consequences of the present course of policy. Explaining the rationale of the strike, Casy states that the fruit pickers walked off their jobs after management cut compensation in half. The decision to offer the strikebreakers a higher wage that will decrease to pre-strike levels after the company wins the dispute reinforces how the working class is divided by the capitalists to perpetuate their control. Casy suggests this function by telling the officers: "You fellas don' know what you're doin'. You're helpin' to starve kids." His demise provides another instance of the repression against the migrants and the consequences of the present socioeconomic order, yet the final sentence articulates the necessity of challenging structures of power even when such actions come at a tremendous cost. Further, the emphasis on the limited responsibility of all involved parallels Tom's slaying of the deputy. Describing the crime, the narrator states that Tom "wrenched the club free. The first time he knew that he had missed and struck a shoulder, but the second time his crushing blow found the head, and as the heavy man sunk down, three more blows found his head" (386). This focus on the mechanical nature of the homicide stresses Tom's physical actions rather than the cognitive processes that gave rise to them. He reinforces this point when he tells Ma, "I didn' know what I was a-doin', no more'n when you take a breath" (392). This scene implies that an economic arrangement which privileges the prerogatives of the affluent will engender widespread dissatisfaction that could culminate in violence when people have no other means to protect their interests.

The concluding sequence of *The Grapes of Wrath* reinforces the central themes of the narrative through Tom's burgeoning political awareness. His separation from his family shows that he has learned from Ma and Casy, shifting from the immediate concerns of the individual to the interests of the people as a whole. Tom asserts: "I been thinkin' a hell of a lot, thinkin' about our people livin' like pigs, an' the good rich lan' layin' fallow, or maybe one fella with a million acres, while a hunderd thousan' good farmers is starvin'. An' I been wonderin' if all our folks got together an' yelled, like them fellas yelled, only a few of 'em at the Hooper ranch—." Tom connects his impulses to the structure of a society that undermines the humanity of the poor, as evidenced through his use of animal imagery, and necessitates concerted action on the part of labor. Describing his conception of such undertakings, Tom states that wherever "they's a fight so hungry people can eat, I'll be there. Wherever they's a cop beatin' up a guy, I'll be there. If Casy knowed, why, I'll be in the way guys yell when they're mad an'—I'll be in the way kids laugh when they're hungry an' they know supper's ready. An' when our folks eat the stuff they raise an' live in the houses they build—why, I'll be there" (419). Through his catalog of specific acts of injustice, Tom articulates the necessity of a more equitable society, evident through the desire for economic self-determination in the final sentence. These assertions reflect a change in consciousness predicated on recognizing the essential unity undermined by exploitative practices, which is a necessary step in pursuit of the concrete objectives of the working class.

Steinbeck juxtaposes Tom's transformation with the further deterioration of the Joads' circumstances because of the floods that undermine the family's fleeting moment of financial security. Chapter 27 foreshadows the impermanence of the Joads' apparent gains. An anonymous speaker states: "Try for God's sake ta save a little money! Winter's comin' fast. They ain't no work at all in California in the winter" (408). The cyclical character of labor in the state compounds the dilemma of the agricultural workers, whose wages do not allow them to save money for the months when their services are not needed. These hardships are compounded by the hostility of the natural world, a representation that Steinbeck based on widespread flooding in Visalia and Nipomo during February 1938, which trapped two thousand migrant workers in the camp where they had assembled for picking season without adequate food or medical supplies. Carey McWilliams, describing pictures of the group, observed that they "are almost incredible in their revelation of the plight of 2,000 starving, dirty, utterly dejected men, women, and children. I know of nothing comparable to these pictures except the scenes of the famine in postwar Europe."[41] This episode provided a compelling illustration of the migrants' plight, which was exacerbated by the landowners' attempts to block shipments of food and medicine from relief agencies to help those trapped in the camp. Describing conditions in the area, Steinbeck wrote: "Four thousand families, drowned out of their tents are really starving to death. . . . The locals are fighting the government bringing in food and medicine. I'm going to try to break the story hard enough so that food and drugs can get moving. Shame and a hatred of publicity will do the job to the miserable local bankers."[42] This suffering highlighted the consequences of consolidating power among a narrow segment of the population and demonstrated how economic self-interest could intensify the detrimental effects of natural disasters. The inclusion of this incident in *The Grapes of Wrath* expresses a return to the enmity of nature that frames the initial chapters, with the added irony that the rain, which would have alleviated the suffering of the Joads in Oklahoma, undermines their brief period of stability in California.

In his presentation of this episode, Steinbeck further juxtaposes an outlook that perpetuates injustice against the collective consciousness that offers a means of combating the restrictions of the deterministic world. Reflecting on the popular response to flooding in chapter 29, the narrator notes that "the comfortable people in tight houses felt pity at first, and then distaste, and finally hatred for migrant people" (434). This response further dramatizes the consequences of a perspective that prioritizes the interests of the individual over the group, one that prevents people from taking action to alleviate suffering, and their hatred provides a pretext for their refusal to assist others. By contrast, the efforts of the migrants illustrate the need for cooperation even against seemingly insurmountable obstacles. When the men attempt to build a dam to prevent the floodwaters from entering the boxcar while Rose of Sharon is in labor, the narrator states that they "heaped the mud up in a long embankment, and those who had no shovels cut live willow whips and wove them into a mat and kicked them into the bank. Over the men came a fury of work, a fury of battle. When one man dropped the shovel, another took it up. . . . They were tired now, and the shovels moved more slowly. And the stream rose slowly" (441). These efforts to keep the deluge at bay suggest the need for individuals to operate as a unit to forestall hostile forces. Such actions are significant in that the men are not building the levee for themselves; instead, they are working past the point of exhaustion for Rose of Sharon, who is in no condition to protect herself.

Steinbeck provides the clearest manifestation of this collective consciousness through Ma and Rose of Sharon. While Tom and Casy both move toward activism, Tom articulates these viewpoints rather than putting them into practice, and Casy's rhetorical formulations often overshadow his self-sacrifice in pursuit of these objectives. Ma Joad, however, operates on the basis of these insights throughout the work, which demonstrates the necessity of a worldview rooted in compassion that prioritizes the needs of other people. John H. Timmerman observes that between "the poles of Tom Joad and Jim Casy, Ma Joad is the lodestar that evinces calm and grants direction. Her concept of the family of man, which she holds intuitively from the start, is the final point at which the others arrive like grim pilgrims, knowing the place for the first time."[43] The matriarch supplies repeated illustrations of this premise, from including Casy in the Joads' journey through sharing some of the family's meager food with the hungry children in the camp. Ma clarifies the value underlying such developments when she asserts that once "the fambly was fust. It ain't so now. It's anybody. Worse off we get, the more we got to do" (445). Throughout *The Grapes of Wrath*, Ma Joad models an outlook that situates the fate of the individual within that of the group, basing her deeds on the requirements of others while indicating that the poor have an obligation to their class since no one else will offer assistance. From these undertakings to benefit the broader human family, Ma presents a counterpoint to perspectives that place individuals over the collective, and her refusal to be bowed by the conditioning forces of life prompts others to do the same.

Steinbeck underscores the significance of Ma Joad's influence through the closing tableau of Rose of Sharon nursing the starving man, which demonstrates the principles that have guided the matriarch throughout the novel.[44] The failure of society to tend to the interests of those who cannot defend themselves emerges through Rose of Sharon's stillborn child, who exemplifies the consequences wrought by greed, and Steinbeck provides a further manifestation through the starving man, with Rose of Sharon showcasing the compassion necessary for the survival of the downtrodden. The narrator notes that Ma Joad "looked at Pa and Uncle John standing helplessly gazing at the sick man. She looked at Rose of Sharon huddled in the comfort. Ma's eyes passed Rose of Sharon's eyes, and then came back to them. And the two women looked deep into each other. The girl's breath came short and gasping" (454). The emphasis on the male characters "helplessly gazing" conveys their inability to adapt to changed circumstances, whereas the glances exchanged between Ma and Rose of Sharon reveal a deeper awareness of the situation, its implications, and the way forward. The young woman's deed at the end of the novel offers a dramatic illustration of the theme that the migrants' progress depends on transcending perspectives based on narrow self-interest. Steinbeck buttresses this idea through the fact that the man is a stranger, which evokes the potential for renewal that results from the alteration of the family dynamic to incorporate the requirements of the human community. In this context, Rose of Sharon's compassion and sympathy denote the values necessary to animate the human experience, and breastfeeding the starving man conveys that people must use the means at their disposal to assist their fellows and to alleviate suffering.

The Grapes of Wrath presents the attributes necessary to address the consequences affected by economic self-interest, and the actions of the characters mirror the dominant impulses underlying Steinbeck's broader project as a novelist. In his Nobel Prize acceptance speech, he asserted that the "writer is delegated to declare and to celebrate man's proven capacity for greatness of heart and spirit—for gallantry in defeat, for courage, compassion, and love. In the endless war against weakness and despair, these are the bright rally flags of hope and of emulation. I hold that a writer who does not passionately believe in the perfectibility of man has no dedication nor any membership in literature."[45] The principals in *The Grapes of Wrath* operate in this context as they demonstrate tremendous courage in their struggles against seemingly insurmountable obstacles. Steinbeck, however, indicates that these forces ultimately can be defeated through a return to the values that exemplify man's "greatness of heart and spirit," ideals that provide a more equitable basis for existence than the financial concerns that too often govern individual behavior. These representations signify that a meaningful social transformation begins with a change in consciousness and that the application of these insights to lived experience could foster a greater range of development for the working class.

CONCLUSION

Social criticism is central to the fiction of Frank Norris, Jack London, and John Steinbeck, which utilizes ideas of economic determinism to illuminate the underlying causes of social injustice for the purpose of their amelioration. These portrayals might seem passé to some readers since legislation has addressed many of the specific concerns expressed by Norris, London, and Steinbeck. For instance, the Sherman Anti-Trust Act dismantled corporate monopolies, the Wagner Act provided workers with the right to bargain collectively, and the Fair Labor Standards Act restricted child labor. Further, the decades following the publication of *The Grapes of Wrath* featured the longest period of sustained growth in U.S. history, one that resulted in a tremendous degree of mobility. However, political and economic developments over the past few decades have brought the central concerns of naturalist fiction back into prominence, reaffirming that individual outcomes often stem from the operations of dominant social institutions. Despite changes to the forms of injustice, the fiscal forces that led to the characters' plight have continued to foster similar consequences in the twenty-first century, which highlights the continuing importance of naturalism.

The social criticism of Norris, London, and Steinbeck emerges through their portrayals of the economic conditions facing their central characters. *The Octopus* traces the tragedies produced by monopoly control over the essential commodities that the principals depend on to survive. The representatives of the Pacific and Southwestern Railroad heighten these consequences through their power over the political, fiscal, and legal structures of California, which causes these agencies to serve the interests of the powerful rather than those of the public. In *The Iron Heel*, London presents a capitalist oligarchy that maintains its authority through the formation of

186

a paramilitary organization to subordinate labor, whereas "The Dream of Debs" emphasizes the practices of employers who profit from an inequitable socioeconomic order and create the circumstances that give rise to the general strike. *In Dubious Battle* and *The Grapes of Wrath* also express how the concentration of resources restricts human progress. *In Dubious Battle* shows how unbridled capitalism adversely impacts laborers, and *The Grapes of Wrath* portrays the causative agents that drive the Joads from their land and necessitate their migration to the West, where the family is exploited by landowners. These texts highlight some of the major economic issues of the nineteenth and twentieth centuries, informing their audience about the harmful effects of the present course of policy with the hope of inspiring the public to action.

The social criticism of Norris, London, and Steinbeck also manifests through their characters' struggles to improve their economic positions. For instance, *McTeague* and *The Octopus* focus on men and women who temporarily attain economic progress, evident through the dentist's ascent from the mines, Trina's lottery winnings, the extensive holdings of Magnus Derrick and his associates, and the harvest that seems to promise even greater returns. The inability to maintain these gains and the characters' subsequent deterioration highlights how conduct is shaped by environmental forces. *Martin Eden* differs from the other texts by centering on a figure who gains affluence through conventional methods of prudence, industry, and thrift. Martin's development offers a cautionary tale, however, for people who define success entirely in materialistic terms as his individualistic aims allow only for acquisition but do not lead to realizing the romantic and intellectual aspirations that he finds to be infinitely more important than money. Instead of portraying figures who experience downward mobility or whose apparent victory evokes a broader failure, Steinbeck presents laborers whose roles in the social hierarchy are largely static. The pickers from *In Dubious Battle* initially work for low wages amid poor conditions, and the book ends with the probable defeat of the strike that might have ameliorated these problems. Through depictions of characters who cannot ultimately influence their fates, Norris, London, and Steinbeck offer a commentary on the limitations to advancement in America, which could cause readers to consider the constraints that govern their own lives.

Norris, London, and Steinbeck buttress these concerns through their refusal to present their characters as innocent victims, and their actions express the problems that result from failing to address social inequities. For example, McTeague and Tom Joad are murderers; the proletarians in "The Apostate," *Martin Eden,* and *In Dubious Battle* are often petty and ignorant individuals; the ranchers in *The Octopus* part with their scruples to pursue their objectives; and the laborers in *The Iron Heel* and *In Dubious Battle* commit acts of violence that call into question the nature of their aspirations. In these depictions, Norris, London, and Steinbeck primarily emphasize the conditions that have contributed to such effects. For instance, Norris frames McTeague's slaying of Trina by reiterating the economic motifs associated with the couple's relationship, which establishes his brutality as the product of his monetary deprivation. In "The Apostate," Johnny is physically and intellectually stunted as a result of his labor in addition to the fact that his education was curtailed so he could enter the workforce. Norris, London, and Steinbeck further contextualize their protagonists' conduct as predictable results of an institutional structure that does not provide any means of redress for their grievances. In *The Octopus,* the ranchers implement the bribery scheme after they discover that the legislative bodies meant to regulate the railroads instead serve their interests; further, the workers' violence in *The Iron Heel* and *In Dubious Battle* occurs in response to the practices of the powerful. These portrayals reinforce that the responsibility for such consequences originates within the socioeconomic system itself, while the alteration of this framework could lead to different outcomes for working people.

Toward this end, these works suggest that the transformation of the socioeconomic order depends on a change in consciousness from the individualistic concerns that have long governed American life to embrace a more collective vision. In *The Octopus,* this growth is discernible through Annixter, who transcends his selfish impulses and learns to consider the needs of others. This newfound interest appears first in his relationship with Hilma Tree and then through his attempts to help Dyke's family, with the implication that Annixter's progression would have continued if not for his death. His viewpoint mirrors that of Jim Casy and Ma Joad, who attempt to balance the welfare of the group with that of individuals. This outlook emerges through Casy's decision to take the blame for attacking a police officer to prevent Tom's arrest, and Steinbeck reinforces this idea through the former preacher's reemergence as a labor leader. Ma Joad prioritizes the well-being of others when she includes Casy in the Joads' journey and later shares the family's meager food with the hungry children in the camp. These characters offer a strategy for easing the disparities within dominant society through the formulation of a collective consciousness that leads to the necessary action to promote common objectives. In *The Iron Heel,* Avis Everhard showcases a similar development. She transcends her privileged class position after witnessing the plight of the working class, which causes her to become a committed revolutionary. This intellectual progression exhibits the necessary trajectory for the readers of naturalist fiction, who should develop a broader awareness of injustice, realize that they have common cause with the victims of injustice, and ultimately work to ameliorate the sources of their plight.

Norris, London, and Steinbeck reinforce this theme by portraying the characters' attempts to address inequitable circumstances, which emerge through both the exertions of individuals that inevitably lead to failure and the collective efforts that have a greater probability of eventual success. *McTeague,* "The Apostate," and *Martin Eden* represent the former category, focusing on protagonists who are concerned only with their own future prospects rather than the conditions facing the majority. *The Octopus* and *In Dubious Battle* express a similar problem. Although both works feature people joining together through the league and the party, these small groups prioritize their financial interests over the broader constituencies that also suffer under the existing socioeconomic structure. In these novels, the defiant conduct of the principals ultimately engenders their demise, yet these results do not signify the futility of struggle and instead articulate the need for broader resistance. London and Steinbeck illustrate the forms that this opposition might take. *The Iron Heel* depicts the collective action that would allow laborers to ultimately remake America for the benefit of all workers, while the victory of the Oligarchy offers a cautionary tale of what might occur if individuals do not find common cause. "The Dream of Debs" presents the general strike as a means of enabling labor to destabilize the hierarchies that have governed American life, with the conclusion of the story indicating that such endeavors must not stop short of the complete transformation of the economic system. *The Grapes of Wrath* also demonstrates the necessity of such struggles. The Joads challenge the prerogatives of private wealth and seek to diminish their adverse effects through acts of compassion, and the undertakings of the migrant family denote the value of concerted action as a vehicle for the downtrodden to combat institutions that misuse their authority. In portraying broader challenges to economic power, Norris, London, and Steinbeck display the resistance that could enable the working class to rectify the power imbalance within dominant society.

The social criticism in these works is strengthened by their artistry, which reinforces the immediate causes of injustice yet also creates greater aesthetic and philosophical complexity. In *McTeague*, Norris undergirds his representation of avarice through motifs of gold and consumption, which are unified through the dentist's gilded molar, to connect his occupation to the greed theme. Steinbeck utilizes symbols associated with the causative agents, evident through the tractors in *The Grapes of Wrath*, which exemplify the societal forces responsible for displacing the poor, or the immediate practices of the powerful, manifest through the destruction of oranges to increase prices. *The Octopus* provides a similar depiction of mechanization through the railroad, which thwarts the ranchers' ambitions. London largely avoids the symbolism of Norris and Steinbeck, instead employing imagery that expresses the constraints responsible for shaping his protagonists, such as the references to mechanization that frame Johnny's exploitation in "The Apostate." Norris, London, and Steinbeck often buttress the main ideas of their fiction through pervasive animal imagery that conveys the principals' struggle for survival. Through such constructs, Norris emphasizes McTeague's reversion due to economic pressures and indicates the ranchers' limited agency in *The Octopus*. London's utilization of such patterns in "The Dream of Debs" underscores the devolution of the ruling class, whereas this imagery in "The Apostate" reflects the loss of Johnny's humanity. Steinbeck's use of similar structures in *The Grapes of Wrath* and *In Dubious Battle* challenges the belief that the laborers are lesser life forms, instead positing that they have been reduced to their subordinate state by the privileged. These elements register the consequences that result from an inequitable economic system, which signal the need to change the underlying causes of injustice to prevent such outcomes.

The works of Norris, London, and Steinbeck remain relevant because they portray issues that continue to shape life in the United States despite the gains for the general population since the 1930s. Although American workers made considerable advances after World War II, this progress resulted from unique historical circumstances: the United States had abundant manufacturing jobs, high marginal tax rates that fueled robust federal spending and reduced inequality, and strict financial regulations that maintained a stable economy.[1] These conditions do not reflect the current situation in the United States. For instance, U.S. manufacturing employment has declined from nearly 19.6 million in 1979 to 11.6 million in 2011 as businesses have moved production overseas.[2] Approximately 1,276 of these positions were purged each day from 2000 to 2012, with companies closing 66,486 factories during this period.[3] There has been a recent resurgence in the manufacturing sector, yet these new jobs are not like the ones that fueled the postwar economic boom, which have been replaced by low-wage positions that often lack union representation and thereby do not offer the same opportunities for mobility.[4] In addition, the tax structure has also changed significantly. From the 1950s through the early 1980s, the maximum tax rate was as high as 94 percent of total compensation; however, the taxes of the uppermost quintile have declined to 39.6 percent, and with deductions, these individuals can pay as little as 16.6 percent.[5] The loss of this revenue has led to cuts in the programs, including components of the New Deal and the Great Society, that once enabled Americans to attain economic security.[6] Finally, the regulations imposed after the Great Depression to prevent another market collapse, such as the Glass-Steagall Act of 1933, were eliminated. As a result, large banks were once again able to engage in risky investments and loans, which caused a global recession in 2008.[7]

As a result of these developments, American society exhibits many of the same problems that appeared in works of American naturalism, including the return of monopoly ownership. According to the Federal Reserve, four banks now control nearly half of all American banking assets, and this figure has increased dramatically since 1990, when the five largest financial institutions possessed under 10 percent of assets, which is comparable to the percentage that Wells Fargo, the third largest entity, has today.[8] The wave of mergers is not limited to the banking industry. As of 2019, three firms control about 80 percent of mobile telecommunications; three companies issue 95 percent of credit card accounts; four airlines provide 70 percent of domestic flights; and four conglomerates are responsible for 85 percent of the sales of corn seed and 75 percent of soy bean seed, up from 60 percent and 50 percent, respectively, in 2000.[9] This concentration has a negative impact on the working class. According to Sally Hubbard from the Open Markets Institute: "Market concentration causes wages to stagnate because it reduces competition for labor. Companies can pay their employees less without having to worry about losing them to competitors. One study found a 17% decline in wages when a labor market goes from the 25th percentile to the 75th percentile in concentration."[10] Through this command over essential resources and industries, these corporations have the ability to determine the fiscal destiny of the nation at the expense of the general population, a situation that parallels the role of monopolies during the times of Norris, London, and Steinbeck.

The continued relevance of naturalist fiction manifests through the rampant economic inequality in modern America, which has reached levels that have not been seen since the early twentieth century. In 1928, 1 percent of the population received nearly 24 percent of income, and this figure declined to 8.9 percent by 1976 yet reached 23.5 percent in 2007.[11] Further, a study from the Congressional Budget Office found that though earnings rose by almost 20 percent for the bottom fifth of the population from 1979 to 2007, the top quintile saw their remuneration swell by 65 percent, with the highest 1 percent realizing an increase of 275 percent, which prompted economist Josh Bivens to assert that "we have now returned to Gilded Age levels of inequality."[12] These gains have correlated with a dramatic expansion in the assets held by those in upper-income brackets as the top 1 percent possesses 39.6 percent of the wealth, while 20 percent has 89.9 percent; in fact, the 3 richest Americans own more than the bottom 160 million individuals combined.[13] These disparities were exacerbated by the Great Recession of 2008. While the net worth of the average American household declined by 36 percent from 2003 to 2013, the wealth of those in the 95th percentile increased by 14 percent during this period.[14] During the early years of the recovery, from 2009 to 2012, the incomes of the top 1 percent grew by 31.4 percent, which equals 95 percent of the total gain during this time, and this group now receives 24 percent of annual compensation.[15] These developments have caused the United States to become, once again, a two-tiered society that concentrates resources among a minority of the population as the advancements made by previous generations continue to erode.

This increasing inequality has resulted in significant economic deprivation in America, which also harks back to the concerns of naturalist fiction. From 1980 to 2014, as the incomes of the top 1 percent grew by 194 percent, the number of people living in poverty in the United States grew from nearly 29.3 million to 46.7 million.[16] Even though this figure decreased to 38.1 million, or 11.8 percent of the population, in 2018, the poverty threshold misrepresents the full extent of economic deprivation in America because the current poverty line is calculated by multiplying a subsistence food budget by three and totals $26,220 for a family of four.[17] By contrast, most industrialized nations set the poverty threshold at half of median disposable income, and using this measure, the Organization for Economic Cooperation and Development estimated that 17.8 percent of Americans were poor in 2019, which is significantly higher than other industrialized countries.[18] Further, many individuals above these poverty thresholds remain close to financial calamity. One study from the Pew Charitable Trusts found that 55 percent of households did not have the savings to replace income for one month, while another noted that of the respondents who had worried about their finances in the previous year, 71 percent were concerned about having enough money to cover regular expenses.[19] In fact, the Federal Reserve discovered that nearly 40 percent of Americans could not cover an expense of four hundred dollars and that they would need to either sell something to raise funds or borrow the money.[20] Economic insecurity creates serious consequences. The impoverished are more likely to commit and be the victims of both violent and property crimes, and they have lower life expectancy as the affluent live ten to fifteen years longer than the poorest Americans.[21] The persistence of poverty in the richest country the world has ever known indicates that the United States has failed to meet its obligations to the most vulnerable.

These developments have produced a social order characterized by limited advancement contrary to conventional formulations of the American Dream. Lawrence Mishel asserts that "most families are stuck in place while economic growth passes them by. In this respect, then, reality does not match the dream. Mobility—movement among economic classes—is far more restricted than in the opportunity-rich ideal of the American Dream. Of course, some families do move up and down the income scale, but most maintain their relative positions, meaning that relative to other families in their age cohort, they remain at or near the income or wealth position in which they started out."[22] Current research indicates both that people's socioeconomic stations are relatively fixed throughout their lifetimes and that the financial growth since the 1970s has not engendered significant intragenerational mobility. In their analysis of twenty-five- to forty-four-year-olds between 1994 and 2004, Gregory Acs and Seth Zimmerman observed that 54.6 percent of those who started in the lowest quintile were still there ten years later and that 80.1 percent did not leave the bottom two-fifths.[23] By contrast, only 8.8 percent reached the middle, 7.6 percent made it to the fourth, and 3.5 percent arrived at the top.[24] These results illustrate that advancement has largely ceased for working people as the United States often confines individuals to the economic position of their birth.

Further, studies that explore fluctuations from one generation to another substantiate the correspondence between a person's eventual rank and the status of their parents. Tom Hertz followed a representative sample of American children from 1968 to 2001, discovering that only 1 percent of youths from the poorest families were able to enter the upper 5 percent of income distribution, and those from the middle had a greater chance of ending up in a lower position as of moving to an elevated one.[25] When the Pew Charitable Trusts examined this group again in 2009, the organization observed that 43 percent of Americans born into the lowest quintile remained there as adults, 70 percent stayed below the midpoint, and only 4 percent arrived at the top.[26] This low degree of economic progress is also evident through intergenerational elasticity (IGE), a measure of the correlation between the wages of parents and those of their offspring, with zero indicating complete mobility and one showing none. The Pew Charitable Trusts found an IGE of .52 for men and .47 for women in the United States.[27] These figures suggest that although upward movement among classes is possible, significant gains are unlikely for those in the bottom quintile. Mishel claims that at an IGE of .5, these children have less than a 60 percent probability of earnings beyond the lowest fifth by adulthood, 22.5 percent of exceeding the median, and only 4.5 percent of reaching the highest bracket.[28] These statistical findings provide a parallel illustration of the limited opportunities over generations and reflect the circumstances that feature in the fiction of Norris, London, and Steinbeck.

The novels of Frank Norris, Jack London, and John Steinbeck call attention to concerns that continue to animate life in the United States. Despite the fact that these writers drew on specific events within precise temporal settings, their texts depict struggles for justice that cannot be confined to a particular historical moment since workers continue to wage the same battles. For this reason, an examination of naturalism in terms of its social criticism supplies an important means to engage with a major literary movement, one that speaks to the tensions of the present through related concerns of the past. Through concentrating on the causative agents that mold the outcomes available to working people, these authors provide a constructive framework to address important issues by focusing not on the failings of individuals or the operations of natural laws but on the practices of dominant institutions.

Further, naturalists display the underlying causes of pressing societal ills that can be overcome through popular pressure. While their characters' resistance cannot alter inequitable conditions, Norris, London, and Steinbeck convey the necessity of these conflicts with the implication that they could facilitate meaningful change if enacted on a broader scale. Through these representations, Norris, London, and Steinbeck express both the necessity for and possibility of creating a more egalitarian society that does not engender the human consequences portrayed in their work. These ideas comprise the enduring contribution of naturalism to American culture.

NOTES

INTRODUCTION

1. Frank Norris, "The Novel with a 'Purpose,'" *World's Work* 4 (May 1902), 2117–19; reprinted in *The Literary Criticism of Frank Norris,* ed. Donald Pizer (Austin: University of Texas Press, 1964), 91.

2. Ibid., 93.

3. Jack London, introduction to *The Cry for Justice,* ed. Upton Sinclair (1915; repr., New York: Barricade Books, 1996), 9.

4. John Steinbeck, "Acceptance," *Nobel Lectures: Literature, 1901–1967,* ed. Horst Frenz (Amsterdam: Elsevier, 1969), 575–76.

5. Quoted in John Steinbeck, *Working Days: The Journals of "The Grapes of Wrath," 1938–1941,* ed. Robert DeMott (New York: Penguin, 1989), 152.

6. Scholars have traditionally dated naturalism from Stephen Crane's *Maggie: A Girl of the Streets* (1893) to Richard Wright's *Native Son* (1940). However, Eric Carl Link's *The Vast and Terrible Drama: American Literary Naturalism in the Nineteenth Century* (2004) expands the boundaries of naturalism through tracing its debt to American romance instead of overemphasizing the influence of realism. Link contends that "lessons taught to the American naturalists by the literary realists, rather than dominating naturalist fiction and dictating genre and convention, were instead used to revise and revive a tradition of American romance that has its roots in the antebellum writings of Charles Brockden Brown, Nathaniel Hawthorne, Edgar Allan Poe, and Herman Melville" and that "our understanding of literary naturalism is enhanced when we take a closer look at how literary naturalism manipulates in positive ways some of the tradition it inherits from earlier authors" (xiv–xv). Link's framework broadens the scope of naturalism to include earlier works, such as Rebecca Harding Davis's *Life in the Iron Mills* (1861) and Oliver Wendell Holmes Sr.'s *Elsie Venner* (1861), and also incorporates utopian fiction, such as Edward Bellamy's *Looking Backward* (1888) and Charlotte Perkins Gilman's *Herland* (1915). This approach creates further avenues to explore the naturalist novel as a vehicle to engage with dominant social problems.

7. Louis J. Budd observes that the "naturalists were the first cohort to consider without surprise the processes that the Civil War had made dominant. They recognized that industrialism

and urbanism, now clearly irreversible, were accelerating; iron mills had expanded into steel mills run by corporations scheming toward monopoly" and that "the conflict between capital and labor was getting bloodier at the seams of a hardened class structure" ("The American Background," in *The Cambridge Companion to American Realism and Naturalism,* ed. Donald Pizer [New York: Cambridge University Press, 1995], 42.)

8. Malcolm Cowley, "Not Men: A Natural History of American Naturalism," *Kenyon Review* 9, no. 3, 1947, 414–35; reprinted in *Documents of American Realism and Naturalism,* ed. Donald Pizer (Carbondale: Southern Illinois University Press, 1998), 235.

9. Ibid., 237.

10. V. L. Parrington, "Naturalism in American Fiction," in Pizer, *Documents of American Realism and Naturalism,* 212. Parrington perceives ideas of social criticism as antithetical to his understanding of naturalism, complaining that Émile Zola, for instance, "abandoned his principles and became a reformer, attacking the church, the capitalistic order, etc.," and noting that this "was the failing of the first group of American naturalists—Frank Norris, Robert Harrick, Jack London" (213).

11. Donald Pizer, *Realism and Naturalism in Nineteenth-Century American Literature* (Carbondale: Southern Illinois University Press, 1964), 31.

12. Donald Pizer, *Twentieth-Century American Literary Naturalism: An Interpretation.* (Carbondale: Southern Illinois University Press, 1982), 13.

13. Walter Benn Michaels, *The Gold Standard and the Logic of Naturalism* (Berkeley: University of California Press, 1987), 27.

14. Ira Wells, *Fighting Words: Polemics and Social Change in Literary Naturalism* (Tuscaloosa: University of Alabama Press, 2013), 11.

15. Cecelia Tichi, *Jack London: A Writer's Fight for a Better America* (Chapel Hill: University of North Carolina Press, 2015), 3–4.

16. Perry Westbrook, *Free Will and Determinism in American Literature* (Madison, NJ: Associated University Presses, 1979), ix.

17. Émile Zola, *The Experimental Novel,* trans. Belle M. Sherman (New York: Haskell House, 1964), 31.

18. George Wilbur Meyer, "The Original Social Purpose of the Naturalist Novel," *Sewanee Review* 50, no. 4 (1942): 570.

19. Nelson Lichtenstein, Susan Strasser, and Roy Rosenzweig, eds., *Who Built America? Working People and the Nation's Economy, Politics, Culture, and Society* (New York: Worth, 2000), 69.

20. Cal Jillson, *Pursuing the American Dream: Opportunity and Exclusion over Four Centuries* (Lawrence: University Press of Kansas, 2004), 122.

21. Alan Trachtenberg, *The Incorporation of America: Culture and Society in the Gilded Age* (New York: Hill and Wang, 1982), 90.

22. Two studies have examined how conditions in California influenced works related to American naturalism: Mary Lawlor's *Recalling the Wild: Naturalism and the Closing of the American West* (2000); and Nicolas S. Witschi's *Traces of Gold: California's Natural Resources and the Claim to Realism in Western American Literature* (2001). Lawlor considers the works of Frank Norris, Jack London, Stephen Crane, and Willa Cather against the romanticized narratives of

the West in American literature. Lawlor, however, provides little discussion of the historical, economic, and political developments in California that serve as the basis for the fiction of London and Norris. Witschi focuses on how the conditions produced by the gold rush influenced California writers, emphasizing the importance of this event to representations of the West and the impact of such texts, especially those of Bret Harte, on American realism rather than the economic themes of naturalist authors.

23. Frank Norris, "An Opening for Novelists: Great Opportunities for Fiction Writers in San Francisco," *Wave* 16, May 22, 1897, 7; reprinted in Pizer, *Literary Criticism of Frank Norris,* 30.

24. Joseph R. McElrath Jr. and Jesse S. Crisler, *Frank Norris: A Life* (Urbana: University of Illinois Press, 2006), 341.

25. Howard Zinn, *A People's History of the United States* (New York: Harper, 1980), 251; and Katherine Adams, *Progressive Politics and the Training of America's Persuaders* (Mahwah, NJ: Lawrence Erlbaum Associates, 1999), 17.

26. Steven T. Dhondt, "'There Is a Good Time Coming': Jack London's Spirit of Proletarian Revolt,'" *Jack London Newsletter* 3, no. 1 (1970): 27–28.

27. Charles N. Watson Jr., *The Novels of Jack London: A Reappraisal* (Madison: University of Wisconsin Press, 1983), 103–12.

28. Jackson J. Benson and Anne Loftis, "John Steinbeck and Farm Labor Unionization: The Background of *In Dubious Battle,*" *American Literature* 52, no. 2 (1980): 202.

29. Frances Fox Piven and Richard Cloward, *Poor People's Movements: Why They Succeed, How They Fail* (New York: Vintage, 1979), 121.

30. DeMott, introduction to Steinbeck, *Working Days,* xxxviii–xlii.

31. Frank Norris, "Zola as Romantic Writer," *Wave* 15, June 27, 1896, 3; reprinted in Pizer, *Literary Criticism of Frank Norris,* 72.

32. Ibid.

33. Naturalists present agency in its philosophical sense, which refers to a person's ability to act, rather than a sociological one, which refers to a person's ability to act in accordance with their free will since naturalists believe that the operations of the will are products of external forces. Ian F. Roberts observes that "free will is most logically and meaningfully defined as the ability to act as one wishes, without denying the fact that one's wishes are themselves determined by one's upbringing, genetics, and circumstances. Hence, a free act is not one that is undetermined, but simply one that is not constrained by certain types of coercion or psychological compulsion" (Ian F. Roberts, "Determinism, Free Will, and Moral Responsibility in American Literary Naturalism," in *The Oxford Handbook of American Literary Naturalism,* ed. Keith Newlin [Oxford: Oxford University Press, 2011], 125).

34. Cecelia Tichi, "The Facts of Life and Literature," in *The Oxford Handbook of Jack London,* ed. Jay Williams (Oxford: Oxford University Press, 2017), 35.

35. Developing the ideas that became the American Dream, John Smith noted that God had created a particularly rich and fertile land, observing that the "mildness of the air, the fertility of the soil, and the situation of the rivers are so propitious to the nature and use of man, as no place is more convenient for pleasure, profit, and man's sustenance" (quoted in Jillson, *Pursuing the American Dream,* 24). This image also appealed to the Puritans, who perceived the Massachusetts Bay Colony as a New Eden, and this view had its clearest expression in "A

Model of Christian Charity" (1630), in which John Winthrop asserted that "we shall be as a city upon a hill, the eyes of all people are upon us. So that if we shall deal falsely with our God in this work we have under-taken and so cause Him to withdraw His present help from us, we shall be made a story and a by-word through the world" (in *Pragmatism and Religion: Classical Sources and Original Essays,* ed. Stuart Rosenbaum [Urbana: University of Illinois Press, 2003], 23). Winthrop argued that the inhabitants of his "city upon a hill" would be a unit joined by the recognition of God's spirit in each other and that all inhabitants must work together for the common good. The Quakers also emphasized a union between the concerns of terrestrial life and the performance of one's religious duty, with material gain as a reward for adhering to moral strictures. As the anonymous writer of *Planter's Speech to His Neighbors* (1684) noted, spiritual peace would result in financial progress "as *trees* are transplanted from one soil to another, to render them more thriving and better bearers, so . . . in peace and secure retirement, under the bountiful protection of God, and in the lap of the least adulterated nature, might everyone the better improve his talent, and bring forth more plenteous fruits, to the glory of God, and pub-lic welfare of the whole creation" (quoted in Frederick B. Tolles, *Meeting House and Counting House: The Quaker Merchants of Colonial Philadelphia, 1682–1763* [New York: Norton, 1963], 33–34). In linking economic benefits to spiritual concerns, the Puritans and Quakers introduced the key concepts of industry, frugality, and prudence that constituted the basis of what schol-ars commonly associate with the American Dream, precepts that have remained at the core of individual and national progress.

36. James Truslow Adams, *The Epic of America* (Garden City, NY: Blue Ribbon Books, 1931), 404.

37. Jennifer Hochschild, *Facing Up to the American Dream: Race, Class, and the Soul of the Nation* (Princeton: Princeton University Press, 1995), 4.

38. Quoted in Malcolm J. Rohrbough, *Days of Gold: The California Gold Rush and the Amer-ican Nation* (Berkeley: University of California Press, 1997), 193.

39. H. W. Brands, *The Age of Gold* (New York: Doubleday, 2002), 442.

1. TWISTED FROM THE ORDINARY

1. Joseph R. McElrath Jr., *Frank Norris Revisited* (New York: Twayne, 1992), 2–3.

2. Ibid., 36.

3. Lawrence E. Hussman, *Harbingers of a Century: The Novels of Frank Norris* (New York: Peter Lang, 1999), 29.

4. For discussions of determinism in *McTeague,* see Donald Pizer, *The Novels of Frank Nor-ris* (New York: Haskell House, 1973), 59–85; Lewis Fried, "The Golden Brotherhood of *McTe-ague,*" *Zeitschrift Für Anglistic und Amerikanistik* 23 (1975): 36–40; George M. Spangler, "The Structure of *McTeague,*" in *Critical Essays on Frank Norris,* ed. Don Graham (Boston: G. K. Hall, 1980), 88–98; Thomas C. Ware, "'Gold to Airy Thinness Beat': The Midas Touch in Frank Nor-ris's *McTeague,*" *Interpretations* 13, no. 1 (1981): 39–47; David McGlynn, "*McTeague*'s Gilded Prison," *Rocky Mountain Review* 62, no. 1 (Spring 2008): 25–44; and Mohamed Zayani, "When Culinary Desire Meets Pecuniary Desire: Passions for Drinks, Appetites for Food, and Orgies of Gold in Frank Norris' *McTeague,*" *Excavatio* 12 (1999): 207–15. Many discussions of *McTe-*

ague have centered on biological determinism, most notably in the formulations of Pizer and Spangler. Pizer argues that "Norris's theme is that man's racial atavism (particularly his brute sexual desires) and man's individual family heritage (alcoholic degeneracy in McTeague's case) can combine as a force toward reversion, toward a return to the emotions and instincts of man's animal past" (*Realism and Naturalism in Nineteenth-Century American Literature* [Carbondale: Southern Illinois University Press, 1966], 16). While such readings have expanded the range of ideas associated with *McTeague,* the animal impulses identified by Pizer and Spangler are triggered by pressures within the characters' environment, which initiates their deterioration. Fried, McGlynn, Ware, and Zayani focus largely on the economic forces operating in the narrative, yet they do not examine the central position of the American Dream in the narrative and the impact of this concept on Norris's handling of economic determinism.

5. Frank Norris to Isaac F. Marcosson, November 22, 1899, in *Frank Norris: Collected Letters,* ed. Jesse S. Crisler (San Francisco: Book Club of California, 1986), 93.

6. Despite his year in France and his fluency in the language, Norris did not appear to have discovered the fiction of Émile Zola until after returning to the United States and enrolling in the University of California in 1889. Norris did not encounter Zola through his coursework at the university as his courses on French literature omitted this author (Joseph R. McElrath Jr. and Jesse S. Crisler, *Frank Norris: A Life* [Urbana: University of Illinois Press, 2006], 109–10).

Some of Norris's classmates, however, recalled seeing him about campus "with a French paper edition of Zola under his arm" and noted that he "was always ready to stop and defend the novelist, who to him embodied strength and truth but to most of them was of interest chiefly because of his obscenity" (quoted in McElrath and Crisler, *Frank Norris,* 151). For further discussion, see Christine Harvey, "Dating Frank Norris' Reading of Zola," *Resources for American Literary Study* 24, no. 2 (1998): 187–206.

7. Frank Norris, "Zola as Romantic Writer," *Wave* 15, June 27, 1896, 3; reprinted in Pizer, *Literary Criticism of Frank Norris,* 72.

8. Earlier in "Zola as Romantic Writer," Norris asserts that Howells's works contain accurate descriptions of "the smaller details of every-day life, things that are likely to happen between lunch and supper, small passions, restricted emotions, dramas of the reception room, tragedies of an afternoon call, crises involving cups of tea" (71).

9. Frank Norris, "A Plea for Romantic Fiction," *Boston Evening Transcript,* December 18, 1901, 14; reprinted in Pizer, *Literary Criticism of Frank Norris,* 76.

10. Norris, "Plea for Romantic Fiction," 78.

11. Frank Norris, "The Novel with a 'Purpose,'" *World's Work* 4 (May 1902): 2117–19; reprinted in Pizer, *Literary Criticism of Frank Norris,* 90.

12. Ibid., 91.

13. Frank Norris, "The Responsibilities of the Novelist," *Critic* 41 (December 1902): 537–40; reprinted in Pizer, *Literary Criticism of Frank Norris,* 97.

14. Frank Norris to William Dean Howells, March 28, 1899, in Crisler, *Frank Norris: Collected Letters,* 73.

15. Frank Norris, "'The Literature of the West': A Reply to W. R. Lighton," *Boston Evening Transcript,* January 8, 1902, 7; reprinted in Pizer, *Literary Criticism of Frank Norris,* 107.

16. Norris, "'Literature of the West,'" 106.

17. Kevin Starr, *California: A History* (New York: Modern Library, 2005), 80.

18. Quoted in Malcolm J. Rohrbough, *Days of Gold: The California Gold Rush and the American Nation* (Berkeley: University of California Press, 1997), 27.

19. Quoted in ibid., 26. The popular imagination has long equated California with the possibility of prosperity framed by abundant natural resources. In 1863, Edward Everett Hale sent a paper to the American Antiquarian Society, which was republished in the *Atlantic Monthly* in March 1864 and identified the source of "California" in Garci Ordóñez de Montalvo's *Las Sergas de Esplandián* (1510). The work chronicled the exploits of Esplandián along with the Californians, who resided on an island of immense wealth and fought with golden weapons. In 1533, a party of Spanish explorers under the command of Hernán Cortés landed on what they believed to be this island in the Pacific Ocean. After 1539, they named their discovery "California" after this locale, and they hoped to find the gold and precious stones described in Montalvo's romance. Cortés arrived in Baja California at La Paz in 1535 and spent two years trying to found a colony due to the prevalent belief that the region contained El Dorado, the fabled city of gold. When this search proved futile, Cortés turned his attention to the North and sent his lieutenant, Francisco Ulloa, to explore the sea between Mexico and the alleged island of California in the hopes of discovering the seven cities of Cíbola. This conception of El Dorado played a central role in the gold rush, with its metaphoric suggestion of being anyplace where fortunes could be rapidly acquired.

20. Starr, *California,* 80.

21. Hubert Howe Bancroft, *The Works of Hubert Howe Bancroft,* 39 vols. (San Francisco: History Co., 1882–90), 23:118.

22. Starr, *California,* 81.

23. Ibid., 83.

24. Walton Bean and James J. Rawls, *California: An Interpretive History* (New York: McGraw-Hill, 1983), 95.

25. Rohrbough, *Days of Gold,* 205–6.

26. Quoted in H. W. Brands, *The Age of Gold* (New York: Doubleday, 2002), 211–12.

27. Mary Hill, *Gold: The California Story* (Berkeley: University of California Press, 1999), 56.

28. David Vaught, *After the Gold Rush: Tarnished Dreams in the Sacramento Valley* (Baltimore: Johns Hopkins University Press, 2007), 5–6.

29. Quoted in Kevin Starr, *Americans and the California Dream, 1850–1915* (Oxford: Oxford University Press, 1973), 55.

30. Quoted in ibid., 56.

31. John Boessenecker, *Gold Dust and Gunsmoke* (New York: John Wiley & Sons, 1999), 324.

32. Ibid., 323–24.

33. Starr, *Americans and the California Dream,* 65–66.

34. Glenn Porter, *The Rise of Big Business, 1860–1920* (Wheeling, IL: Harlan Davidson, 2006), 4.

35. Ray Ginger, *The Age of Excess: The United States from 1877 to 1914* (New York: Macmillan, 1975), 20; and Walter Licht, *Industrializing America: The Nineteenth Century* (Baltimore: Johns Hopkins University Press, 1995), xvi.

36. "Twenty-Nine Fatal Wounds," *San Francisco Examiner,* October 10, 1893, 12.

37. "Collins' Shirt Found," *San Francisco Chronicle,* October 12, 1893, 4.

38. "He Was Born for the Rope," *San Francisco Examiner,* October 14, 1893, 8.

39. Ibid., 8.

40. Frank Norris, *A Novelist in the Making: A Collection of Student Themes and the Novels "Blix" and "Vandover and the Brute,"* ed. James D. Hart (Cambridge: Harvard University Press, 1970), 88–89.

41. Frank Norris, *McTeague: A Story of San Francisco,* ed. Donald Pizer (1899; repr., New York: Norton, 1997), 5–6. All further quotations from this edition will be cited parenthetically in the text.

42. Hugh Dawson, "McTeague as Ethnic Stereotype," *American Literary Realism* 20, no. 1 (1987): 34–44.

43. For a discussion of the imagery in *McTeague,* see Suzy Bernstein Goldman, "*McTeague:* The Imagistic Network," *Western American Literature* 7, no. 2 (1972): 83–99.

44. Keith S. Sheppard, "A New Note for McTeague's Canary," *Western American Literature* 9, no. 3 (1974): 217.

45. Nan Morelli-White, "The Damnation of *McTeague:* Frank Norris's Morality Play," *Frank Norris Studies* 13 (1992): 5.

46. McGlynn, "*McTeague*'s Gilded Prison," 26.

47. Norris found the inspiration for this object in the large gilded molar that hung outside the offices of Dr. L. A. Teague, a prominent dentist in San Francisco who practiced at the corner of Geary and Kearney during the 1890s. For identifications of other elements of San Francisco that Norris incorporated into the novel, see Robert D. Lundy, "The Making of *McTeague* and *The Octopus"* (PhD diss., Berkeley: University of California, 1956), 145–53; and Jesse S. Crisler, "A Critical and Textual Study of Frank Norris's *McTeague"* (PhD diss., University of South Carolina, 1973), 39–62.

48. Spangler, "Structure of *McTeague,"* 88–89.

49. For further discussion of the lottery, see Fried, "Golden Brotherhood of *McTeague,"* 38–39.

50. Don Graham, *The Fiction of Frank Norris: The Aesthetic Context* (Columbia: University of Missouri Press, 1978), 57.

51. Burton J. Bledstein, *The Culture of Professionalism: The Middle Class and the Development of Higher Education in America* (New York: Norton, 1976), 84.

52. For contrasting viewpoints, see Maria F. Brandt, "'For His Own Satisfaction': Eliminating the New Woman Figure in *McTeague,"* *American Transcendental Quarterly* 18, no. 1 (2004): 5–23; and Denise H. Long, "A Dentist No More: The Destruction of Masculinity in *McTeague,"* *Midamerica* 32 (2005): 67–77. These articles provide valuable readings of *McTeague* by examining how the protagonist's violence toward Trina results from an inversion of patriarchal gender roles, though Norris often prioritizes the economic context of McTeague's brutality.

53. In his early review of *McTeague,* Howells argued that Norris's "one folly is the insistence on the love-making of those silly elders" ("A Case in Point," in *Criticism and Fiction and Other Essays,* ed. Clara Marburg Kirk and Rudolf Kirk [New York: New York University Press, 1959], 282), an argument seconded by Pizer, who finds this episode to be "thematically and dramati-

cally weak" (*Novels of Frank Norris,* 74). For further discussion of this subplot, see Donna M. Campbell, "Frank Norris' 'Drama of a Broken Teacup': The Old Grannis–Miss Baker Plot in *McTeague," American Literary Realism* 26, no. 1 (1993): 40–49.

54. McGlynn, "*McTeague's* Gilded Prison," 34.

55. Graham, *Fiction of Frank Norris,* 61–62. Graham devotes primary attention to the lithograph and its reflection of a traditional world in the context of his discussion of Norris's aesthetic sensibilities with only a secondary emphasis on the other elements in relation to his economic themes.

56. Crisler, *Frank Norris: Collected Letters,* 73. For discussions of the ending of *McTeague,* see George K. Johnson, "The Frontier behind Frank Norris's *McTeague," Huntington Library Quarterly* 26 (1962): 91–104; and William J. Hug, "*McTeague* as Metafiction? Frank Norris' Parodies of Bret Harte and the Dime Novel," *Western American Literature* 26, no. 3 (1991): 219–28. For explanations about how the concluding chapters operate within the context of the structural patterns of the novel, see Graham, *Fiction of Frank Norris,* 60–65; Pizer, *Novels of Frank Norris,* 81–82; and Hussman, *Harbingers of a Century,* 75–79.

57. See Donald Pizer, "The Biological Determinism of *McTeague* in Our Time," *American Literary Realism* 29, no. 2 (1997): 27–32. Pizer argues that recent scholarship in biology and the social sciences offers a partial confirmation of Norris's view in *McTeague.* Pizer effectively addresses the issue of McTeague's inherited alcoholism, examining research that has found a hereditary influence to such behavior. Pizer's claims are less effective in his discussion of the "born criminal." While he cites quite a few studies that discern a genetic link to crime, two of these stress the role of environmental factors in shaping the actions of the individual, which seems to discredit a biological interpretation of criminality (28–29).

2. TENTACLES OF CAPITAL

1. Frank Norris to William Dean Howells, March 28, 1899; and Frank Norris to Harry Manville Wright, April 5, 1899, both in *Frank Norris: Collected Letters,* ed. Jesse S. Crisler (San Francisco: Book Club of California, 1986), 73 and 75.

2. While most studies of the work include a cursory overview of the Mussel Slough tragedy, this subject has seldom been the topic of sustained discussion. For some notable exceptions, see Joseph R. McElrath Jr. and Jesse S. Crisler, *Frank Norris: A Life* (Urbana: University of Illinois Press, 2006), 347–55; and Robert D. Lundy, "The Making of *McTeague* and *The Octopus*" (PhD diss., University of California, Berkeley, 1956), 203–30. For readings that devote primary attention to the social themes of the novel, see George Wilbur Meyer, "A New Interpretation of *The Octopus," College English* 4, no. 6 (1943): 351–59; James K. Folsom, "Social Darwinism or Social Protest? The 'Philosophy' of *The Octopus," Modern Fiction Studies* 8, no. 4 (1963): 393–400; Richard Allan Davison, "Frank Norris and the Arts of Social Criticism," *American Literary Realism* 14, no. 1 (1981): 77–89; and Clare Virginia Eby, "*The Octopus:* Big Business as Art," *American Literary Realism* 26, no. 1 (1994): 33–51. Meyer argues that Norris juxtaposes the immutable world of nature with the excesses of capitalism and highlights the need for reform to create a society that does not violently clash with the natural world. Eby, by contrast, asserts

that the narrative reaches toward an aesthetic informed by, and not opposed to, the present economic system.

3. Carey McWilliams, *Factories in the Field* (1935; repr., Berkeley: University of California Press, 1999), 15–17.

4. Richard J. Orsi, *Sunset Limited: The Southern Pacific Railroad and the Development of the American West, 1850–1930* (Berkeley: University of California Press, 2005), 94–95.

5. "A Collision," *San Francisco Chronicle,* May 12, 1880, 3.

6. "The Settlers vs. the Railway," *San Francisco Chronicle,* May 13, 1880, 3.

7. "Collision," 3.

8. For analyses of Norris's treatment of the Mussel Slough tragedy, see William Deverell, *Railroad Crossing: Californians and the Railroad, 1850–1910* (Berkeley: University of California Press, 1994), 137–48; and Orsi, *Sunset Limited,* 92–104. Deverell states that the "novel's depiction of the circumstances surrounding the outbreak of violence at Mussel Slough is woefully inadequate as history, and it is both unfair and misleading to term the novel a history of that particular conflict" (142), and Orsi asserts that *The Octopus* is "a fanciful, fictional account that bears virtually no resemblance to the actual event" (92). Deverell does not effectively develop his claims about factual issues in Norris's handling of the event, and his argument is marred by misreadings of the text. Orsi provides a more sophisticated account of Mussel Slough, challenging the conventional assumptions about this episode with Norris as a mere spokesman for anti-railroad sentiment. However, Orsi bases his argument on documents from executives that present the actions of the Southern Pacific company in the most favorable light, in stark contrast to coverage in the *Chronicle* and *Examiner.* While Norris compressed the time frame of events and radically altered the geography of the San Joaquin Valley, his representation of the Mussel Slough tragedy coheres with periodical accounts. It is also important to note that Norris was not the first author to write a novel that centered on this conflict, which was also the subject of four other works: William C. Morrow's *Blood Money* (1882); Charles Cyril Post's *Driven from Sea to Sea* (1884); Josiah Royce's *The Feud of Oakville Creek: A Novel of California* (1887); and May Merrill Miller's *First the Blade* (1938). For discussion of these works, see Terry Beers, introduction to *Gunfight at Mussel Slough: Evolution of a Western Myth* (Berkeley: Heyday Books, 2004), 1–35.

9. McElrath and Crisler, *Frank Norris,* 343.

10. Ibid., 341.

11. Lundy, "Making of *McTeague* and *The Octopus,*" 212.

12. Franklin Walker, *Frank Norris: A Biography* (Garden City, NY: Doubleday, Doran, 1932), 286.

13. "Southern Pacific Railroad Completes New Orleans to California Route," *History.com,* November 16, 2019, https://www.history.com/this-day-in-history/southern-pacific-railroad -completes-sunset-route#:~:text=The%20Southern%20Pacific%20Railroad%20completes, rail%20traffic%20to%20the%20Pacific.

14. McWilliams, *Factories in the Field,* 15.

15. Ibid., 17.

16. George Mowry, *The California Progressives* (Berkeley: University of California Press, 1951), 9.

17. Kenneth Howe, "Rise and Fall of a Railroad: Southern Pacific Shaped California," *San Francisco Chronicle,* July 8, 1996, https://www.sfgate.com/business/article/RISE-AND-FALL -OF-A-RAILROAD-Southern-Pacific-2974892.php.

18. Mowry, *California Progressives,* 16.

19. Ibid., 9.

20. Quoted in Walton Bean and James J. Rawls, *California: An Interpretive History* (New York: McGraw-Hill, 1983), 247.

21. Spencer C. Olin, *California's Prodigal Sons: Hiram Johnson and the Progressives, 1911– 1917* (Berkeley: University of California Press, 1968), 4–9.

22. Mowry, *California Progressives,* 18.

23. Ibid.

24. Walter Licht, *Industrializing America: The Nineteenth Century* (Baltimore: Johns Hopkins University Press, 1995), 158; and Naomi R. Lamoreaux, *The Great Merger Movement in American Business, 1895–1904* (London: Cambridge University Press, 1985), 108.

25. Howard Zinn, *A People's History of the United States* (New York: Harper, 1980), 252.

26. Ray Ginger, *The Age of Excess: The United States from 1877 to 1914* (New York: Macmillan, 1975), 97.

27. Matthew Josephson, *The Robber Barons* (New York: Harcourt, 1934).

28. William M. Wiecek, *The Lost World of Classical Legal Thought: Law and Ideology in America, 1889–1937* (Oxford: Oxford University Press, 1998), 147.

29. Lamoreaux, *Great Merger Movement,* 165–66.

30. Licht, *Industrializing America,* 159.

31. Frank Norris, *The Octopus: A Story of California* (1901; repr., New York: Penguin, 1986), 67. All further quotations from this edition will be cited parenthetically in the text.

32. Eby, "*Octopus,*" 42. For further discussion of Norris's use of maps in the narrative, see Leigh Ann Litwiller Berte, "Mapping *The Octopus:* Frank Norris' Naturalist Geography," *American Literary Realism* 37, no. 3 (2005): 202–24.

33. "Collision," 3.

34. Ibid.

35. Kevin Starr, *California: A History* (New York: Modern Library, 2005), 167.

36. For further discussion of the importance of water to both *The Octopus* and California, see Paul Formisano, "Presley's Pauses: Unearthing Force in California's Land and Water Regimes and Frank Norris's *The Octopus,*" *Journal of Ecocriticism* 7 (2015): 1–18.

37. John Locke, *Two Treatises of Civil Government* (1690; repr., London: J. M. Dent, 1991), 130.

38. For further discussions of the ranchers, see Hamlin Garland, "The Work of Frank Norris," *Critic* 42 (1903): 216–18; Meyer, "New Interpretation of *The Octopus,*" 353–55; Donald Pizer, *The Novels of Frank Norris* (New York: Haskell House, 1973), 140–41; and Joseph R. McElrath Jr., "Frank Norris's *The Octopus:* The Christian Ethic as Pragmatic Response," in *Critical Essays on Frank Norris,* ed. Don Graham (Boston: G. K. Hall, 1980), 140–43.

39. Norris differentiates Derrick from his fellow ranchers. Annixter, for instance, advances an alternate conception of nature than Magnus, critiquing his view of the soil as a commodity to be exploited in the service of maximizing returns. Annixter states that Magnus "thinks he's still running his mine, and that the same principles will apply to getting grain out of the earth

as to getting gold. . . . Get the guts out of your land; work it to death; never give it a rest. Never alternate your crop, and then when your soil is exhausted, sit down and roar about hard times" (28–29). Annixter highlights the problems posed for the land as a result of the perspectives that reduce the value of earth to the profits that one can extract from it heedless of the long-term consequences engendered by such undertakings. This passage highlights the need for a reciprocal relationship with the soil, one based on the preservation of resources to engender their continued fertility and growth.

40. John J. Powell, *The Golden State and Its Resources* (San Francisco: Bacon & Co., 1874), 76–77.

41. Ibid., 36.

42. Ibid., 35.

43. For further discussion of freight rates in *The Octopus,* see Robert A. Emery, "Railroad Rates in *The Octopus:* A Literary Footnote," *Journal of Transportation Law, Logistics, and Policy* 64 (1997): 298–304.

44. California Public Utilities Commission, *Biennial Report of the Board of Railroad Commissioners of the State of California* (Sacramento: California State Printing Office, 1896), 378.

45. An article in Norris's notebook contains the information that "a corps of Southern Pacific freight clerks made out the new figures for rates, and were very busy in doing so the past five or six weeks" ("I. Notes," Frank Norris Collection of Papers and Related Materials, BANC MSS C-H 80, Bancroft Library, University of California, Berkeley, 8).

46. J. L. Brown, *The Mussel Slough Tragedy* (n.p.: by the author, 1958), 54.

47. "An Appeal to the People," *Visalia (CA) Weekly Delta,* May 7, 1880, 2.

48. "Collision," 3.

49. "Appeal to the People," 2.

50. McElrath and Crisler, *Frank Norris,* 348.

51. Quoted in Brown, *Mussel Slough Tragedy,* 42.

52. Members of the league were also accused of using intimidation and threats of violence toward those who attempted to gain control over the disputed land. The league and the San Francisco papers denied such claims, with a writer for the *Chronicle* asserting that "parties who have been thought unfriendly to the interests of the settlers have left for fear that their lives are not safe; but there is no good evidence to show that the Settlers' League, as an organization, has warned any one of them to leave, though irresponsible persons may have done so" ("Gloom in Tulare," May 14, 1880, 3). Regarding these allegations, the anonymous correspondent observes that representatives of the league "think that it was the work of those who wished to create public sentiment against the organization and to misrepresent its purpose" (3).

53. Brown, *Mussel Slough Tragedy,* 55.

54. "Tulare and Fresno Settlers," *San Francisco Chronicle,* December 16, 1879, 4.

55. "Tulare Settler," *San Francisco Chronicle,* September 12, 1880, 5.

56. For further discussion of Norris's treatment of political solutions, see James Dorson, "Rates, Romance, and Regulated Monopoly in Frank Norris's *The Octopus," Studies in American Naturalism* 12, no. 1 (2017): 50–69.

57. Frank Norris to Isaac F. Marcosson, November 22, 1899, in Crisler, *Frank Norris: Collected Letters,* 93.

58. Ibid.

59. Norris, "I. Notes," 7.

60. Ibid., 1. Norris may also have drawn on the actions of John Sontag, a former railroad brakeman, and Chris Evans, who were notorious train robbers during the late 1880s and early 1890s. Like Dyke, they were embittered toward the Southern Pacific, dynamited trains, and evaded capture in the surrounding mountains before being apprehended by a posse.

61. Ibid.

62. "The Deadly Feud," *Morning Call* (San Francisco), May 13, 1880, 3.

63. "Tulare's Troubles," *San Francisco Chronicle,* May 13, 1880, 3.

64. Ibid.

65. "Deadly Feud," 3.

66. "The Tulare Tragedy," *San Francisco Examiner,* May 13, 1880, 3.

67. "Deadly Feud," 3; "Tulare's Troubles," 3; and "The Tulare Feud," *San Francisco Examiner,* May 12, 1880, 3.

68. "Deadly Feud," 3.

69. Ibid.

70. Ibid.

71. For further discussion of the role of chance in American naturalism, see Patti Luedecke, "Chance, Positivism, and the Arctic in Frank Norris's *A Man's Woman*," *Studies in American Naturalism* 15, no. 1 (2020): 111–34.

72. "Tulare Tragedy," 3.

73. French claims that *The Octopus* reveals "a transcendent romantic faith in the grand design of a benevolent nature" and that the characters suffer "because of their selfish efforts to thwart nature's benevolent intentions" (*Frank Norris* [New Haven, CT: College and University Press, 1962], 9). Pizer views the work in the context of evolutionary theism as an illustration of the idea that evil "was therefore an inevitable but negligible and transient factor if one kept in view the larger cosmic movement toward good" ("The Concept of Nature in Frank Norris' 'The Octopus,'" *American Quarterly* 14, no. 1 [1962]: 74). For readings that conflate Norris with Presley, see Torsten Pettersson, "Deterministic Acceptance versus Moral Outrage: A Problem of Literary Naturalism in Frank Norris's *The Octopus*," *Orbis Litterarum* 42, no. 1 (1987): 77–95; Thomas Austenfeld, "A Happy Naturalist? Jeremy Bentham and the Cosmic Morality of *The Octopus*," *Studies in American Naturalism* 2, no. 1 (2007): 33–45; and Daniel J. Mrozowski, "How to Kill a Corporation: Frank Norris's *The Octopus* and the Embodiment of American Business," *Studies in American Naturalism* 6, no. 2 (2011): 161–84. These readings largely overlook Norris's use of indirect discourse and the representations of Presley's instability.

74. Joseph R. McElrath Jr., *Frank Norris Revisited* (New York: Twayne, 1992), 100.

75. See Graham, *Fiction of Frank Norris*, 97–104; Davison, "Frank Norris," 77–82; Joseph R. McElrath Jr., "Edwin Markham in Frank Norris's *The Octopus*," *Frank Norris Studies* 13 (1992): 10–11; and Steven Frye, "Presley's Pretense: Irony and Epic Convention in Frank Norris' *The Octopus*," *American Literary Realism* 39, no. 3 (2007): 213–21.

76. "Character Sketches," Frank Norris Collection of Papers and Related Materials, BANC MSS C-H 80, Bancroft Library, University of California, Berkeley, 8.

77. For further discussion of Shelgrim, including how Norris drew on newspaper interviews with Collis P. Huntington in the depiction of his fictional railroad magnate, see Donald Pizer,

"Collis P. Huntington, William S. Rainsford, and the Conclusion of Frank Norris's *The Octopus*," *Studies in American Naturalism* 5, no. 2 (2010): 133–50; and Dennis Drabelle, *The Great American Railroad War: How Ambrose Bierce and Frank Norris Took on the Notorious Central Pacific Railroad* (New York: St. Martin's, 2012).

78. Norris, "I. Notes," 3.

79. Ibid., 17.

80. For further discussion of Presley, see Donald Pizer, "Another Look at 'The Octopus,'" *Nineteenth-Century Fiction* 10, no. 3 (1955): 217–24; and Charles Duncan, "'If Your View Be Large Enough': Narrative Growth in *The Octopus*," *American Literary Realism* 25, no. 2 (1993): 56–66.

81. For a related discussion of Annixter, see McElrath, "Frank Norris's *The Octopus*," 145–48. McElrath primarily focuses on the character's development in the context of the Sermon on the Mount.

82. Frank Norris to George Henry Sargent, June 9, 1901, in Crisler, *Frank Norris: Collected Letters*, 157–59.

3. INJURY TO ONE

1. Philip S. Foner, "Jack London: American Rebel," in *The Social Writings of Jack London*, ed. Philip S. Foner (Secaucus, NJ: Citadel Press, 1964), 3.

2. Leonard Cassuto and Jeanne Campbell Reesman, "Introduction: Jack London, a Representative Man," in *Rereading Jack London*, ed. Leonard Cassuto and Jeanne Campbell Reesman (Stanford: Stanford University Press, 1996), 5–6.

3. Jack London, *John Barleycorn* (1913; repr., New York: Modern Library, 2001), 114.

4. Ibid., 121.

5. James L. Haley, *Wolf: The Lives of Jack London* (New York: Basic Books, 2010), 60.

6. For contextual information about London's period on the road, see Todd DePastino, introduction to *The Road*, by Jack London (1907; repr., New Brunswick, NJ: Rutgers University Press, 2006), ix–xlix.

7. Jack London, "How I Became a Socialist," *Comrade* 2 (March 1903): 122–23; reprinted in Foner, *Social Writings of Jack London*, 364.

8. London, *John Barleycorn*, 124.

9. Haley, *Wolf*, 113.

10. Jack London to George P. Brett, March 25, 1903, in *The Letters of Jack London*, ed. Earle Labor, Robert C. Leitz III, and I. Milo Shepard (Stanford: Stanford University Press, 1988), 1:358. For more discussion of London's early literary success, see Earle Labor, *Jack London: An American Life* (New York: Farrar, Straus, and Giroux, 2013), 133–86.

11. Stephan Thernstrom, *The Other Bostonians: Poverty and Progress in the American Metropolis, 1880–1970* (Cambridge: Harvard University Press, 1973), 257.

12. Michael R. Haines, "Poverty, Economic Stress, and the Family in a Late Nineteenth-Century American City: Whites in Philadelphia, 1880," in *Philadelphia: Work, Space, Family, and Group Experience in the 19th Century: Essays toward an Interdisciplinary History of the City*, ed. Theodore Hershberg (New York: Oxford University Press, 1981), 260.

13. Thernstrom, *Other Bostonians*, 241.

14. James I. McClintock, *Jack London's Strong Truths* (East Lansing: Michigan State University Press, 1997), 129; and Jeanne Campbell Reesman, *Jack London: A Study of the Short Fiction* (New York: Twayne, 1999), 87. For further critical discussion of "The Apostate," see Steven T. Dhondt, "'There Is a Good Time Coming': Jack London's Spirit of Proletarian Revolt," *Jack London Newsletter* 3, no. 1 (1970): 25–34; Leonard Cassuto, "Jack London's Class-Based Grotesque," in *Literature and the Grotesque*, ed. Michael J. Meyer (Amsterdam: Rodopi, 1995), 113–28; and Jeanne Campbell Reesman, "Frank Norris and Jack London," in *A Companion to the American Short Story*, ed. Alfred Bendixen and James Nagel (West Sussex, UK: Wiley-Blackwell, 2010), 171–86. Dhondt views the story as an illustration of "the abominable conditions under which the working class lived in London's time" and examines his use of satire to illuminate the causes of injustice (25), Cassuto argues that the protagonist is "a human whose grip on his humanity has been systematically loosened by the physical and mental effects of his unceasing toil" (118), and Reesman presents the work in conjunction with Frank Norris's "*Fantaisie Printanière*" to explicate the central tendencies of American naturalism.

15. Haley, *Wolf*, 235.

16. Jack London to Mabel Applegarth, November 30, 1898, *Letters*, 1:25.

17. London, *John Barleycorn*, 39.

18. London's marginalia and precise references express the connections among these articles and the story, which he completed on March 29, 1906.

19. Jack London, "The Apostate," reprinted in Foner, *Social Writings of Jack London*, 222. All further quotations from this story will be cited parenthetically in the text. Horatio Alger, *Ragged Dick; or, Street Life in New York with the Boot Blacks* (Boston: Loring, 1868), 9.

20. Owen R. Lovejoy, "The Modern Slaughter of the Innocents," *Men and Women* 3 (October 1905): 4; Jack London Subject File: Socialism, Jack London Collection, Henry E. Huntington Library, San Marino, CA, box 555, JLE 1554.

21. "Child Labor Legislation: Owen R. Lovejoy's Address to Factory Inspectors," in Jack London Subject File: Socialism, Jack London Collection, Henry E. Huntington Library, San Marino, CA, box 555, JLE 1523, 1.

22. "To Protect Childhood," in Jack London Subject File: Socialism, Jack London Collection, Henry E. Huntington Library, San Marino, CA, box 555, JLE 1529, 1.

23. "Child Labor Legislation," 1.

24. Juliet Wilbor Tompkins, "Turning Children into Dollars," *Success Magazine*, January 1906, 15; Jack London Subject File: Socialism, Jack London Collection, Henry E. Huntington Library, San Marino, CA, box 555, JLE 1579.

25. Joan Hedrick, *Solitary Comrade: Jack London and His Work* (Chapel Hill: University of North Carolina Press, 1982), 171.

26. Dhondt, "'There Is a Good Time Coming,'" 30.

27. Prior to the Fair Labor Standards Act, the Supreme Court blocked two attempts to implement federal laws regarding the employment of children: the Keating-Owen Act of 1916 and the Pomerene Amendment to the Revenue Bill of 1919. The Executive Committee of Southern Cotton Manufacturers mounted a legal challenge to the first measure, which banned commodities produced by youths under the age of fourteen from interstate commerce, and the Supreme

Court ruled in *Hammer v. Dagenhart* that Congress did not have the authority to regulate articles of trade based on the conditions of their production (Hugh D. Hindman, *Child Labor: An American History* [Armonk, NY: M. E. Sharpe, 2002], 68–69). In *Drexel Furniture v. J. W. Bailey,* the Supreme Court struck down the second measure, which imposed a 10 percent excise tax on goods made by children, on constitutional grounds (72–73). In response to these defeats, Congress proposed an amendment to the Constitution that would outlaw child labor, yet this proposal met with little support at the state level.

28. Tompkins, "Turning Children into Dollars," 17.

29. Ibid.

30. Quoted in Charmian London, *The Book of Jack London* (New York: Century, 1921), 2:49–50.

31. Franklin Walker, "Jack London: *Martin Eden,*" in *The American Novel from James Fennimore Cooper to William Faulkner,* ed. Wallace Stegner (New York: Basic Books, 1965), 143. For negative appraisals of the novel, see Charles Child Walcutt, *Jack London* (Minneapolis: University of Minnesota Press, 1966), 41–44; and John DeCaire, "The Boys' Book of Despair," *Southwest Review* 88, nos. 2–3 (2003): 277–90. For readings that examine the artistic and thematic complexities of the work, see Charles N. Watson Jr., *The Novels of Jack London: A Reappraisal* (Madison: University of Wisconsin Press, 1983), 123–64; and Earle Labor and Jeanne Campbell Reesman, *Jack London* (New York: Twayne, 1994), 76–82.

32. For discussions of upward mobility in *Martin Eden,* see N. E. Dunn and Pamela Wilson, "The Significance of Upward Mobility in *Martin Eden,*" *Jack London Newsletter* 5, no. 1 (1972): 1–8; Watson, *Novels of Jack London,* 129–32; Renny Christopher, "Rags to Riches to Suicide: Unhappy Narratives of Upward Mobility: *Martin Eden, Bread Givers, Delia's Song,* and *Hunger of Memory,*" *College Literature* 29, no. 4 (2002): 79–108. While most of these articles address the national success story in the context of broader arguments, Christopher provides an in-depth analysis of this concept, focusing largely on the psychological dimensions of Martin's struggle for mobility and his growing estrangement from his working-class background. Dunn and Wilson also devote attention to London's emphasis on advancement, viewing the narrative in the context of the author's own struggles to become a successful novelist. For discussion of issues of economic class in the novel, see Loren Glass, "Nobody's Renown: Plagiarism and Publicity in the Career of Jack London," *American Literature* 71, no. 3 (1999): 536–45.

33. Jack London, "Notebook of Story Plots," Jack London Collection, Henry E. Huntington Library, San Marino, CA, JL 1004, 106.

34. Quoted in Watson, *Novels of Jack London,* 125.

35. Quoted in ibid., 126.

36. Quoted in ibid., 126–27.

37. Jack London, "What Life Means to Me," *Cosmopolitan* 41, March 1906, 526–30; reprinted in Foner, *Social Writings of Jack London,* 392.

38. Ibid., 397–98.

39. Ibid., 396.

40. On February 27, London notified Brett that he "will shortly receive, by express, the manuscript of my new novel. It is some 142,000 words long. In case *Success* is already a copyrighted

title, I give you herewith three titles which I prefer in the following order: (1) *Success* (2) *Star-Dust* (3) *Martin Eden.*" London's original title exhibits the fundamental irony of the narrative, with its juxtaposition of accomplishments defined by economic values against Martin's romantic and aesthetic aims. London further noted: "I don't know what you will think of this novel; I don't know what to think of it myself. But at any rate, I think you will find it fresh and original" (*Letters*, 2:738).

41. For the centrality of the sea and nautical imagery to *Martin Eden*, see Anita Duneer, "Crafting the Sea: Romance and Realism in Jack London's *Martin Eden*," *American Literary Realism* 47, no. 3 (2015): 250–71.

42. Jack London, *Martin Eden* (1909; repr., New York: Penguin, 1984), 31. All further quotations from this edition will be cited parenthetically in the text.

43. For additional discussion regarding the significance of the painting, see Thomas R. Tietze, "Teaching Aesthetics: Art and the Artist on Jack London's *Martin Eden*," *Eureka Studies in Teaching Short Fiction* 5, no. 1 (2004): 79.

44. For further examination of London's allusions to Swinburne, see Roy L. Weitzel, "Toward a 'Bright White Light': London's Use of Swinburne in *Martin Eden*," *Jack London Newsletter* 7, no. 1 (1974): 1–8.

45. For an analysis of sexual determinism in the novel, see George M. Spangler, "Divided Self and World in *Martin Eden*," *Jack London Newsletter* 9, no. 3 (1976): 121–22.

46. For contrasting viewpoints about the representation of Ruth, see Kim Moreland, "The Attack on the Nineteenth-Century Heroine Reconsidered: Women in Jack London's *Martin Eden*," *Markham Review* 13 (1983): 16–20; and Lisa Anderson, "Justice to Ruth Morse: The Devolution of a Character in *Martin Eden*," *Call* 10, nos. 1–2 (2008): 11–14.

47. For criticisms of the ending, see Sam S. Baskett, introduction to *Martin Eden*, by Jack London (New York: Holt, Rinehart, and Winston, 1956), xi–xii; Walker, "Jack London: *Martin Eden*," 139–42; and William Haney, "*Martin Eden*: The Failure of Individualism," *Jack London Newsletter* 12 (1979): 38–41. These readings overlook the patterns of imagery that anticipate Martin's suicide.

48. London to Fannie K. Hamilton, December 6, 1909, *Letters*, 2:847. London further contends that "had he taken Neal Brissenden's advice and tied himself to life by embracing socialism, he would have found there were a few million others to live & fight for" (847). For analysis of London's reading of *Martin Eden*, see Richard Morgan, "Naturalism, Socialism, and Jack London's *Martin Eden*," *Jack London Newsletter* 10, no. 1 (1977): 19–20; and Joseph R. McElrath Jr., "Jack London's *Martin Eden*: The Multiple Dimensions of a Literary Masterpiece," in *Jack London: One Hundred Years a Writer*, ed. Sara S. Hodson and Jeanne Campbell Reesman (San Marino, CA: Huntington Library, 2002), 93–96. Morgan asserts that the "lack of a socialist 'model' casts further doubt on the existence, at least on an effective level, of an anti-individualist basis to the book" (19), and McElrath argues that "despite the lip service he gave to socialism after he completed *Martin Eden*, he had strayed from the path of party-line virtue while writing it" (95). While the novel advances a critique of individualism, London does not present the Socialist characters in favorable terms, which undermines his view of *Martin Eden* as a testament to his ideology.

49. London, "What Life Means to Me," 399.

4. WAR OF THE CLASSES

1. Cecelia Tichi, "The Facts of Literature and Life," in *The Oxford Handbook of Jack London,* ed. Jay Williams (New York: Oxford University Press, 2017), 30.

2. Paul Douglas, *Real Wages in the United States, 1890–1926* (Boston: Houghton Mifflin, 1930), 177–79.

3. Melvyn Dubofsky, *When Workers Organize: New York City in the Progressive Era* (Amherst: University of Massachusetts Press, 1968), 12.

4. Ibid.

5. Ibid.

6. Philip S. Foner, *History of the Labor Movement in the United States,* 10 vols. (New York: International Publishers, 1947), 1:439.

7. Ibid.

8. Matthew Josephson, *The Robber Barons* (New York: Harcourt, 1934), 172–73.

9. Eric T. L. Love, *Race over Empire: Racism and U.S. Imperialism, 1865–1900* (Chapel Hill: University of North Carolina Press, 2004), 80.

10. Nell Irvin Painter, *Standing at Armageddon: The United States, 1877–1919* (New York: Norton, 1987), 116.

11. Alan Trachtenberg, *The Incorporation of America: Culture and Society in the Gilded Age* (New York: Hill and Wang, 1982), 99.

12. Nelson Lichtenstein, Susan Strasser, and Roy Rosenzweig, eds., *Who Built America? Working People and the Nation's Economy, Politics, Culture, and Society* (New York: Worth, 2000), 123.

13. Jeremy Brecher, *Strike!* (Boston: South End Press, 1997), 47. For a further discussion of the Great Upheaval, see Philip S. Foner, *The Great Labor Uprising of 1877* (New York: Monad Press, 1977). For concise overviews of this dispute, see Foner, *History of the Labor Movement,* 1:464–74; and Brecher, *Strike,* 13–37. For a detailed analysis of the strikes of 1885–86, see James Green, *Death in the Haymarket: The Story of Chicago, the First Labor Movement, and the Bombing That Divided Gilded Age America* (New York: Pantheon, 2006); and Theresa A. Case, *The Great Southwest Railroad Strike and Free Labor* (College Station: Texas A&M University Press, 2010). For condensed versions, see Foner, *History of the Labor Movement,* 2:93–114; and Brecher, *Strike,* 39–68.

14. Brecher, *Strike,* 56.

15. For a discussion of the Homestead strike, see Paul Krause, *The Battle for Homestead, 1880–1892: Politics, Culture, and Steel* (Pittsburgh: University of Pittsburgh Press, 1992); Foner, *History of the Labor Movement,* 2:206–18; and Brecher, *Strike,* 69–80. For an overview of the Pullman boycott, see Jack Kelly, *The Edge of Anarchy: The Railroad Barons, the Gilded Age, and the Greatest Labor Uprising in America* (New York: St. Martin's, 2019); Foner, *History of the Labor Movement,* 2:261–78; and Brecher, *Strike,* 96–114.

16. Jack London, "What Socialism Is," *San Francisco Examiner,* December 25, 1895; reprinted in *The Radical Jack London: Writings on War and Revolution,* ed. Jonah Raskin (Berkeley: University of California Press, 2008), 57.

17. Emanuel Haldeman-Julius, "The Pessimism of Jack London," *Western Comrade,* May 28, 1913, 92.

18. Jack London, "Revolution," *Contemporary Review* 93 (January 1908): 17–31; reprinted in *The Social Writings of Jack London,* ed. Philip S. Foner (Secaucus, NJ: Citadel Press, 1964), 499.

19. Jack London, "The Class Struggle," *Independent* 55, November 5, 1903, 2903–10; reprinted in Foner, *Social Writings of Jack London,* 448.

20. Many critics have called attention to the contradictory nature of London's socialism, most notably Joan Hedrick, *Solitary Comrade: Jack London and His Work* (Chapel Hill: University of North Carolina Press, 1982); and Carolyn Johnston, *Jack London—An American Radical?* (Westport, CT: Greenwood Press, 1984). London accumulated material possessions as quickly as he could; he lived on the sprawling acreage of his Beauty Ranch, complete with a valet and house servants. However, he did not view these developments as being inconsistent with his critique of capitalism, feeling that he had earned these luxuries through his own labor and not through the exploitation of others. For further discussion of London's socialism, see Jonah Raskin, "Jack London: The Orphan at the Abyss," in Raskin, *Radical Jack London,* 1–49; and Jay Williams, "Jack London and Socialism," in *Approaches to Teaching the Works of Jack London,* ed. Kenneth K. Brandt and Jeanne Campbell Reesman (New York: Modern Language Association of America, 2015), 59–68.

21. Jack London to the Members of Local Glen Ellen, Socialist Labor Party, March 7, 1916, in *The Letters of Jack London,* ed. Earle Labor, Robert C. Leitz III, and I. Milo Shepard (Stanford: Stanford University Press, 1988), 3:1538.

22. Some commentators have viewed the work as a prophecy that anticipates the rise of fascism. For example, Leon Trotsky asserted that *The Iron Heel* is "precisely the picture of fascism, of its economy, of its governmental technique, its political psychology! The fact is incontestable: in 1907 Jack London already foresaw and described the fascist regime as the inevitable result of the defeat of the proletarian revolution" (*Literature and Revolution: Writings on Literature, Politics, and Culture,* ed. Paul N. Siegel [New York: Pathfinder Press, 1970], 224). London advanced a different view of the book, stating: "I didn't write the thing as a prophecy at all. I really don't think these things are going to happen in the United States. I believe the increasing socialist vote will prevent—hope for it, anyhow. But I will say that I sent out, in *The Iron Heel,* a warning of what I think might happen if they don't look to their votes" (quoted in Charmian London, *Book of Jack London,* 2:138–39). The novel, however, seems to discount the ability of the workers to transform society by electoral means due to the wealth and power of the capitalists, and London expressed this idea in his interview with Emanuel Haldeman-Julius in 1913.

23. Earle Labor and Jeanne Campbell Reesman, *Jack London* (New York: Twayne, 1994), 66.

24. Nathaniel Teich, "Marxist Dialectics in Content, Form, and Point of View: Structures in Jack London's *The Iron Heel,*" *Modern Fiction Studies* 22, no. 1 (1976): 85; and Paul Stein, "Jack London's *The Iron Heel:* Art as Manifesto," *Studies in American Fiction* 6, no. 1 (1978): 78. While Teich bases his reading of *The Iron Heel* on London's approximation of Marxism, Stein examines the relationship between the structure of the narrative and its ideological content.

25. Jack London, "Notebook of Story Plots," Jack London Collection, Henry E. Huntington Library, San Marino, CA, JL 1004, 51.

26. Jack London, "Notes for *The Iron Heel,*" Jack London Collection, Henry E. Huntington Library, San Marino, CA, JL 833, envelope 1, 30.

27. The novel received negative reviews from many Socialists. For instance, John Spargo asserted that the novel "tends to weaken the political Socialist movement by discrediting the ballot and to encourage the chimerical and reactionary notion of physical force, so alluring to a certain type of mind" (quoted in Joan London, *Jack London and His Times: An Unconventional Biography* [1938; repr., Seattle: University of Washington Press, 1968], 310). Whereas London discredits the effectiveness of electoral solutions to pressing social ills, he presents violence not as a preferential alternative but as the logical outcome of the current course of policy.

28. Jack London, "Explanation of the Great Socialist Vote of 1904," in Foner, *Social Writings of Jack London*, 404.

29. Ibid.

30. Ibid., 406.

31. Abraham Ascher, *The Revolution of 1905: Russia in Disarray* (Stanford: Stanford University Press, 1988), 90–98. For further discussion about Bloody Sunday, see Andrew M. Verner, *The Crisis of Russian Autocracy: Nicholas II and the 1905 Revolution* (Princeton: Princeton University Press, 1990), 141–83.

32. Ascher, *Revolution of 1905*, 92–94 and 162–65.

33. Verner, *Crisis of Russian Autocracy*, 326–50.

34. Haldeman-Julius, "Pessimism of Jack London," 92. For additional explanation of the impact of the 1905 Revolution on London, see Joan London, *Jack London and His Times*, 264–80.

35. W. J. Ghent, *Our Benevolent Feudalism* (New York: Macmillan, 1902), 181–82. For London's discussion of this work, see "A Review," in *War of the Classes* (1905; repr., New York: Macmillan, 1975), 195–214. London confined himself to presenting a broad overview of Ghent's argument in relation to John Graham Brooks's *The Social Unrest* (1903), examining the broader affinity of these works despite the fact that Ghent was a proponent of socialism and Brooks was a defender of capitalism.

36. Jack London, *The Iron Heel* (1908; repr., in *Jack London: Novels and Social Writings*, ed. Donald Pizer, New York: Library of America, 1982), 464. All further quotations from this edition will be cited parenthetically in the text.

37. In this context, *The Iron Heel* serves as a criticism of the utopian novels of the nineteenth century, most notably Edward Bellamy's *Looking Backward* (1888), William Morris's *News from Nowhere* (1890), and William Dean Howells's *A Traveler from Altruria* (1894), which represent a peaceful transfer of power from the capitalists to the workers that creates socialistic societies. For further discussion of this point, see Gorman Beauchamp, "*The Iron Heel* and *Looking Backward:* Two Paths to Utopia," *American Literary Realism* 9, no. 4 (1976): 307–14; and Erica Briscoe, "*The Iron Heel:* How Not to Write a Popular Novel," *Jack London Journal* 5 (1998): 19–21.

38. London advances a similar strategy when Ernest explains the seemingly inevitable collapse of capitalism in relation to Marx's theory of surplus value, the process of paying workers less in wages than the value created by their labor, which prevents them from consuming excess production. Ernest, in a speech that echoes London's "The Question of the Maximum," asserts that when "every country stands with an unconsumed and unsalable surplus on its hands, the capitalist system will break down under the terrific structure of profits that it itself has reared. ... The United States, and the whole world for that matter, will enter upon a new and tremendous

era" (420). The narrative, however, undercuts the inevitability of this development by illustrating the ability of the Iron Heel to adapt to changed circumstances through their efforts to dispose of this surplus, which manifests in the construction of their wonder cities and massive public works projects that forestall the revolution for three hundred years. Though Ernest anticipates these events and Meredith again applauds the protagonist's foresight, the actions of the oligarchs complicate conventional narratives of progress by accentuating the strategies employed by the wealthy to maintain their power, developments that necessitate militant rather than electoral action to facilitate social change.

39. Paul Lauter, "Teaching *The Iron Heel,*" in Brandt and Reesman, *Approaches to Teaching the Works of Jack London,* 70.

40. Jude Davies, "Naturalism and Class," in *The Oxford Handbook of American Literary Naturalism,* ed. Keith Newlin (Oxford: Oxford University Press, 2011), 309.

41. Kathy Knapp, "*The Iron Heel* and the Contemporary Bourgeois Novel," in Newlin, *Oxford Handbook of Jack London,* 316.

42. For further discussion of this episode, see Francis Shor, "Power, Gender, and Ideological Discourse in *The Iron Heel,*" in *Rereading Jack London,* ed. Leonard Cassuto and Jeanne Campbell Reesman (Stanford: Stanford University Press, 1996), 80–82.

43. Jocelyn Lewis, "Was It Worthwhile?" *Outlook* 18, August 18, 1906, 902–4. Watson also identifies *Our Benevolent Feudalism* as London's source for the journalist who refuses to publish Avis's article, noting several close correspondences with an anonymous reporter cited by Ghent (*Novels of Jack London,* 105–6).

44. Jack London, "Disappearing Class," Jack London Collection, Henry E. Huntington Library, San Marino, CA, JL 602, 3.

45. London, "Disappearing Class," 4.

46. Quoted in Foner, *History of the Labor Movement,* 2:264–65.

47. Ibid., 2:385.

48. Ibid., 2:386.

49. In response to writs filed on behalf of imprisoned miners, Bell stated, "Habeas corpus be damned . . . we'll give 'em post mortems" (quoted in Peter Carlson, *Roughneck: The Life and Times of Big Bill Haywood* [New York: Norton, 1983], 62).

50. Robert Edward Lee Knight, *Industrial Relations in the San Francisco Bay Area, 1900–1918* (Berkeley: University of California Press, 1960), 152, 187–88.

51. For discussion of these labor disputes, see Brecher, *Strike.*

52. Foner, *History of the Labor Movement,* 2:106.

53. Ibid., 2:110–11.

54. Ibid., 3:398.

55. George G. Suggs, *Colorado's War on Militant Unionism: James H. Peabody and the Western Federation of Miners* (Norman: University of Oklahoma Press, 1972), 110–12.

56. Elizabeth Jameson, *All That Glitters: Class, Conflict, and Community in Cripple Creek* (Urbana: University of Illinois Press, 1998), 230–31.

57. "The Dream of Debs" has received little critical attention. Labor and Reesman mention the story only in passing (*Jack London,* 66), Johnston limits her discussion to a brief summary

of the work (*Jack London,* 131–32), and Foner merely posits that London's handling of events reveals that he "had done considerable reading on the tactics of a general strike" ("Jack London," 106). James I. McClintock examines the propagandistic nature of the text, asserting that as "interesting as the story is as a socialist argument, it is an artistic failure," yet basing his analysis on the intentions of the author and the responses of his readers (*Jack London's Strong Truths* [East Lansing: Michigan State University Press, 1997], 128). Hedrick also focuses on problems that emerge through London's narrative method, claiming that "London's use of an upper-class narrator who is victimized by the strike denies the reader direct participation in the working-class victory, and his dead-pan narration kills much of the vitality of the story" (176). Reesman advances the most perceptive reading of "The Dream of Debs" as she interprets it in the context of London's major themes and observes that this tale represents one of the few examples of successful working-class revolt in his oeuvre (*Jack London: A Study of the Short Fiction* [New York: Twayne, 1999], 84–85).

58. Stephen Naft, *The Social General Strike,* trans. Arnold Roller (Chicago: Debating Club No. 1, 1905), 7. Although chapter 13 of *The Iron Heel* features a similar work stoppage that provides the impetus for more repressive measures from the Oligarchy, this occurrence does not undermine the potential power of the industrial action in the story since it involves more detailed planning and creates greater consequences for capital, which contributes to the victory of labor.

59. London considered a number of potential titles, including "The Great Labor Day," "The Chaos of Order," and "The Dream of Labor," before settling on the final version ("Notes for 'The Dream of Debs,'" Jack London Collection, Henry E. Huntington Library, San Marino, CA, JL 615, 1).

60. Eugene Victor Debs, "Unionism and Socialism," *Debs: His Life, Writings, and Speeches* (Chicago: Charles H. Kerr & Co., 1908), 134.

61. Describing the formation of the union in the story, London wrote that the "larger aggregations of capital that combined and defeated the big combinations of laborers—the I. W. W. had combined with the W. F. of M. and the A. F. of L." ("Notes for 'The Dream of Debs,'" 5). For discussion of the IWW, see Foner, *History of the Labor Movement,* vol. 4.

62. Quoted in Howard Zinn, *A People's History of the United States* (New York: Harper, 1980), 322.

63. Jack London, "The Dream of Debs," reprinted in Foner, *Social Writings of Jack London,* 253. All further quotations from this story will be cited parenthetically in the text.

64. Laurence H. Shoup, *Rulers & Rebels: A People's History of Early California, 1769–1901* (New York: iUniverse, 2010), 430–32. London was familiar with the 1901 waterfront strike as his folder for "Disappearing Class" includes articles about this conflict.

65. "The Fight of the Employers against the Unions," *San Francisco Examiner,* August 7, 1901, 1; Jack London Subject File: Trade Unionism, Jack London Collection, Henry E. Huntington Library, San Marino, CA, box 557, JLE 1657.

66. Knight, *Industrial Relations,* 72–77.

67. Ibid., 84–85.

68. Jack London, "Something Rotten in Idaho," reprinted in Foner, *Social Writings of Jack London,* 409.

69. J. Anthony Lukas, *Big Trouble: A Murder in a Small Western Town Sets Off a Struggle for the Soul of America* (New York: Simon & Schuster, 1998), 378. For further discussion of the case, see Foner, *History of the Labor Movement*, 4:40–59; and Carlson, *Roughneck*, 87–135.

70. Quoted in Foner, *History of the Labor Movement*, 4:55–56.

71. Exodus 10:3–5.

72. Eugene Victor Debs, "Revolutionary Unionism," *Debs: His Life, Writings, and Speeches*, 427.

5. SOLIDARITY FOREVER

1. Jackson J. Benson and Anne Loftis, "John Steinbeck and Farm Labor Unionization: The Background of *In Dubious Battle*," *American Literature* 52, no. 2 (1980): 194–223. Benson and Loftis examine how Steinbeck incorporated elements of these strikes into *In Dubious Battle*, yet they do not present this information in the context of an interpretation of the work. For a fascinating discussion of the history of Tagus Ranch, see Matthew Ford, "I Ain't Gonna Work on Merritt's Farm No More: A Brief History of Central California's Forgotten Empire," *Public Seminar*, October 11, 2019, http://publicseminar.org/essays/i-aint-gonna-work-on-merritts-farm-no-more. For further analysis of the historical sources of the novel, see Will Watson, "'Written in Disorder': John Steinbeck's *In Dubious Battle* and 'The Big Strike,'" *Genre* 49, nos. 1–2 (2009): 33–60. Watson views the San Francisco general strike of 1934 as an antecedent for the book, analyzing Steinbeck's labor dispute in relation to Antonio Negri's conception of revolutionary time. While this work stoppage undoubtedly shaped the representation of events in the novel, the strikes identified by Benson and Loftis provide the main historical tether for *In Dubious Battle*, supplying Steinbeck with the raw materials for both the broader contours of the walkout and pivotal episodes in the clash between capital and labor.

2. Warren French, *John Steinbeck* (Boston: Twayne, 1975), 76.

3. John H. Timmerman, *John Steinbeck's Fiction: The Aesthetics of the Road Taken* (Norman: University of Oklahoma Press, 1986), 87.

4. For readings that examine Steinbeck's economic themes, see Jerry W. Wilson, "*In Dubious Battle:* Engagement in Collectivity," *Steinbeck Quarterly* 13, nos. 1–2 (1980): 31–42; and Richard S. Pressman, "Individualists or Collectivists? Steinbeck's *In Dubious Battle* and Hemingway's *To Have and Have Not*," *Steinbeck Quarterly* 25, nos. 3–4 (1992): 119–33. Pressman and Wilson also analyze the representation of the organizers in the context of Steinbeck's sympathy for agricultural workers; however, these critics do not connect these insights to the disputes that provide the historical background for the novel.

5. For further discussion of the relationship between Steinbeck and Ricketts, see Richard Astro, *John Steinbeck and Edward F. Ricketts: The Shaping of a Novelist* (Minneapolis: University of Minnesota Press, 1973).

6. Frederick Bracher, "John Steinbeck and the Biological View of Man," in *Steinbeck and His Critics: A Record of Twenty-Five Years*, ed. E. W. Tedlock and C. V. Wicker (Albuquerque: University of New Mexico Press, 1957), 184.

7. John Steinbeck and Edward F. Ricketts, *Sea of Cortez: A Leisurely Journal of Travel and Research* (1941; repr., Mount Vernon: Paul P. Appel, 1989), 135. While this formulation has been

commonly associated with Steinbeck, non-teleological thinking is actually the philosophy of his collaborator. As Richard Astro observes, the Easter Sermon in *The Sea of Cortez* comes almost verbatim from Ricketts's unpublished writings (*John Steinbeck and Edward F. Ricketts,* 14). As such, these ideas are not necessarily indicative of Steinbeck's position toward his material as his fiction devoted considerable attention to basic principles of causation and attributed blame for social injustice, positions that do not suggest objective detachment.

8. Although Steinbeck's fiction often highlights the need for popular pressure to address injustice, it is important to note that he did not profess radical beliefs. Steinbeck had a lifelong hostility toward communism, which he referred to as the "pseudo right that calls itself left" and that was "about as revolutionary as the Daughters of the American Revolution" (John Steinbeck, "I Am a Revolutionary," in *America and Americans and Selected Nonfiction,* ed. Susan Shillinglaw and Jackson J. Benson [New York: Penguin, 2002], 89. Instead, he was a New Deal Democrat who objected to a consolidation of resources that endangered vulnerable members of society.

9. Quoted in *Working Days: The Journals of "The Grapes of Wrath," 1938–1941,* ed. Robert DeMott (New York: Penguin, 1989), 152.

10. Quoted in Susan Shillinglaw, *On Reading "The Grapes of Wrath"* (New York: Penguin, 2014), 92–93.

11. Quoted in Jackson J. Benson, *The True Adventures of John Steinbeck, Writer* (New York: Penguin, 1984), 386.

12. Gwendolyn Mink and Alice O'Connor, *Poverty in the United States: An Encyclopedia of History, Politics, and Policy* (Santa Barbara, CA: ABC-CLIO, 2004), 26.

13. Robert S. McElvaine, *The Great Depression: America, 1929–1941* (New York: Times Books, 1994), 38; and Meyer Weinberg, *A Short History of American Capitalism* (New York: New History Press, 2002), 209–10.

14. Lizabeth Cohen, *Making a New Deal: Industrial Workers in Chicago, 1919–1939* (New York: Cambridge University Press, 1990), 102.

15. Mink and O'Connor, *Poverty in the United States,* 26.

16. Nelson Lichtenstein, Susan Strasser, and Roy Rosenzweig, eds., *Who Built America? Working People and the Nation's Economy, Politics, Culture, and Society* (New York: Worth, 2000), 325.

17. John Kenneth Galbraith, *The Great Crash, 1929* (1955; repr., Boston: Mariner Books, 2009), 168–69.

18. Ibid., 177–86.

19. Mink and O'Connor, *Poverty in the United States,* 26.

20. McElvaine, *Great Depression,* 75.

21. Ibid.

22. Howard Zinn, *A People's History of the United States* (New York: Harper, 1980), 378.

23. Melvyn Dubofsky, *Industrialism and the American Worker, 1865–1920* (Wheeling, IL: Harlan Davidson, 1996), 40.

24. Frances Fox Piven and Richard Cloward, *Poor People's Movements: Why They Succeed, How They Fail* (New York: Vintage, 1979), 121.

25. Jeremy Brecher, *Strike!* (Boston: South End Press, 1997), 166–74.

26. For further discussion, see Sidney Fine, *Sit-Down: The General Motors Strike of 1936–1937* (Ann Arbor: University of Michigan Press, 1969).

27. Carey McWilliams, *Factories in the Field* (1935; repr., Berkeley: University of California Press, 1999), 199.

28. Daniel Cornford, "Editor's Introduction," in *Working People of California,* ed. Daniel Cornford (Berkeley: University of California Press, 1995), 208.

29. McWilliams, *Factories in the Field,* 230–39.

30. T. H. Watkins, *The Hungry Years: A Narrative History of the Great Depression in America* (New York: Henry Holt, 1999), 440–41.

31. For discussions of the CAWIU, see McWilliams, *Factories in the Field,* 214–29; and Cletus E. Daniel, *Bitter Harvest: A History of California Farmworkers, 1870–1941* (Ithaca, NY: Cornell University Press, 1981), 105–40.

32. "Tagus Strike Not Expected to Be Serious," *Visalia (CA) Times-Delta,* August 12, 1933, 1; and Daniel, *Bitter Harvest,* 156–57.

33. "Statewide Walkout in Orchards Threatened by Strikers Unless Growers Meet Wage Demands," *Visalia (CA) Times-Delta,* August 18, 1933, 1; and "NRA to Aid Rolph Settle Strike," *San Francisco Chronicle,* August 17, 1933, 1.

34. "NRA to Aid Rolph Settle Farm Strike," 1; and "Walkout Averted as New Price Set for Field Labor," *Visalia (CA) Times-Delta,* August 19, 1933, 1.

35. Daniel, *Bitter Harvest,* 158.

36. Ibid., 179.

37. Ibid., 181, 194.

38. "4 Slain in State Strike," *San Francisco Chronicle,* October 11, 1933, 1, 9.

39. "75 Cent Rate Fixed by Commission," *Visalia (CA) Times-Delta,* October 23, 1933, 1.

40. "Cotton Strikers Defy U.S.!" *San Francisco Chronicle,* October 26, 1933, 1; and "Cotton Strikers Capitulate Row," *Visalia (CA) Times-Delta,* October 27, 1933, 4.

41. Quoted in Peter Lisca, *The Wide World of John Steinbeck* (New Brunswick, NJ: Rutgers University Press, 1958), 112.

42. Benson and Loftis, "John Steinbeck and Farm Labor Unionization," 202.

43. Quoted in Lisca, *Wide World of John Steinbeck,* 113.

44. Benson and Loftis, "John Steinbeck and Farm Labor Unionization," 200–201.

45. When Steinbeck initially submitted the manuscript to Covici-Friede, an editor at the firm, Harry Black, declined the work because of qualms about its ideological stance. This appraisal was forwarded to Steinbeck, who wrote Mavis McIntosh in April 1935 that he was "deeply shocked by the attitude of Covici.... Answering the complaint that the ideology is incorrect, this is the silliest of criticism. There are as many communist systems as there are communists" (in *Steinbeck: A Life in Letters,* ed. Elaine Steinbeck and Robert Wallsten [New York: Penguin, 1989], 107). After this rejection, Bobbs-Merrill quickly accepted *In Dubious Battle.* When Pascal Covici returned to New York and learned what had happened, he immediately fired Black, mailed an apologetic note to Steinbeck, and asked to publish the book.

46. John Steinbeck to George Albee, January 15, 1935, in Steinbeck and Wallsten, *Steinbeck,* 98.

47. Ibid.

48. John Steinbeck, *In Dubious Battle* (1936; repr., New York: Bantam, 1972), 121. All further quotations from this edition will be cited parenthetically in the text.

49. Daniel, *Bitter Harvest,* 180.

50. Ibid., 157.

51. "State Labor War Spreading; Strike Affects 20,000," *San Francisco Chronicle*, October 10, 1933, 1.

52. Benson and Loftis, "John Steinbeck and Farm Labor Unionization," 211.

53. "Cotton Strikers Capitulate Row," 4.

54. "State Labor War Spreading," 13.

55. "Infant Starves in Strike Camp," *San Francisco Chronicle*, October 11, 1933, 9.

56. Ella Winter, *And Not to Yield: An Autobiography* (New York: Harcourt, Brace, and World, 1963), 196–97.

57. "NRA to Aid Rolph Settle Farm Strike," 6.

58. "Police Dump Household Goods of Strikers," *Visalia (CA) Times-Delta*, August 15, 1933, 1.

59. "NRA to AID Rolph Settle Farm Strike," 6.

60. "Wave of Unrest among Workers Halts Agriculture," *Visalia (CA) Times-Delta*, October 10, 1933, 1.

61. "Martial Law Call Hinted in Cotton Strike," *San Francisco Chronicle*, October 21, 1933, 11.

62. "State Labor War Spreading," 1.

63. "Strikers Demand Murder Charge," *Visalia (CA) Times-Delta*, October 11, 1933, 1; "Grand Jury to Consider Pixley Cotton Rioting," *Visalia (CA) Times-Delta*, October 11, 1933, 6; "4 Slain in State Strike Riots," 1; and Daniel, *Bitter Harvest*, 196.

64. "Strikers Demand Murder Charge," 1; and "4 Slain in State Strike Riots," 1.

65. Steinbeck also changed the ethnicity of the workers involved in the disputes: the majority of the strikers at the Tagus Ranch and in the cotton fields were Mexican, yet Steinbeck's characters are white. Louis Owens contends that Steinbeck made this change because the introduction of the role played by minorities "would have complicated the simple picture of group-man he wished to show, and to have introduced the complexities of race and gender would have blurred the single focus he sought" ("Writing in Costume: The Missing Voices of *In Dubious Battle*," in *John Steinbeck: The Years of Greatness, 1936–1939*, ed. Tetsumaro Hayashi [Tuscaloosa: University of Alabama Press, 1993], 86).

66. Quoted in Daniel, *Bitter Harvest*, 159–60.

67. "Creel May Take Personal Charge in Cotton Strike," *Visalia (CA) Times-Delta*, October 17, 1933, 6.

68. "Maintain Order in the Strike Area," *Visalia (CA) Times-Delta*, October 24, 1933, 6.

69. Ibid.; and "Starving Strikers to Be Fed," *San Francisco Chronicle*, October 13, 1933, 10.

70. Jeffrey Wayne Yeager, "The Social Mind: John Elof Boodin's Influence on John Steinbeck's Phalanx Writings, 1935–1941," *Steinbeck Review* 10, no. 1 (2013): 45.

71. John Steinbeck to Carlton A. Sheffield, June 21, 1933, in Steinbeck and Wallsten, *Steinbeck*, 76.

72. Quoted in Astro, *John Steinbeck and Edward F. Ricketts*, 65.

73. "Martial Law Faces Cotton Strike Area," *San Francisco Chronicle*, October 15, 1933, 3.

74. For criticisms of Mac, see Peter W. Yancey, "Steinbeck's Relationship to Proletarian Literature," *Steinbeck Review* 9, no. 1 (2012): 39–53; Lisca, *Wide World of John Steinbeck*, 124–25; and Abby H. P. Werlock, "Looking at Lisa: The Function of the Feminine in Steinbeck's *In Dubious Battle*," in Hayashi, *John Steinbeck*, 53–54. Yancey contrasts Steinbeck with the labor

organizer, observing that for the novelist, agricultural workers "are real people with real needs, not pawns in a larger political struggle" ("Steinbeck's Relationship to Proletarian Literature," 44). In a related vein, Lisca asserts that "Mac's actions make it increasingly evident that he is exploiting the workers for party agitation rather than helping them" (*Wide World of John Steinbeck,* 125), and Werlock examines the organizer in relation to Lisa, who "becomes the first of many individuals Mac views as useful objects; as such she illuminates Mac's inhumanity" ("Looking at Lisa," 54). For contrasting arguments, see Linda Ray Pratt, "In Defense of Mac's Dubious Battle," *Steinbeck Quarterly* 10, no. 2 (1977): 36–44; and Wilson, "*In Dubious Battle,*" 38–42.

75. Lisca argues that Doc Burton provides "an objective chorus" and possesses an outlook that "is very close to Steinbeck's (*Wide World of John Steinbeck,* 125–26). Owens opines that "Doc is the spokesman for Steinbeck's point of view in this novel; his detached, intellectual position of noncommitment mirrors the novelist's relationship to his materials" (*John Steinbeck's Re-Vision of America* [Athens: University of Georgia Press, 1985], 96). Such interpretations do not take into account how Steinbeck undermines Doc's perspective. For further discussion, see Barry Sarchett, "*In Dubious Battle:* A Revaluation," *Steinbeck Quarterly* 13, nos. 3–4 (1980): 91–95.

76. For further discussion of this point, see Owens, *John Steinbeck's Re-Vision of America,* 97–99.

77. See, for instance, Howard Levant, "The Unity of *In Dubious Battle:* Violence and Dehumanization," *Modern Fiction Studies* 11 (1965): 25; and Alan Henry Rose, "Steinbeck and the Complexity of the Self in *In Dubious Battle,*" *Steinbeck Quarterly* 9, no. 1 (1976): 17–18. For a contrasting view, see Sarchett, "*In Dubious Battle,*" 89–90.

78. In *The Harvest Gypsies,* Steinbeck discussed the scope of the Associated Farmers. He observed that this group drew its membership from "officials of banks, publishers of newspapers and politicians; and through close association with the State Chamber of Commerce they have interlocking associations with shipowners' associations, public utilities corporations and transportation companies." Through this organization, the growers, whose ventures "are organized as closely and are as centrally directed in their labor policy as are the industries and shipping, the banking and public utilities," could shape agricultural production and dictate the circumstances facing workers (*The Harvest Gypsies: On the Road to "The Grapes of Wrath,"* ed. Charles Wollenberg [Berkeley: Heyday Books, 1988], 33). This authority provided the Associated Farmers with the means to suppress labor and correlates to the causative agents that Steinbeck presents in *The Grapes of Wrath.*

79. McWilliams, *Factories in the Field,* 224–26.

80. Daniel, *Bitter Harvest,* 249–57; McWilliams, *Factories in the Field,* 226–28.

81. McWilliams, *Factories in the Field,* 240–60.

82. John Steinbeck, "Dubious Battle in California," *Nation,* September 12, 1936, 304.

6. A REVOLUTION OF VALUES

1. Louis Owens, *John Steinbeck's Re-Vision of America* (Athens: University of Georgia Press, 1985), 3.

2. For discussions of *The Grapes of Wrath* in relation to the American Dream, see ibid., 129–39; and Warren French, "John Steinbeck and American Literature," *San Jose Studies* 13,

no. 2 (1987): 35–48. Owens offers a perceptive reading of *The Grapes of Wrath* that focuses largely on its representation of the Eden myth. For analyses of the economic themes of *The Grapes of Wrath,* see Richard S. Pressman, "'Them's Horses—We're Men': Social Tendency and Counter-Tendency in *The Grapes of Wrath," Steinbeck Quarterly* 19, nos. 3–4 (1986): 71–79; William J. Beck and Edward Erickson, "The Emergence of Class Consciousness in *Germinal* and *The Grapes of Wrath," Comparatist* 12 (1988): 44–57; Michael G. Barry, "Degrees of Mediation and Their Political Value in Steinbeck's *The Grapes of Wrath,*" in *The Steinbeck Question: New Essays in Criticism,* ed. Donald R. Noble (Troy: Whitston Publishing, 1993): 108–24; and Keith Windschuttle, "Steinbeck's Myth of the Okies," *New Criterion* 20, no. 10 (2002): 24–32. These articles largely overlook the relationship between the American Dream and *The Grapes of Wrath* or the association between the novel and naturalist fiction, which frames Steinbeck's handling of the economic forces that undermine individual progress in this book.

3. Charles L. Etheridge Jr., *"The Grapes of Wrath* and Literary Naturalism," in *"The Grapes of Wrath": A Re-Consideration,* ed. Michael J. Meyer (Amsterdam: Rodopi, 2009), 2:653.

4. Alan Gibb, "Naturalism and Steinbeck's 'Curious Compromise' in *The Grapes of Wrath,*" in Meyer, *"Grapes of Wrath,"* 2:689.

5. Quoted in Donald Worster, *Dust Bowl: The Southern Plains in the 1930s* (Oxford: Oxford University Press, 1979), 59.

6. Ibid., 89–94.

7. Ibid., 94.

8. Nelson Lichtenstein, Susan Strasser, and Roy Rosenzweig, eds., *Who Built America? Working People and the Nation's Economy, Politics, Culture, and Society* (New York: Worth, 2000), 376.

9. Worster, *Dust Bowl,* 60. These problems resulted in the increasing concentration of agrarian ownership and the monopolistic control that these conglomerates exerted over the economy. By 1930, half of the farms in the nation were responsible for almost 90 percent of all cash crops, and the resulting inability of small producers to sell their produce caused a surge in foreclosures and forced many people off their property (Lichtenstein, Strasser, and Rosenzweig, *Who Built America,* 344). As a result, the majority of the nation's farmland fell under the control of a handful of individuals and corporations, who organized agricultural production in line with conventional methods of industrial management.

10. Worster, *Dust Bowl,* 83–90. For further information about the causes of the Dust Bowl, see Sara Gregg, "From Bread Breadbasket to Dust Bowl: Rural Credit, the World War I Plow-Up, and the Transformation of American Agriculture," *Great Plains Quarterly* 35, no. 2 (2015): 129–66.

11. Lichtenstein, Strasser, and Rosenzweig, *Who Built America,* 377–78.

12. James M. Gregory, *American Exodus: The Dust Bowl Migration and Okie Culture in California* (Oxford: Oxford University Press, 1989), 9–10.

13. Ibid., 11.

14. Ibid., 11–13.

15. For further discussion of the Oklahoma chapters of *The Grapes of Wrath,* see Arthur Krim, "Right near Sallisaw," *Steinbeck Newsletter* 12, no. 1 (1999): 1–4.

16. John Steinbeck, *The Harvest Gypsies: On the Road to "The Grapes of Wrath,"* ed. Charles Wollenberg (Berkeley: Heyday Books, 1988), 25.

17. For discussion of Tom Collins and his role in *The Grapes of Wrath,* see Jackson J. Benson, "'To Tom, Who Lived It': John Steinbeck and the Man from Weedpatch," *Journal of Modern Literature* 5, no. 2 (1976): 151–210.

18. Robert Demott, introduction to *Working Days: The Journals of "The Grapes of Wrath," 1938–1941* (New York: Penguin, 1989), xxxvi.

19. Quoted in ibid., xl.

20. Jay Parini, *John Steinbeck: A Biography* (New York: Henry Holt, 1995), 226. To avoid potential libel charges, Steinbeck removed Joan Crawford's name from the discussion of the syphilitic actress in chapter 15 and omitted William Randolph Hearst's name from Casy's comments about the large landowner who was dead inside in chapter 19. Steinbeck also added three paragraphs on a separate sheet following page 87 to explain the disappearance of Noah Joad in chapter 18, and he deleted a lengthy passage in chapter 21 that compared the arrival of the migrants in California with the invasion of Rome by German hordes. For further discussion, see Roy S. Simmonds, "The Original Manuscript," *San Jose Studies* 16, no. 1 (1990): 117–32.

21. John Steinbeck, *The Grapes of Wrath* (1939; repr., New York: Penguin, 2006), 1. All further quotations from this edition will be cited parenthetically in the text.

22. Owens, *John Steinbeck's Re-Vision of America,* 131. Steinbeck explained the purpose of these chapters in a letter to a student at Columbia University, writing: "You say the inner chapters were counterpoint and so they were—that they were pace changers and they were that too but their basic purpose was to hit the reader below the belt. With the rhythms and symbols of poetry one can get into a reader—and open him up and while he is open—introduce things on a [*sic*] intellectual level which he would not or could not receive unless he were opened up" (quoted in Phyllis T. Dircks, "Steinbeck's Statement on the Inner Chapters of *The Grapes of Wrath,*" *Steinbeck Quarterly* 24, nos. 3–4 [1991]: 87).

23. For further discussion, see Elin Käck, "'They fix 'em so you can't win nothing': Agency in *The Grapes of Wrath,*" *Steinbeck Review* 14, no. 2 (2017): 184–200.

24. Barbara A. Heavilin, "A Sacred Bond Broken: The People versus the Land in *The Grapes of Wrath,*" *Steinbeck Review* 14, no. 1 (2017): 35.

25. For further discussion, see Louis Owens, *"The Grapes of Wrath": Trouble in the Promised Land* (Boston: Twayne, 1989), 58–64.

26. For discussions of Casy, see Martin Shockley, "Christian Symbolism in *The Grapes of Wrath,*" *College English* 18, no. 2 (1956): 87–90; Helen Lojek, "Jim Casy: Politico of the New Jerusalem," *Steinbeck Quarterly* 15, nos. 1–2 (1982): 30–37; Stephen Bullivant, "'That's Him. That Shiny Bastard': Jim Casy and Christology," *Steinbeck Studies* 16, nos. 1–2 (2005): 14–31; Kelly MacPhail, "'He's—a kind of man': Jim Casy's Spiritual Journey in *The Grapes of Wrath,*" in Meyer, *"Grapes of Wrath,"* 1:99–127.

27. Frederic I. Carpenter, "The Philosophical Joads," *College English* 2, no. 4 (1941): 316–18.

28. For discussions about Ma Joad, see Warren Motley, "From Patriarchy to Matriarchy: Ma Joad's Role in *The Grapes of Wrath,*" *American Literature* 54, no. 3 (1982): 397–412; Nellie McKay, "Happy(?)-Wife-and-Motherdom: The Portrayal of Ma Joad in John Steinbeck's *The Grapes of Wrath,*" in *New Essays on John Steinbeck's "The Grapes of Wrath,"* ed. David Wyatt (Cambridge: Cambridge University Press, 1990), 47–70; and Lorelei Cederstrom, "The 'Great Mother' in *The Grapes of Wrath,*" in *Steinbeck and the Environment: Interdisciplinary Approaches,*

ed. Susan F. Beegel, Susan Shillinglaw, and Wesley N. Tiffney Jr. (Tuscaloosa: University of Alabama Press, 1997), 76–91.

29. Owens, *John Steinbeck's Re-Vision of America,* 133–36.

30. Critics have often interpreted the Joads' travels to California in the context of both the Book of Exodus and broader patterns of religious imagery in the novel. For further discussion, see John H. Timmerman, "John Steinbeck's Use of the Bible: A Descriptive Bibliography of the Critical Tradition," *Steinbeck Quarterly* 21, nos. 1–2 (1988): 24–39; and John Clark Pratt, "Religion in *The Grapes of Wrath:* A Reader's Guide," in Meyer, *"Grapes of Wrath,* 1:149–59. For a contrasting argument, see Ken Eckert, "Exodus Inverted: A New Look at *The Grapes of Wrath,"* *Religion and the Arts* 13, no. 4 (2009): 340–57. Eckert argues that the journey suggests an inversion of Exodus with California as Egypt rather than Canaan, which coheres with the representation of this state and highlights the problems with readings that rely too heavily on biblical parallels (341). Eckert, however, presents Oklahoma as the Promised Land, an interpretation that does not have adequate grounding in the novel, and the religious readings of *The Grapes of Wrath* largely elide the economic arguments at the center of the narrative.

31. Kevin Starr notes that many landowners in California did not embrace such practices; in fact, the Associated Farmers even placed ads in newspapers in Kansas, Nebraska, and Oklahoma warning migrants to stay away. Further, when cotton growers in Arizona distributed leaflets encouraging migration, the California Chamber of Commerce protested under the assumption that these workers would continue westward (Starr, *Endangered Dreams: The Great Depression in California* [Oxford: Oxford University Press, 1996], 259).

32. Thomas Collins, "Report for Week Ending July 11, 1936," Weekly Narrative Reports, 1935–1936, Arvin File Code 918-01, box 23, National Archives and Records Administration—Pacific Region, San Bruno, CA, 4–5.

33. Carey McWilliams, *Factories in the Field* (1935; repr., Berkeley: University of California Press, 1999), 158.

34. John Steinbeck to Elizabeth Otis, September 10, 1938, in *John Steinbeck: A Life in Letters,* ed. Elaine Steinbeck and Robert Wallsten (New York: Penguin, 1989), 171.

35. John Steinbeck to Pascal Covici, January 1, 1939, in Steinbeck and Wallsten, *Steinbeck,* 174.

36. Sanora Babb and Dorothy Babb, *On the Dirty Plate Trail: Remembering the Dust Bowl Refugee Camps,* ed. Douglas Wixson (Austin: University of Texas Press, 2007), 64.

37. For further discussion of this point, see Gregory, *American Exodus,* 79–112.

38. Steinbeck, *Harvest Gypsies,* 39.

39. Steinbeck advanced a similar argument in "Starvation under the Orange Trees." He observed that "the people who picked the cotton, and cut the peaches and apricots, who crawled all day in the rows of lettuce and beans, are hungry. The men who harvested the crops of California, the women and girls who stood all day and half the night in canneries, are starving," and Steinbeck claimed that such problems would continue "until the rich produce of California can be grown and harvested on some other basis than that of stupidity and greed" ("Starvation under the Orange Trees," *Monterey Trader,* April 15, 1938, 1, 4; reprinted in *America and Americans and Selected Nonfiction,* ed. Susan Shillinglaw and Jackson J. Benson [New York: Penguin, 2002], 83). The contrast between the abundance of the state and the poverty of the laborers highlights

the structural inequality that pervaded the agricultural industry in addition to the irrationality of an economic order that could not assist those people most in need. Steinbeck presents the farmworkers' plight within a broader pattern of exploitation that could engender an increasing number of disturbances.

40. Susan Shillinglaw, *On Reading "The Grapes of Wrath"* (New York: Penguin, 2014), 147.

41. McWilliams, *Factories in the Field*, 312–13.

42. John Steinbeck to Elizabeth Otis, February 14, 1938, in Steinbeck and Wallsten, *Steinbeck*, 159.

43. John H. Timmerman, *John Steinbeck's Fiction: The Aesthetics of the Road Taken* (Norman: University of Oklahoma Press, 1986), 119.

44. The conclusion has been the source of controversy since Steinbeck first submitted the typescript of *The Grapes of Wrath* to Pascal Covici, who encouraged Steinbeck to change the ending or to incorporate the stranger into the novel prior to the final scene. Steinbeck refused to do so, writing his editor on January 16, 1939, that the final tableau "is casual—there is no fruity climax, it is not more important than any other part of the book—if there is a symbol, it is a survival symbol not a love symbol, it must be an accident, it must be a stranger, and it must be quick. To build this stranger into the structure of the book would be to warp the whole meaning of this book. The fact that the Joads don't know him, don't care about him, have no ties to him—that is the emphasis" (in Steinbeck and Wallsten, *Steinbeck*, 178). For further discussions of the ending, see Martha Heasley Cox, "The Conclusion of *The Grapes of Wrath:* Steinbeck's Conception and Execution," *San Jose Studies* 1, no. 3 (1975): 73–81; and Edward John Royston, "The Emotional and Narrative Significance of Rose of Sharon's Mysterious Smile," *Steinbeck Review* 10, no. 2 (2013): 152–59.

45. John Steinbeck, "Acceptance," *Nobel Lectures: Literature, 1901–1967,* ed. Horst Frenz (Amsterdam: Elsevier, 1969), 575–76.

CONCLUSION

1. These advancements are discernible through the fates of refugees from the Dust Bowl, whose circumstances did not improve because of an expansion of the FSA camp program as Steinbeck envisioned or through a proletarian revolution. Instead, itinerant workers saw their living standards rise exponentially after the outbreak of World War II. Because of its strategic importance, the West Coast became a vital center for the war effort, and the defense industry provided employment for many migrants, who continued to progress throughout the early 1940s as pay increased by 22 percent in California during this period (Gerald D. Nash, *The American West Transformed: The Impact of the Second World War* [Lincoln: University of Nebraska Press, 1985], 221). The advances made by the employees in this region paralleled improvements for the workforce throughout the nation. Real wages rose by 27 percent during World War II, with compensation at the bottom of the social scale escalating more rapidly than for those at the top (Nelson Lichtenstein, Susan Strasser, and Roy Rosenzweig, eds., *Who Built America? Working People and the Nation's Economy, Politics, Culture, and Society* [New York: Worth, 2000], 506–7). The necessity of production facilitated a climate favorable to unionization, with membership swelling from 10.5 million in 1941 to 14.75 million in 1945 (Christopher J. Tassava, "The American Economy during World War II," *EH.Net Encyclopedia*, February 10, 2008, https://eh.net

/encyclopedia/the-american-economy-during-world-war-ii). This prosperity continued in the decades after World War II, which featured the longest sustained financial expansion in American history. An economic boom during this era raised compensation and contributed to the growth of the middle class as family income nearly doubled between 1941 and 1969 (Juliann Sivulka, *Soap, Sex, and Cigarettes: A Cultural History of American Advertising* [New York: Wadsworth Publishing, 2011], 209). These higher earnings and improved conditions resulted in a degree of mobility that would seem to reduce the relevance of naturalist fiction for modern audiences.

2. Donald L. Barlett and James B. Steele, *The Betrayal of the American Dream* (New York: Public Affairs, 2012), 40, 45.

3. Robert D. Atkinson et al. *Worse than the Great Depression: What Experts Are Missing about American Manufacturing Decline* (Washington, DC: Information Technology and Innovation Foundation, 2012), 5.

4. "Politicians Cannot Bring Back Old-Fashioned Factory Jobs," *Economist,* January 14, 2017, https://www.economist.com/briefing/2017/01/14/politicians-cannot-bring-back-old-fashioned-factory-jobs; Kate Trafecante, "The Myth of the Manufacturing Jobs Renaissance," *CNN,* February 9, 2020, https://www.cnn.com/2020/02/08/economy/manufacturing-jobs/index.html.

5. Barlett and Steele, *Betrayal of the American Dream,* 129–32.

6. For a discussion of this period, see Cal Jillson, *Pursuing the American Dream: Opportunity and Exclusion over Four Centuries* (Lawrence: University Press of Kansas, 2004), 231–60; for a discussion of American society in the context of the Great Recession, see Josh Bivens, *Failure by Design: The Story behind America's Broken Economy* (Ithaca, NY: ILR Press, 2011).

7. Sewell Chan, "Financial Crisis Was Avoidable, Inquiry Finds," *New York Times,* January 25, 2011, A1.

8. Alicia Phaneuf, "Here Is a List of the Largest Banks in the United States by Assets in 2021," *Business Insider,* December 22, 2020, https://www.businessinsider.com/largest-banks-us-list; and Samantha Schaefer, "Five Biggest U.S. Banks Control Nearly Half Industry's $15 Trillion in Assets," *Forbes,* December 3, 2014, https://www.forbes.com/sites/steveschaefer/2014/12/03/five-biggest-banks-trillion-jpmorgan-citi-bankamerica/#1db3cc68b539.

9. John Mauldin, "America Has a Monopoly Problem," *Forbes,* April 11, 2019, https://www.forbes.com/sites/johnmauldin/2019/04/11/america-has-a-monopoly-problem/#649c4ddf2972.

10. Sally Hubbard, "Monopolies Are Killing the American Dream: We Must Keep Them in Check," *CNN,* July 2, 2019, https://www.cnn.com/2019/07/01/perspectives/monopolies-candidates-antitrust/index.html.

11. Emmanuel Saez, "Striking It Richer: The Evolution of Top Incomes in the United States," Department of Economics, University of California, Berkeley, September 3, 2013, http://eml.berkeley.edu/~saez/saez-UStopincomes-2012.pdf.

12. Alexander Eichler and Michael McAuliff, "Income Inequality Reaches Gilded Age Levels, Congressional Report Finds," *Huffington Post,* October 26, 2011, http://www.huffington post.com/2011/10/26/income-inequality_n_1032632.html.

13. Edward N. Wolff, *Household Wealth Trends in the United States, 1962 to 2016: Has Middle Class Wealth Recovered?* (Cambridge, MA: National Bureau of Economic Research,

2017), 9; and Noah Kirsch, "The 3 Richest Americans Hold More Wealth than Bottom 50% of the Country, Study Finds," *Forbes,* November 11, 2017, https://www.forbes.com/sites/noah-kirsch/2017/11/09/the-3-richest-americans-hold-more-wealth-than-bottom-50-of-country-study-finds/#799e4b523cf8.

14. Sam Frizell, "The Average American Family Is Poorer than It Was 10 Years Ago," *Time,* July 27, 2014, http://time.com/3042924/american-wealth-inequality.

15. Brenda Cronin, "Some 95% of 2009–2012 Income Gains Went to Wealthiest 1%," *Wall Street Journal,* September 10, 2013, http://blogs.wsj.com/economics/2013/09/10/some-95-of-2009-2012-income-gains-went-to-wealthiest-1; and Wolff, *Household Wealth Trends,* 11.

16. Jay Shambaugh et al., *Who Is Poor in the United States? A Hamilton Project Annual Report* (Washington, DC: Brookings Institution, 2017), 1.

17. Jessica Semega et al., "Income and Poverty in the United States: 2018," United States Census Bureau, September 10, 2019, https://www.census.gov/library/publications/2019/ demo/ p60–266.html#:~:text=Poverty%3A,14.8%20percent%20to%2011.8%20percent.

18. "Poverty Rate," Organization for Economic Cooperation and Development (OECD), 2019, https://data.oecd.org/inequality/poverty-rate.htm. According to the OECD, Iceland has the lowest poverty rate, at 5.9 percent, and the United States fares worse than other G7 nations, which range from France, at 8.5 percent, and Germany, at 10.4 percent, to Canada, at 11.8 percent. In fact, the poverty rate in the United States is comparable to those of Latvia, Lithuania, and Romania.

19. *The Precarious State of Family Balance Sheets* (Washington, DC: Pew Charitable Trusts, 2015), 12; and *Americans' Financial Security: Perception and Reality* (Washington, DC: Pew Charitable Trusts, 2015), 5.

20. Board of Governors of the Federal Reserve System, "Report on the Economic Well-Being of U.S. Households in 2018," May 2019, https://www.federalreserve.gov/publications/ 2019-eco nomic-well-being-of-us-households-in-2018-dealing-with-unexpected-expenses.htm.

21. Katie Butriago et al., *Cycle of Risk: The Intersection of Poverty, Violence, and Trauma* (Chicago: Heartland Alliance, 2017); and Roge Karma, "The Gross Inequality of Death in America," *New Republic,* May 10, 2019, https://newrepublic.com/ article/153870/inequality-death-america-life-expectancy-gap.

22. Lawrence Mishel et al., *The State of Working America,* 12th ed. (Washington, DC: Economic Policy Institute), 139–40.

23. Gregory Acs and Seth Zimmerman, *U.S. Intragenerational Economic Mobility from 1984 to 2004: Trends and Implications* (Washington, DC: Pew Charitable Trusts, 2008), 5.

24. Ibid.

25. Tom Hertz, *Understanding Economic Mobility in America* (Washington, DC: Center for American Progress, 2006), i.

26. *Pursuing the American Dream: Economic Mobility across Generations* (Washington, DC: Pew Charitable Trusts, 2012), 2.

27. Pablo A. Mitnik and David B. Grusky, *Economic Mobility in the United States* (Washington, DC: Pew Charitable Trusts, 2015), 4.

28. Mishel et al., *State of Working America,* 150.

BIBLIOGRAPHY

Acs, Gregory, and Seth Zimmerman. *U.S. Intragenerational Economic Mobility from 1984 to 2004: Trends and Implications.* Washington, DC: Pew Charitable Trust, 2008.

Adams, James Truslow. *The Epic of America.* Garden City, NY: Blue Ribbon Books, 1931.

Adams, Katherine H. *Progressive Politics and the Training of America's Persuaders.* Mahwah, NJ: Lawrence Erlbaum Associates, 1999.

Alger, Horatio. *Ragged Dick; or, Street Life in New York with the Boot Blacks.* Boston: Loring, 1867.

Anderson, Lisa. "Justice to Ruth Morse: The Devolution of a Character in *Martin Eden.*" *Call* 10, nos. 1–2 (2008): 11–14.

Ascher, Abraham. *The Revolution of 1905: Russia in Disarray.* Stanford: Stanford University Press, 1988.

Astro, Richard. *John Steinbeck and Edward F. Ricketts: The Shaping of a Novelist.* Minneapolis: University of Minnesota Press, 1973.

Atkinson, Robert D., et al. *Worse than the Great Depression: What Experts Are Missing about American Manufacturing Decline.* Washington, DC: Information Technology and Innovation Foundation, 2012.

Austenfeld, Thomas. "A Happy Naturalist? Jeremy Bentham and the Cosmic Morality of *The Octopus.*" *Studies in American Naturalism* 2, no. 1 (2007): 33–45.

Babb, Sanora, and Dorothy Babb. *On the Dirty Plate Trail: Remembering the Dust Bowl Refugee Camps.* Edited by Donald Wixson. Austin: University of Texas Press, 2007.

Bancroft, Hubert Howe. *The Works of Hubert Howe Bancroft.* 39 vols. San Francisco: History Co., 1882–90.

Barlett, Donald L., and James B. Steele. *The Betrayal of the American Dream.* New York: Public Affairs, 2012.

Barry, Michael G. "Degrees of Mediation and Their Political Value in Steinbeck's *The Grapes of Wrath.*" In *The Steinbeck Question: New Essays in Criticism,* edited by Donald R. Noble, 108–24. Troy, NY: Whitston Publishing, 1993.

Baskett, Sam S. Introduction to *Martin Eden,* by Jack London. New York: Holt, Rinehart, and Winston, 1956.

Bean, Walton, and James J. Rawls. *California: An Interpretive History.* New York: McGraw-Hill, 1983.

Beauchamp, Gorman. "*The Iron Heel* and *Looking Backward:* Two Paths to Utopia." *American Literary Realism* 9, no. 4 (1976): 307–14.

Beck, William J., and Edward Erickson. "The Emergence of Class Consciousness in *Germinal* and *The Grapes of Wrath.*" *Comparatist* 12 (1988): 44–57.

Beers, Terry, ed. *Gunfight at Mussel Slough: Evolution of a Western Myth.* Berkeley: Heyday Books, 2004.

Benson, Jackson J. "'To Tom, Who Lived It': John Steinbeck and the Man from Weedpatch." *Journal of Modern Literature* 5, no. 2 (1976): 151–210.

———. *The True Adventures of John Steinbeck, Writer.* New York: Penguin, 1984.

Benson, Jackson J., and Anne Loftis. "John Steinbeck and Farm Labor Unionization: The Background of *In Dubious Battle.*" *American Literature* 52, no. 2 (1980): 194–223.

Berte, Leigh Ann Litwiller. "Mapping *The Octopus:* Frank Norris' Naturalist Geography." *American Literary Realism* 37, no. 3 (2005): 202–24.

Bledstein, Burton J. *The Culture of Professionalism: The Middle Class and the Development of Higher Education in America.* New York: Norton, 1976.

Boessenecker, John. *Gold Dust and Gunsmoke.* New York: John Wiley & Sons, 1999.

Bracher, Frederick. "John Steinbeck and the Biological View of Man." In *Steinbeck and His Critics: A Record of Twenty-Five Years,* edited by E. W. Tedlock and C. V. Wicker, 183–96. Albuquerque: University of New Mexico Press, 1957.

Brands, H. W. *The Age of Gold.* New York: Doubleday, 2002.

Brandt, Maria F. "'For His Own Satisfaction': Eliminating the New Woman Figure in *McTeague.*" *American Transcendental Quarterly* 18, no. 1 (2004): 5–23.

Brecher, Jeremy. *Strike!* Boston: South End Press, 1997.

Briscoe, Erica. "*The Iron Heel:* How Not to Write a Popular Novel." *Jack London Journal* 5 (1998): 5–38.

Brown, J. L. *The Mussel Slough Tragedy.* N.p.: by the author, 1958.

Budd, Louis J. "The American Background." In *The Cambridge Companion to American Realism and Naturalism,* edited by Donald Pizer, 21–46. Cambridge: Cambridge University Press, 1995.

Bullivant, Stephen. "'That's Him. That Shiny Bastard': Jim Casy and Christology." *Steinbeck Studies* 16, nos. 1–2 (2005): 14–31.

Bureau of Labor Statistics. *BLS Spotlight on Statistics: The Recession of 2007–2009.* Washington, DC: Government Printing Office, 2012.

Butriago, Katie, Amy Rynell, and Samantha Tuttle. *Cycle of Risk: The Intersection of Poverty, Violence, and Trauma.* Chicago: Heartland Alliance, 2017.

California Public Utilities Commission. *Biennial Report of the Board of Railroad Commissioners of the State of California.* Sacramento: California State Printing Office, 1896.

Campbell, Donna M. "Frank Norris' 'Drama of a Broken Teacup': The Old Grannis–Miss Baker Plot in *McTeague.*" *American Literary Realism* 26, no. 1 (1993): 40–49.

Carlson, Peter. *Roughneck: The Life and Times of Big Bill Haywood.* New York: Norton, 1983.

Carpenter, Frederic I. "The Philosophical Joads." *College English* 2, no. 4 (1941): 315–25.

Case, Theresa A. *The Great Southwest Railroad Strike and Free Labor.* College Station: Texas A&M University Press, 2010.

Cassuto, Leonard. "Jack London's Class-Based Grotesque." In *Literature and the Grotesque,* edited by Michael J. Meyer, 113–28. Amsterdam: Rodopi, 1995.

Cassuto, Leonard, and Jeanne Campbell Reesman. "Introduction: Jack London, a Representative Man." In *Rereading Jack London,* edited by Leonard Cassuto and Jeanne Campbell Reesman, 1–9. Stanford: Stanford University Press, 1996.

Cederstrom, Lorelei. "The 'Great Mother' in *The Grapes of Wrath.*" In *Steinbeck and the Environment: Interdisciplinary Approaches,* edited by Susan F. Beegel, Susan Shillinglaw, and Wesley N. Tiffney Jr., 76–91. Tuscaloosa: University of Alabama Press, 1997.

Christopher, Renny. "Rags to Riches to Suicide: Unhappy Narratives of Upward Mobility: *Martin Eden, Bread Givers, Delia's Song,* and *Hunger of Memory.*" *College Literature* 29, no. 4 (2002): 79–108.

Cohen, Lizabeth. *Making a New Deal: Industrial Workers in Chicago, 1919–1939.* New York: Cambridge University Press, 1990.

Collins, Thomas. "Report for Week Ending July 11, 1936." Weekly Narrative Reports, 1935–1936. Arvin File Code 918-01. Box 23. National Archives and Records Administration—Pacific Region, San Bruno, CA.

Corak, Miles. "Do Poor Children Become Poor Adults? Lessons from a Cross Country Comparison of Generational Earnings Mobility." *Research on Economic Inequality* 13, no. 1 (2006): 143–88.

Cornford, Daniel, ed. *Working People of California.* Berkeley: University of California Press, 1995.

Cox, Martha Heasley. "The Conclusion of *The Grapes of Wrath:* Steinbeck's Conception and Execution." *San Jose Studies* 1, no. 3 (1975): 73–81.

Crisler, Jesse S. "A Critical and Textual Study of Frank Norris's *McTeague.*" PhD diss. University of South Carolina, 1973.

Daniel, Cletus E. *Bitter Harvest: A History of California Farmworkers, 1870–1941.* Ithaca, NY: Cornell University Press, 1981.

Davies, Jude. "Naturalism and Class." In *The Oxford Handbook of American Literary Naturalism,* edited by Keith Newlin, 307–21. Oxford: Oxford University Press, 2011.

Davison, Richard Allan. "Frank Norris and the Arts of Social Criticism." *American Literary Realism* 14, no. 1 (1981): 77–89.

Dawson, Hugh. "McTeague as Ethnic Stereotype." *American Literary Realism* 20, no. 1 (1987): 34–44.

Debs, Eugene Victor. *Debs: His Life, Writings, and Speeches.* Chicago: Charles H. Kerr & Co., 1908.

DeCaire, John. "The Boys' Book of Despair." *Southwest Review* 88, nos. 2–3 (2003): 277–90.

Deverell, William. *Railroad Crossing: Californians and the Railroad, 1850–1910.* Berkeley: University of California Press, 1994.

Dhondt, Steven T. "'There Is a Good Time Coming': Jack London's Spirit of Proletarian Revolt.'" *Jack London Newsletter* 3, no. 1 (1970): 25–34.

Dircks, Phyllis T. "Steinbeck's Statement on the Inner Chapters of *The Grapes of Wrath.*" *Steinbeck Quarterly* 24, nos. 3–4 (1991): 86–94.

Dorson, James. "Rates, Romance, and Regulated Monopoly in Frank Norris's *The Octopus.*" *Studies in American Naturalism* 12, no. 1 (2017): 50–69.

Douglas, Paul. *Real Wages in the United States, 1890–1926.* Boston: Houghton Mifflin, 1930.

Drabelle, Dennis. *The Great American Railroad War: How Ambrose Bierce and Frank Norris Took on the Notorious Central Pacific Railroad.* New York: St. Martin's, 2012.

Dubofsky, Melvyn. *Industrialism and the American Worker, 1865–1920.* Wheeling, IL: Harlan Davidson, 1996.

———. *When Workers Organize: New York City in the Progressive Era.* Amherst: University of Massachusetts Press, 1968.

Duncan, Charles. "'If Your View Be Large Enough': Narrative Growth in *The Octopus.*" *American Literary Realism* 25, no. 2 (1993): 56–66.

Duneer, Anita. "Crafting the Sea: Romance and Realism in Jack London's *Martin Eden.*" *American Literary Realism* 47, no. 3 (2015): 250–71.

Dunn, N. E., and Pamela Wilson. "The Significance of Upward Mobility in *Martin Eden.*" *Jack London Newsletter* 5, no. 1 (1972): 1–8.

Eby, Clare. "*The Octopus:* Big Business as Art." *American Literary Realism* 26, no. 1 (1994): 33–51.

Eckert, Ken. "Exodus Inverted: A New Look at *The Grapes of Wrath.*" *Religion and the Arts* 13, no. 4 (2009): 340–57.

Emery, Robert A. "Railroad Rates in *The Octopus:* A Literary Footnote." *Journal of Transportation Law, Logistics, and Policy* 64 (1997): 298–304.

Etheridge, Charles L. "*The Grapes of Wrath* and Literary Naturalism." In "*The Grapes of Wrath*": *A Re-Consideration,* edited by Michael J. Meyer, 2:653–86. Amsterdam: Rodopi, 2009.

Fine, Sidney. *Sit-Down: The General Motors Strike of 1936–1937.* Ann Arbor: University of Michigan Press, 1969.

Folsom, James K. "Social Darwinism or Social Protest? The 'Philosophy' of *The Octopus.*" *Modern Fiction Studies* 8, no. 4 (1963): 393–400.

Foner, Philip S. *The Great Labor Uprising of 1877.* New York: Monad Press, 1977.

——. *History of the Labor Movement in the United States.* 10 vols. New York: International Publishers, 1947.

——. "Jack London: American Rebel." In *The Social Writings of Jack London,* edited by Philip S. Foner, 3–130. Secaucus, NJ: Citadel Press, 1964.

Ford, Matthew. "I Ain't Gonna Work on Merritt's Farm No More: A Brief History of Central California's Forgotten Empire." *Public Seminar,* October 11, 2019. http://publicseminar.org/essays/i-aint-gonna-work-on-merritts-farm-no-more.

Formisano, Paul. "Presley's Pauses: Unearthing Force in California's Land and Water Regimes and Frank Norris's *The Octopus.*" *Journal of Ecocriticism* 7 (2015): 1–18.

French, Warren. *Frank Norris.* New Haven, CT: College and University Press, 1962.

——. *John Steinbeck.* Boston: Twayne, 1975.

——. "John Steinbeck and American Literature." *San Jose Studies* 13, no. 2 (1987): 35–48.

Fried, Lewis. "The Golden Brotherhood of *McTeague.*" *Zeitschrift für Anglistic und Amerikanistik* 23 (1975): 36–40.

Frye, Steven. "Presley's Pretense: Irony and Epic Convention in Frank Norris' *The Octopus.*" *American Literary Realism* 39, no. 3 (2007): 213–21.

Galbraith, John Kenneth. *The Great Crash, 1929.* Boston: Mariner Books, 2009.

Garland, Hamlin. "The Work of Frank Norris." *Critic* 42 (1903): 216–18.

Gibb, Alan. "Naturalism and Steinbeck's 'Curious Compromise' in *The Grapes of Wrath.*" In "*The Grapes of Wrath*": *A Re-Consideration,* edited by Michael J. Meyer, 2:687–704. Amsterdam: Rodopi, 2009.

Ginger, Ray. *The Age of Excess: The United States from 1877 to 1914.* New York: Macmillan, 1975.

Glass, Loren. "Nobody's Renown: Plagiarism and Publicity in the Career of Jack London." *American Literature* 71, no. 3 (1999): 529–49.

Goldman, Suzy Bernstein. "*McTeague:* The Imagistic Network." *Western American Literature* 7, no. 2 (1972): 83–99.

Graham, Don. *The Fiction of Frank Norris: The Aesthetic Context.* Columbia: University of Missouri Press, 1978.

Green, James. *Death in the Haymarket: The Story of Chicago, the First Labor Movement, and the Bombing That Divided Gilded Age America.* New York: Pantheon, 2006.

Gregg, Sara. "From Bread Breadbasket to Dust Bowl: Rural Credit, the World War I Plow-Up, and the Transformation of American Agriculture." *Great Plains Quarterly* 35, no. 2 (2015): 129–66.

Gregory, James M. *American Exodus: The Dust Bowl Migration and Okie Culture in California.* Oxford: Oxford University Press, 1989.

Haldeman-Julius, Emanuel. "The Pessimism of Jack London." *Western Comrade,* May 28, 1913, 90–92.

Haley, James L. *Wolf: The Lives of Jack London.* New York: Basic Books, 2010.

Haney, William. "*Martin Eden:* The Failure of Individualism." *Jack London Newsletter* 12 (1979): 38–41.

Hart, Richard E. "Steinbeck on Man and Nature: A Philosophical Reflection." In *Steinbeck and the Environment: Interdisciplinary Approaches,* edited by Susan F. Beegel, Susan Shillinglaw, and Wesley N. Tiffney Jr., 43–54. Tuscaloosa: University of Alabama Press, 1997.

Harvey, Christine. "Dating Frank Norris' Reading of Zola." *Resources for American Literary Study* 24, no. 2 (1998): 187–206.

Heavilin, Barbara A. "A Sacred Bond Broken: The People versus the Land in *The Grapes of Wrath.*" *Steinbeck Review* 14, no. 1 (2017): 23–38.

Hedrick, Joan. *Solitary Comrade: Jack London and His Work.* Chapel Hill: University of North Carolina Press, 1982.

Hertz, Tom. *Understanding Economic Mobility in America.* Washington, DC: Center for American Progress, 2006.

Hill, Mary. *Gold: The California Story.* Berkeley: University of California Press, 1999.

Hindman, Hugh D. *Child Labor: An American History.* Armonk, NY: M. E. Sharpe, 2002.

Hochschild, Jennifer. *Facing Up to the American Dream: Race, Class, and the Soul of the Nation.* Princeton: Princeton University Press, 1995.

Howard, June. *Form and History in American Literary Naturalism.* Chapel Hill: University of North Carolina Press, 1985.

Howells, William Dean. *Criticism and Fiction and Other Essays.* Edited by Clara Marburg Kirk and Rudolf Kirk. New York: New York University Press, 1959.

Hug, William J. "*McTeague* as Metafiction? Frank Norris' Parodies of Bret Harte and the Dime Novel." *Western American Literature* 26, no. 3 (1991): 219–28.

Hussman, Lawrence E. *Harbingers of a Century: The Novels of Frank Norris.* New York: Peter Lang, 1999.

Jameson, Elizabeth. *All That Glitters: Class, Conflict, and Community in Cripple Creek.* Urbana: University of Illinois Press, 1998.

Jillson, Cal. *Pursuing the American Dream: Opportunity and Exclusion over Four Centuries.* Lawrence: University Press of Kansas, 2004.

Johnson, George K. "The Frontier behind Frank Norris's *McTeague.*" *Huntington Library Quarterly* 26 (1962): 91–104.

Johnston, Carolyn. *Jack London—An American Radical?* Westport, CT: Greenwood Press, 1984.

Josephson, Matthew. *The Robber Barons.* New York: Harcourt, 1934.

Käck, Elin. "They fix 'em so you can't win nothing': Agency in *The Grapes of Wrath.*" *Steinbeck Review* 14, no. 2 (2017): 184–200.

Kelly, Jack. *The Edge of Anarchy: The Railroad Barons, the Gilded Age, and the Greatest Labor Uprising in America.* New York: St. Martin's, 2019.

Knapp, Kathy "*The Iron Heel* and the Contemporary Bourgeois Novel." In *The Oxford Handbook of Jack London,* edited by Jay Williams, 316–29. New York: Oxford University Press, 2017.

Knight, Robert Edward Lee. *Industrial Relations in the San Francisco Bay Area, 1900–1918.* Berkeley: University of California Press, 1960.

Krause, Paul. *The Battle for Homestead, 1880–1892: Politics, Culture, and Steel.* Pittsburgh: University of Pittsburgh Press, 1992.

Krim, Arthur "Right near Sallisaw." *Steinbeck Newsletter* 12, no. 1 (1999): 1–4.

Labor, Earle. *Jack London: An American Life.* New York: Farrar, Straus, and Giroux, 2013.

Labor, Earle, and Jeanne Campbell Reesman. *Jack London.* New York: Twayne, 1994.

Lamoreaux, Naomi R. *The Great Merger Movement in American Business, 1895–1904.* London: Cambridge University Press, 1985.

Lauter, Paul. "Teaching *The Iron Heel.*" In *Approaches to Teaching the Works of Jack London,* edited by Kenneth K. Brandt and Jeanne Campbell Reesman, 69–76. New York: Modern Language Association of America, 2015.

Lawlor, Mary. *Recalling the Wild: Naturalism and the Closing of the American West.* New Brunswick, NJ: Rutgers University Press, 2000.

Levant, Howard. "The Unity of *In Dubious Battle:* Violence and Dehumanization." *Modern Fiction Studies* 11 (1965): 21–33.

Lewis, Jocelyn. "Was It Worthwhile?" *Outlook* 18, August 18, 1906, 902–4.

Licht, Walter. *Industrializing America: The Nineteenth Century.* Baltimore: Johns Hopkins University Press, 1995.

Lichtenstein, Nelson, Susan Strasser, and Roy Rosenzweig, eds. *Who Built America? Working People and the Nation's Economy, Politics, Culture, and Society.* New York: Worth, 2000.

Link, Eric Carl. *The Vast and Terrible Drama: American Literary Naturalism in the Late Nineteenth Century.* Tuscaloosa: University of Alabama Press, 2004.

Lisca, Peter. *The Wide World of John Steinbeck.* New Brunswick, NJ: Rutgers University Press, 1958.

Locke, John. *Two Treatises of Civil Government.* 1690. London: J. M. Dent, 1991.

Lojek, Helen. "Jim Casy: Politico of the New Jerusalem." *Steinbeck Quarterly* 15, nos. 1–2 (1982): 30–37.

London, Charmian. *The Book of Jack London.* 2 vols. New York: Century, 1921.

London, Jack. "Disappearing Class." Jack London Collection. Henry E. Huntington Library. San Marino, CA, JL 602.

——. *The Iron Heel.* 1908. In *Jack London: Novels and Social Writings,* edited by Donald Pizer. New York: Library of America, 1982.

——. *John Barleycorn.* 1913. New York: Modern Library, 2001.

——. *The Letters of Jack London.* 3 vols. Edited by Earle Labor, Robert C. Leitz III, and I. Milo Shepard. Stanford: Stanford University Press, 1988.

——. *Martin Eden.* 1909. New York: Penguin, 1984.

——. "Notebook of Story Plots." Jack London Collection. Henry E. Huntington Library. San Marino, CA, JL 1004.

——. "Notes for 'The Dream of Debs.'" Jack London Collection. Henry E. Huntington Library. San Marino, CA, JL 615.

——. "Notes for *The Iron Heel.*" Jack London Collection. Henry E. Huntington Library. San Marino, CA, JL 833.

——. "The Octopus," *Impressions Quarterly* 2 (June 1901): 45–47.

——. *The Social Writings of Jack London.* Edited by Philip S. Foner. Secaucus, NJ: Citadel Press, 1964.

——. *War of the Classes.* New York: Macmillan, 1905.

London, Joan. *Jack London and His Times: An Unconventional Biography.* Seattle: University of Washington Press, 1968.

Long, Denise H. "A Dentist No More: The Destruction of Masculinity in *McTeague.*" *Midamerica* 32 (2005): 67–77.

Love, Eric T. L. *Race over Empire: Racism and U.S. Imperialism, 1865–1900.* Chapel Hill: University of North Carolina Press, 2004.

Lovejoy, Owen R. "The Modern Slaughter of the Innocents." *Men and Women* 3 (October 1905): 1, 4; Jack London Subject File: Socialism. Jack London Collection. Henry E. Huntington Library. San Marino, CA. Box 555. JLE 1554.

Luedecke, Patti. "Chance, Positivism, and the Arctic in Frank Norris's *A Man's Woman.*" *Studies in American Naturalism* 15, no. 1 (2020): 111–34.

Lukas, J. Anthony. *Big Trouble: A Murder in a Small Western Town Sets Off a Struggle for the Soul of America.* New York: Simon & Schuster, 1998.

Lundy, Robert D. "The Making of *McTeague* and *The Octopus.*" PhD diss., University of California, Berkeley, 1956.

MacPhail, Kelly. "'He's—a kind of man': Jim Casy's Spiritual Journey in *The Grapes of Wrath.*" In *"The Grapes of Wrath": A Re-Consideration,* edited by Michael J. Meyer, 1:99–128. Amsterdam: Rodopi, 2009.

McClintock, James I. *Jack London's Strong Truths.* East Lansing: Michigan State University Press, 1997.

McElrath, Joseph R., Jr. "Edwin Markham in Frank Norris's *The Octopus.*" *Frank Norris Studies* 13 (1992): 10–11.

——. *Frank Norris Revisited.* New York: Twayne, 1992.

——. "Frank Norris's *The Octopus:* The Christian Ethic as Pragmatic Response." In *Critical Essays on Frank Norris,* edited by Don Graham, 138–52. Boston: G. K. Hall, 1980.

——. "Jack London's *Martin Eden:* The Multiple Dimensions of a Literary Masterpiece." In *Jack London: One Hundred Years a Writer,* edited by Sara S. Hodson and Jeanne Campbell Reesman, 77–97. San Marino, CA: Huntington Library, 2002.

McElrath, Joseph R., Jr., and Jesse S. Crisler. *Frank Norris: A Life.* Urbana: University of Illinois Press, 2006.

McElvaine, Robert S. *The Great Depression: America, 1929–1941.* New York: Times Books, 1994.

McGlynn, David. "*McTeague*'s Gilded Prison." *Rocky Mountain Review* 62, no. 1 (Spring 2008): 25–44.

McKay, Nellie. "Happy(?)-Wife-and-Motherdom: The Portrayal of Ma Joad in John Steinbeck's *The Grapes of Wrath.*" In *New Essays on John Steinbeck's "The Grapes of Wrath,"* edited by David Wyatt, 47–70. Cambridge: Cambridge University Press, 1990.

McWilliams, Carey. *Factories in the Field: The Story of Migratory Farm Labor in California.* Berkeley: University of California Press, 2000.

Meyer, George Wilbur. "A New Interpretation of *The Octopus.*" *College English* 4, no. 6 (1943): 351–59.

——. "The Original Social Purpose of the Naturalist Novel." *Sewanee Review* 50, no. 4 (1942): 563–70.

Meyer, Michael J., ed. *"The Grapes of Wrath": A Re-Consideration.* Amsterdam: Rodopi, 2009.

——. "Misnomers and Misunderstandings: Tenets of Naturalism in the Work of John Steinbeck." In *John Steinbeck: A Centennial Tribute,* edited by Mashkoor Ali Syed, 146–69. Jaipur, India: Surabhi Publications, 2004.

Michaels, Walter Benn. *The Gold Standard and the Logic of Naturalism.* Berkeley: University of California Press, 1987.

Mink, Gwendolyn, and Alice O'Connor. *Poverty in the United States: An Encyclopedia of History, Politics, and Policy.* Santa Barbara, CA: ABC-CLIO, 2004.

Mishel, Lawrence, et al. *The State of Working America.* 12th ed. Washington, DC: Economic Policy Institute.

Mitchell, Lee Clark. *Determined Fictions.* New York: Columbia University Press, 1989.

Mitnik, Pablo A., and David B. Grusky. *Economic Mobility in the United* States. Washington, DC: Pew Charitable Trusts, 2015.

Moreland, Kim. "The Attack on the Nineteenth-Century Heroine Reconsidered: Women in Jack London's *Martin Eden.*" *Markham Review* 13 (1983): 16–20.

Morelli-White, Nan. "The Damnation of *McTeague:* Frank Norris's Morality Play." *Frank Norris Studies* 13 (1992): 5–10.

Morgan, Richard. "Naturalism, Socialism, and Jack London's *Martin Eden*." *Jack London Newsletter* 10, no. 1 (1977): 13–22.

Motley, Warren. "From Patriarchy to Matriarchy: Ma Joad's Role in *The Grapes of Wrath*." *American Literature* 54, no. 3 (1982): 397–412.

Mowry, George. *The California Progressives*. Berkeley: University of California Press, 1951.

Mrozowski, Daniel J. "How to Kill a Corporation: Frank Norris's *The Octopus* and the Embodiment of American Business." *Studies in American Naturalism* 6, no. 2 (2011): 161–84.

Naft, Stephen. *The Social General Strike*. Translated by Arnold Roller. Chicago: Debating Club No. 1, 1905.

Nash, Gerald D. *The American West Transformed: The Impact of the Second World War*. Lincoln: University of Nebraska Press, 1985.

Norris, Frank. "Character Sketches." Frank Norris Collection of Papers and Related Materials. BANC MSS C-H 80. Bancroft Library. University of California, Berkeley.

——. *Frank Norris: Collected Letters*. Edited by Jesse S. Crisler. San Francisco: Book Club of California, 1986.

——. "I. Notes." Frank Norris Collection of Papers and Related Materials. BANC MSS C-H 80. Bancroft Library. University of California, Berkeley.

——. *The Literary Criticism of Frank Norris*. Edited by Donald Pizer. Austin: University of Texas Press, 1964.

——. *McTeague: A Story of San Francisco*. 1899. Edited by Donald Pizer. New York: Norton, 1997.

——. *A Novelist in the Making: A Collection of Student Themes and the Novels "Blix" and "Vandover and the Brute."* Edited by James D. Hart. Cambridge: Harvard University Press, 1970.

——. *The Octopus: A Story of California*. 1901. New York: Penguin, 1986.

Olin, Spencer C. *California's Prodigal Sons: Hiram Johnson and the Progressives, 1911–1917*. Berkeley: University of California Press, 1968.

Orsi, Richard J. *Sunset Limited: The Southern Pacific Railroad and the Development of the American West, 1850–1930*. Berkeley: University of California Press, 2005.

Owens, Louis. *"The Grapes of Wrath": Trouble in the Promised Land*. Boston: Twayne, 1989.

——. *John Steinbeck's Re-Vision of America*. Athens: University of Georgia Press, 1985.

——. "Writing in Costume: The Missing Voices of *In Dubious Battle*." In *John Steinbeck: The Years of Greatness, 1936–1939*, edited by Tetsumaro Hayashi, 77–94. Tuscaloosa: University of Alabama Press, 1993.

Painter, Nell Irvin. *Standing at Armageddon: The United States, 1877–1919*. New York: Norton, 1987.

Parini, Jay. *John Steinbeck: A Biography.* New York: Henry Holt, 1995.

Pettersson, Torsten. "Deterministic Acceptance versus Moral Outrage: A Problem of Literary Naturalism in Frank Norris's *The Octopus.*" *Orbis Litterarum* 42, no. 1 (1987): 77–95.

Pew Charitable Trusts. *Americans' Financial Security: Perception and Reality.* Washington, DC: Pew Charitable Trusts, 2015.

———. *The Precarious State of Family Balance Sheets.* Washington, DC: Pew Charitable Trusts, 2015.

———. *Pursuing the American Dream: Economic Mobility across Generations.* Washington, DC: Pew Charitable Trusts, 2012.

Pizer, Donald. "Another Look at 'The Octopus.'" *Nineteenth-Century Fiction* 10, no. 3 (1955): 217–24.

———. "The Biological Determinism of *McTeague* in Our Time." *American Literary Realism* 29, no. 2 (1997): 27–32.

———. "Collis P. Huntington, William S. Rainsford, and the Conclusion of Frank Norris's *The Octopus.*" *Studies in American Naturalism* 5, no. 2 (2010): 133–50.

———. "The Concept of Nature in Frank Norris' 'The Octopus.'" *American Quarterly* 14, no. 1 (1962): 73–80.

———. *The Novels of Frank Norris.* New York: Haskell House, 1973.

———. *Realism and Naturalism in Nineteenth-Century American Literature.* Carbondale: Southern Illinois University Press, 1964.

———. *Twentieth-Century American Literary Naturalism: An Interpretation.* Carbondale: Southern Illinois University Press, 1982.

Porter, Glenn. *The Rise of Big Business, 1860–1920.* Wheeling, IL: Harlan Davidson, 2006.

Powell, John J. *The Golden State and Its Resources.* San Francisco: Bacon & Co., 1874.

Pratt, John Clark. "Religion in *The Grapes of Wrath:* A Reader's Guide." In *"The Grapes of Wrath": A Re-Consideration,* edited by Michael J. Meyer, 1:149–59. Amsterdam: Rodopi, 2009.

Pratt, Linda Ray. "In Defense of Mac's Dubious Battle." *Steinbeck Quarterly* 10, no. 2 (1977): 36–44.

Pressman, Richard S. "Individualists or Collectivists? Steinbeck's *In Dubious Battle* and Hemingway's *To Have and Have Not.*" *Steinbeck Quarterly* 25, nos. 3–4 (1992): 119–33.

———. "'Them's Horses—We're Men': Social Tendency and Counter-Tendency in *The Grapes of Wrath.*" *Steinbeck Quarterly* 19, nos. 3–4 (1986): 71–79.

Raskin, Jonah. "Jack London: The Orphan at the Abyss." In *The Radical Jack London: Writings on War and Revolution,* edited by Jonah Raskin, 1–49. Berkeley: University of California Press, 2008.

Reesman, Jeanne Campbell. "Frank Norris and Jack London." In *A Companion to the American Short Story,* edited by Alfred Bendixen and James Nagel, 171–86. West Sussex, UK: Wiley-Blackwell, 2010.

——. *Jack London: A Study of the Short Fiction*. New York: Twayne, 1999.

Roberts, Ian F. "Determinism, Free Will, and Moral Responsibility in American Literary Naturalism." In *The Oxford Handbook of American Literary Naturalism*, edited by Keith Newlin, 121–38. Oxford: Oxford University Press, 2011.

Rohrbough, Malcolm J. *Days of Gold: The California Gold Rush and the American Nation*. Berkeley: University of California Press, 1997.

Rose, Alan Henry. "Steinbeck and the Complexity of the Self in *In Dubious Battle*." *Steinbeck Quarterly* 9, no. 1 (1976): 15–19.

Royston, Edward John. "The Emotional and Narrative Significance of Rose of Sharon's Mysterious Smile." *Steinbeck Review* 10, no. 2 (2013): 152–59.

Saez, Emmanuel. "Striking It Richer: The Evolution of Top Incomes in the United States." Department of Economics, University of California, Berkeley, September 3, 2013, http://eml.berkeley.edu/~saez/saez-UStopincomes-2012.pdf.

Sarchett, Barry. "*In Dubious Battle:* A Revaluation." *Steinbeck Quarterly* 13, nos. 3–4 (1980): 87–97.

Shambaugh, Jay, Lauren Bauer, and Audrey Breitwieser. *Who Is Poor in the United States? A Hamilton Project Annual Report*. Washington, DC: Brookings Institution, 2017.

Sheppard, Keith S. "A New Note for McTeague's Canary." *Western American Literature* 9, no. 3 (1974): 217–18.

Shillinglaw, Susan. *On Reading "The Grapes of Wrath."* New York: Penguin, 2014.

Shockley, Martin. "Christian Symbolism in *The Grapes of Wrath*." *College English* 18, no. 2 (1956): 87–90.

Shor, Francis. "Power, Gender, and Ideological Discourse in *The Iron Heel*." In *Rereading Jack London,* edited by Leonard Cassuto and Jeanne Campbell Reesman, 75–91. Stanford: Stanford University Press, 1996.

Shoup, Laurence H. *Rulers and Rebels: A People's History of Early California, 1769–1901*. New York: iUniverse, 2010.

Simmonds, Roy S. "The Original Manuscript." *San Jose Studies* 16, no. 1 (1990): 117–32.

Sivulka, Juliann. *Soap, Sex, and Cigarettes: A Cultural History of American Advertising*. New York: Wadsworth Publishing, 2011.

Spangler, George M. "Divided Self and World in *Martin Eden*." *Jack London Newsletter* 9, no. 3 (1976): 118–26.

——. "The Structure of *McTeague*." In *Critical Essays on Frank Norris,* edited by Don Graham, 88–98. Boston: G. K. Hall, 1980.

Starr, Kevin. *Americans and the California Dream, 1850–1915*. Oxford: Oxford University Press, 1973.

——. *California: A History*. New York: Modern Library, 2005.

——. *Endangered Dreams: The Great Depression in California*. Oxford: Oxford University Press, 1996.

Stein, Paul. "Jack London's *The Iron Heel:* Art as Manifesto." *Studies in American Fiction* 6, no. 1 (1978): 77–92.

Steinbeck, John. "Acceptance." In *Nobel Lectures: Literature, 1901–1967,* edited by Horst Frenz, 575–77. Amsterdam: Elsevier, 1969.

——. *America and Americans and Selected Nonfiction.* Edited by Susan Shillinglaw and Jackson J. Benson, New York: Penguin, 2002.

——. "Dubious Battle in California." *Nation,* September 12, 1936, 302–4.

——. *The Grapes of Wrath.* 1939. New York: Penguin, 2006.

——. *The Harvest Gypsies: On the Road to "The Grapes of Wrath."* Edited by Charles Wollenberg. Berkeley: Heyday Books, 1988.

——. *In Dubious Battle.* 1936. New York: Bantam, 1972.

——. *Steinbeck: A Life in Letters.* Edited by Elaine Steinbeck and Robert Wallsten. New York: Penguin, 1989.

——. *Working Days: The Journals of "The Grapes of Wrath," 1938–1941.* Edited by Robert DeMott. New York: Penguin, 1989.

Steinbeck, John, and Edward F. Ricketts, *Sea of Cortez: A Leisurely Journal of Travel and Research.* 1941. Mount Vernon, NY: Paul P. Appel, 1989.

Suggs, George G. *Colorado's War on Militant Unionism: James H. Peabody and the Western Federation of Miners.* Norman: University of Oklahoma Press, 1972.

Teich, Nathaniel. "Marxist Dialectics in Content, Form, and Point of View: Structures in Jack London's *The Iron Heel.*" *Modern Fiction Studies* 22, no. 1 (1976): 85–100.

Thernstrom, Stephan. *The Other Bostonians: Poverty and Progress in the American Metropolis, 1880–1970.* Cambridge: Harvard University Press, 1973.

Tichi, Cecelia. "The Facts of Life and Literature." In *The Oxford Handbook of Jack London,* edited by Jay Williams, 27–39. New York: Oxford University Press, 2017.

——. *Jack London: A Writer's Fight for a Better America.* Chapel Hill: University of North Carolina Press, 2015.

Tietze, Thomas R. "Teaching Aesthetics: Art and the Artist on Jack London's *Martin Eden.*" *Eureka Studies in Teaching Short Fiction* 5, no. 1 (2004): 78–88.

Timmerman, John H. *John Steinbeck's Fiction: The Aesthetics of the Road Taken.* Norman: University of Oklahoma Press, 1986.

——. "John Steinbeck's Use of the Bible: A Descriptive Bibliography of the Critical Tradition." *Steinbeck Quarterly* 21, nos. 1–2 (1988): 24–39.

——. "Ma Joad as Thematic Center." In *Readings on "The Grapes of Wrath,"* edited by Gary Wiener, 76. San Diego: Greenhaven, 1999.

Tolles, Frederick B. *Meeting House and Counting House: The Quaker Merchants of Colonial Philadelphia, 1682–1763.* New York: Norton, 1963.

Tompkins, Juliet Wilbor. "Turning Children into Dollars." *Success Magazine* (January 1906): 15–17, 45–46; Jack London Subject File: Socialism. Jack London Collection. Henry E. Huntington Library. San Marino, CA. Box 555. JLE 1579.

"To Protect Childhood." Jack London Subject File: Socialism. Jack London Collection. Henry E. Huntington Library. San Marino, CA. Box 555. JLE 1529.

Trachtenberg, Alan. *The Incorporation of America: Culture and Society in the Gilded Age.* New York: Hill and Wang, 1982.

Trotsky, Leon. *Literature and Revolution: Writings on Literature, Politics, and Culture.* Edited by Paul N. Siegel. New York: Pathfinder Press, 1970.

Vaught, David. *After the Gold Rush: Tarnished Dreams in the Sacramento Valley.* Baltimore: Johns Hopkins University Press, 2007.

Verner, Andrew M. *The Crisis of Russian Autocracy: Nicholas II and the 1905 Revolution.* Princeton: Princeton University Press, 1990.

Walcutt, Charles Child. *American Literary Naturalism: A Divided Stream.* Minneapolis: University of Minnesota Press, 1956.

Walker, Franklin. *Frank Norris: A Biography.* Garden City, NY: Doubleday, Doran, 1932.

———. "Jack London: *Martin Eden.*" In *The American Novel from James Fennimore Cooper to William Faulkner,* edited by Wallace Stegner, 133–43. New York: Basic Books, 1965.

Walther, Louis. "Oklahomans Steinbeck's Theme." *San Jose Mercury Herald,* January 8, 1938 12.

Ware, Thomas C. "'Gold to Airy Thinness Beat': The Midas Touch in Frank Norris's *McTeague.*" *Interpretations* 13, no. 1 (1981): 39–47.

Watson, Charles N., Jr. *The Novels of Jack London: A Reappraisal.* Madison: University of Wisconsin Press, 1983.

Watson, Will. "'Written in Disorder': John Steinbeck's *In Dubious Battle* and 'The Big Strike.'" *Genre* 49, nos. 1–2 (2009): 33–60.

Weinberg, Meyer. *A Short History of American Capitalism.* New York: New History Press, 2002.

Weitzel, Roy L. "Toward a 'Bright White Light': London's Use of Swinburne in *Martin Eden.*" *Jack London Newsletter* 7, no. 1 (1974): 1–8.

Wells, Ira. *Fighting Words: Polemics and Social Change in Literary Naturalism.* Tuscaloosa: University of Alabama Press, 2013.

Werlock, Abby H. P. "Looking at Lisa: The Function of the Feminine in Steinbeck's *In Dubious Battle.*" In *John Steinbeck: The Years of Greatness, 1936–1939,* edited by Tetsumaro Hayashi, 46–63. Tuscaloosa: University of Alabama Press, 1993.

Westbrook, Perry D. *Free Will and Determinism in American Literature.* Madison, NJ: Associated University Presses, 1979.

Wiecek, William M. *The Lost World of Classical Legal Thought: Law and Ideology in America, 1889–1937.* Oxford: Oxford University Press, 1998.

Williams, Jay. "Jack London and Socialism." In *Approaches to Teaching the Works of Jack London,* edited by Kenneth K. Brandt and Jeanne Campbell Reesman, 59–68. New York: Modern Language Association of America, 2015.

Wilson, Jerry W. *"In Dubious Battle:* Engagement in Collectivity." *Steinbeck Quarterly* 13, nos. 1–2 (1980): 31–42.

Windschuttle, Keith. "Steinbeck's Myth of the Okies." *New Criterion* 20, no. 10 (2002): 24–32.

Winter, Ella. *And Not to Yield: An Autobiography.* New York: Harcourt, Brace, and World, 1963.

Winthrop, John. "A Model of Christian Charity." 1630. In *Pragmatism and Religion: Classical Sources and Original Essays,* edited by Stuart Rosenbaum, 21–23. Urbana: University of Chicago Press, 2003.

Witschi, Nicolas S. *Traces of Gold: California's Natural Resources and the Claim to Realism in Western American Literature.* Tuscaloosa: University of Alabama Press, 2001.

Wolff, Edward N. *Household Wealth Trends in the United States, 1962 to 2016: Has Middle Class Wealth Recovered?* Cambridge, MA: National Bureau of Economic Research, 2017.

Worster, Donald. *Dust Bowl: The Southern Plains in the 1930s.* Oxford: Oxford University Press, 1979.

Yancey, Peter W. "Steinbeck's Relationship to Proletarian Literature." *Steinbeck Review* 9, no. 1 (2012): 39–53.

Yeager, Jeffrey Wayne. "The Social Mind: John Elof Boodin's Influence on John Steinbeck's Phalanx Writings, 1935–1941." *Steinbeck Review* 10, no. 1 (2013): 31–46.

Zayani, Mohamed. "When Culinary Desire Meets Pecuniary Desire: Passions for Drinks, Appetites for Food, and Orgies of Gold in Frank Norris' *McTeague." Excavatio* 12 (1999): 207–15.

Zieger, Robert. *American Workers, American Unions.* Baltimore: Johns Hopkins University Press, 1994.

Zinn, Howard. *A People's History of the United States.* New York: Harper, 1980.

Zola, Émile. *The Experimental Novel.* 1880. Translated by Belle M. Sherman. New York: Haskell House, 1964.

INDEX

Acs, Gregory, 193

Adams, James Truslow, 12

Agriculture: conditions in nineteenth century, 6; conditions in twentieth century, 50, 142, 177; monopoly ownership, 191, 223n9; John Steinbeck and, 164; wages, 143–44, 163, 177

Albee, George, 145

Alger, Horatio, Jr., 73–74

Agricultural Labor Bureau of the San Joaquin Valley, 146

Amalgamated Association of Iron and Steel Workers, 109

American Dream, 12–14, 187–88, 199–200n35; "Apostate, The," 73–75, 80, 84; "Dream of Debs, The," 130; *Grapes of Wrath, The,* 162, 168, 173–74; *In Dubious Battle,* 155–56; *Iron Heel, The,* 121; London, Jack, 69–71; *McTeague,* 15, 22–23, 27–30; *Martin Eden,* 84, 88–91, 93–98, 101–4; nineteenth century, during, 71–72; *Octopus, The,* 47–50; twentieth century, during, 107, 190–91; twenty-first century, during, 192–94

American Federation of Labor (AFL), 122

American Railway Union (ARU), 108–9, 128

American Tobacco, 44

"Apostate, The," 8, 10, 13, 69, 97, 106, 136, 188–90; American dream, 73–75, 80, 84;

background/ sources, 72–73, 75–78, 81; child labor, 71–73, 75, 78, 81; critique of capitalism, 72, 74, 77, 79, 81–84; dehumanization of protagonist, 76–78; determinism, 74, 77, 80, 81–84; nature, 82–83; physical decline of protagonist, 75–76, 79, 83–84

Appeal to Reason, 117

"Appeal to the People, An," 53

Arthur, Peter M., 122

Arvin Sanitary Camp, 164, 178

Associated Farmers of California, 143, 160, 222n78

Astro, Richard, 219n7

Babb, Sanora, 177

Bancroft, Hubert Howe, 18

"Battle Hymn of the Republic, The," 176

Bell, Sherman, 123, 216n49

Benson, Jackson J., 138, 144, 148

Bivens, Josh, 192

Black, Harry, 220n45

Boessenecker, John, 19–20

Braden, William, 58

Brands, H. W., 13

Brett, George P., 112, 211n40

Brewer, Henry, 58

Brotherhood of Locomotive Engineers, 122

Budd, Louis J., 197n7

245

9 780807 177129